THE
TELEVISION
SERIES

Andrew Davies

MANCHEStER
1824

Manchester University Press

THE TELEVISION SERIES

series editors

SARAH CARDWELL
JONATHAN BIGNELL

already published

Terry Nation JONATHAN BIGNELL AND ANDREW O'DAY

Jimmy Perry and David Croft SIMON MORGAN-RUSSELL

SARAH CARDWELL

Andrew Davies

Manchester University Press

MANCHESTER AND NEW YORK

distributed exclusively in the USA by Palgrave

Published by Manchester University Press
Oxford Road, Manchester M13 9NR, UK
and Room 400, 175 Fifth Avenue, New York, NY 10010, USA
www.manchesteruniversitypress.co.uk

Distributed exclusively in the USA by
Palgrave, 175 Fifth Avenue, New York, NY 10010, USA

Distributed exclusively in Canada by
UBC Press, University of British Columbia, 2029 West Mall, Vancouver, BC, Canada V6T 1Z2

British Library Cataloguing-in-Publication Data
A catalogue record for this book is available from the British Library

Library of Congress Cataloging-in-Publication Data applied for

ISBN 0 7190 6491 0 hardback
EAN 978 0 7190 6491 3
ISBN 0 7190 6492 9 paperback
EAN 978 0 7190 6492 0

First published 2005

14 13 12 11 10 09 08 07 06 05   10 9 8 7 6 5 4 3 2 1

Typeset in Scala with Meta display
by Koinonia, Manchester
Printed in Great Britain
by Bell & Bain Limited, Glasgow

Contents

List of illustrations

General editors' preface

Television is part of our everyday experience, and is one of the most significant features of our cultural lives today. Yet its practitioners and its artistic and cultural achievements remain relatively unacknowledged. The books in this series aim to remedy this by addressing the work of major television writers and creators. Each volume provides an authoritative and accessible guide to a particular practitioner's body of work, and assesses his or her contribution to television over the years. Many of the volumes draw on original sources, such as specially conducted interviews and archive material, and all of them list relevant bibliographic sources and provide full details of the programmes discussed. The author of each book makes a case for the importance of the work considered therein, and the series includes books on neglected or overlooked practitioners alongside well-known ones.

In comparison with some related disciplines, Television Studies scholarship is still relatively young, and the series aims to contribute to establishing the subject as a vigorous and evolving field. This series provides resources for critical thinking about television. While maintaining a clear focus on the writers, on the creators and on the programmes themselves, the books in this series also take account of key critical concepts and theories in Television Studies. Each book is written from a particular critical or theoretical perspective, with reference to pertinent issues, and the approaches included in the series are varied and sometimes dissenting. Each author explicitly outlines the reasons for his or her particular focus, methodology or perspective. Readers are invited to think critically about the subject matter and approach covered in each book.

Although the series is addressed primarily to students and scholars of television, the books will also appeal to the many people who are interested in how television programmes have been commissioned, made and enjoyed. Since television has been so much a part of personal and public life in the twentieth and twenty-first centuries, we hope that the series will engage with, and sometimes challenge, a broad and diverse readership.

Sarah Cardwell
Jonathan Bignell

Acknowledgements

First and foremost, I would like to express my gratitude to Andrew Davies, who provided me with interview material, lent me precious lone copies of some of his earlier work, and answered all my questions with alacrity and openness. Above all, it is his work that provided me with the reason to undertake this project in the first place, and with many hours of enjoyable television viewing. Thank you.

The University of Kent provided me with a term's sabbatical; the Arts and Humanities Research Board then funded me to take a second term's leave. Without this help from Kent and from the AHRB this book would certainly not have been finished within a reasonable period. I am therefore extremely grateful for the support of both these institutions. The School of Drama, Film and Visual Arts Research Board and the University of Kent Colyer-Fergusson Fund contributed valuable funds towards the costs of viewing archive materials; I am similarly indebted to them for this help.

Particular individuals have helped me during the preparation of this manuscript. My co-editor and friend Dr Jonathan Bignell was there with advice and support, and encouraged me to see more clearly how I might shape the book. Others who have contributed to the research process include Kathleen Dickson at the British Film Institute, who has been invaluable in aiding the search for the necessary archive material; Steve Tollervey (blue-eyed Steve), also of the BFI, who organised all my viewing sessions, and who kept my spirits up during those long hours in the BFI basement; Dave Rolinson, at the University of Hull, who provided me with additional written resources and tapes of some of Davies's more obscure work; Chris Ward, from the University of Kent library, who has gone out of her way on many occasions to seek resources for my research; and Conor Ryan, Film Technician at Kent, who compiled the frame grabs used in this book. I must also acknowledge the assistance of Steve Bayley and his colleagues at PC World in Canterbury, who saved an entire chapter of the manuscript when the laptop I was using gave up the ghost, and Jon Davies, who valiantly proof-read the final draft and spotted the errors I would otherwise have missed.

My colleagues at Kent continue to provide much-appreciated support, and I would especially like to thank Dr Katie Grant and Dr Elizabeth Cowie for their interest and encouragement; Jan Langbein for her kindness and helpfulness; Michael Grant for his wit, honesty and inspiration; and Steve Peacock, for his enthusiasm and good humour, and for running my television aesthetics course in my absence.

On a more personal level, there are a number of people who sustained my motivation for this project through the long period of its genesis. I thank my parents, as ever, for their unwavering encouragement, reassurance and high expectations. Elisabeth Cardwell helped me rediscover my enthusiasm for the project during a slow period of research, with her animated discussion of *The Way We Live Now*; Charles Cardwell has been equally supportive in making repeated and continuing offers of dinner (I hope one day to be able to attend!). I would like to thank Matthew Frost for his plain-talking editorial advice and, more importantly, his ongoing and special friendship. Dr Neil Sinyard's e-mails kept me in good humour, and Dr Howard Bowman, Alan Payne and Ian Banks helped to sustain the research process through their supportive friendship and their willingness to discuss the subject with me. My partner Jon Davies continues to be an inspiring lead not only in the Argentine tango but in so much more besides. Thank you.

This book is dedicated to a very special fan of Andrew Davies's *Pride and Prejudice* – my sister Elisabeth, and also to my brother Charles.

Introduction

Andrew Davies is one of today's most prolific television screenwriters. He has written plays for radio and the stage, books for children and adults, and cinematic screenplays. However, the majority of his work – and that for which he is best known – has been created for television. Davies's work is not just critically appreciated but also tenderly regarded by television audiences. Programmes such as *The Signalman, To Serve Them All My Days, A Very Peculiar Practice, Pride and Prejudice* and *Othello* are cherished as examples of classic British television. Again and again, audiences discern in Davies's oeuvre admirable qualities that engage and entertain them: wit, warmth, boldness, freshness, originality, insightfulness and intelligence. If only for these reasons, his work warrants critical attention; one of the central aims of this book, then, is to explore and evaluate his output. The second is concurrently to explore the issue of television authorship as it relates to Davies's particular case.

Many of Davies's best-known and best-loved works are adaptations from literature – in particular, from 'classic' literature. Indeed, my own interest in Davies arose because of my long-standing fascination with screen versions of literary sources. While researching my previous book, which dealt with television adaptations of classic novels, I found that Davies's programmes provided a rich source of inspiration, and determined to discover more about this man's work. Further research revealed a staggering range of output, and closer inspection exposed the development of a clearly discernible authorial signature (characterised herein through reference to a world view, voice and sensibility) across his oeuvre.

At the centre of this project, then, stands the interpretation and evaluation of particular, key examples of Davies's work. For this reason, the central methodology employed here is the close textual analysis of television programmes, incorporating the study of narrative structure, visual composition, editing, performance and sound design. Certain texts are selected as 'case studies', and explored in particular detail. I would contend that in undertaking such criticism one should hope to achieve what Noël Carroll calls 'sympathetic disinterest'.[1] Underlying this book is a reflection upon what 'sympathetic' might mean in this context. In my opinion, it highlights the desirable close link between the work and the critic. This book recognises that the variety in Davies's work requires from the critic a concomitant flexibility in critical approaches. So, while close textual analysis is my chosen methodology, this is modified according to the characteristic features of each individual programme and, in the case of adaptations, the influence of the source text and its medium.

At one level, the purpose of this approach (close textual analysis) is straightforwardly to illuminate and critique Davies's oeuvre, exploring his work in some detail, and sharing with the reader my own inter-pretations of those texts. At a second level, though, the analyses offered are part of my broader aim: to explore Davies's 'authorship' of his work. For this reason, I shall pay attention to the recurrence and development of thematic and stylistic motifs. Thus in subjecting Davies's work to a critical review, I simultaneously trace the process of negotiating and asserting 'authorship' within the particular example of his television oeuvre.

The reasons for and implications of this focus on authorship, are explored in Chapter 2, following the biographical sketch proffered in Chapter 1. Davies constitutes a particularly intriguing example of a television 'author', especially given the eclecticism of his work and the dominance of adapted texts in his oeuvre. Chapter 2 introduces the topic of authorship, and explores it within the context of television, with reference to factors such as television's collaborative production process; the relatively lesser status of the director in comparison with film; the view of television as 'entertainment' rather than an art form, and so on. Chapter 2 also considers the theoretical and conceptual challenges that have arisen to undermine widely held notions of authorship.

Chapter 3 presents the programmes for which Davies wrote 'original' (non-adapted) screenplays, and recalls some of his earliest works, which will no doubt be familiar to many readers, but which are not always readily available to view on video or DVD. I hope that readers will also enjoy discovering some of Davies's less well-known works, covered in this chapter. Davies's non-adapted work exhibits a coherent 'world view' – an attitude to the world and its inhabitants – which constitutes the most basic starting point of his authorial signature. Chapter 3 elucidates that world view through close attention to specific instances of its manifestation.

Chapters 4 and 5 explore Davies's numerous adaptations, and reveal behind them an extremely talented writer of adapted screenplays. The skill of adapting is frequently undervalued and yet, especially in the case of classic-novel adaptations, the screenwriter is under immense pressure from those who already value the literary source and who seem determined to find fault with the television version. These chapters rest upon an assumption that a strict 'fidelity-orientated' approach is ordinarily inadequate to the task of critical appreciation of television adaptations,[2] and instead they critique the programmes as individual artworks – sometimes with reference to their adaptive contexts, and sometimes in relation to other more pertinent contexts, depending on the particular work. The adaptations are also regarded in terms of Davies's authorship, seeking to understand what Davies's work can tell us about the relation of adapting to authoring, and how his adaptations ask us to comprehend their authorship. Incrementally, an argument is constructed that posits Davies as the author of his adaptations as much as he is the author of his original drama. In particular, the notion of authorial voice becomes increasingly salient in my analyses of his more recent programmes.

Chapter 6 addresses Davies's adaptations from other kinds of sources (theatrical and filmic), and emphasises the televisual nature of his work as a fundamental feature of his authorial sensibility. Davies's willingness to experiment and to challenge existing conventions and traditions, seen most clearly in his desire to innovate within generic boundaries, has resulted in a significant contribution to the art form of television. It may seem ironic that a writer whose work is so frequently adapted from non-televisual sources has contributed so much to the development of truly 'televisual' aesthetic devices, but Chapter 6 contends that this is precisely the case.

Chapter 7 concludes the book by reflecting upon the implications of Davies's work for the critic of it, drawing together the central ideas presented herein, and offering some thoughts regarding the critical project that has been undertaken, and its potential conceptual implications.

I have gained great pleasure from exploring Davies's work, discovering unfamiliar texts and revisiting favourite, familiar ones. In viewing his oeuvre, I have not only been able to observe the development of an important television practitioner; I have also, simultaneously, experienced in a concentrated form the gradual artistic development of the televisual medium, its genres and forms. I hope that this book will communicate to readers some of the enjoyment with which Davies's work has provided me, and encourage them to re-experience that work for themselves.

Notes

1 In his article 'Art and the domain of the aesthetic', Carroll describes the necessary attitude of the critic to the artwork as 'disinterested and sympathetic attention' (Carroll, 2000: 195).

2 This assumption is based on the conceptual/theoretical work laid out in *Adaptation Revisited* (Cardwell, 2002); I do not reiterate the arguments here. However, I do briefly return to the implications and consequences of a 'comparative' approach to adaptation, in Chapter 7, when I discuss the opening sequence of *The Way We Live Now*.

Biographical sketch

Andrew Wynford Davies was born on 20 September 1936 in Cardiff, Wales. He attended Whitchurch Grammar School in Cardiff, and then University College London, receiving a BA Honours degree in English in 1957. His primary career was as a teacher and lecturer: beginning in London, he taught at St Clement Danes Grammar School (1958–61) and then at Woodberry Down Comprehensive School (1961–63), before moving on to two lectureships. The first of these was at Coventry College of Education (1963–71), and the second at the University of Warwick, which absorbed Coventry College; Davies remained here for sixteen years, eventually giving up his teaching career to focus on his writing in 1987.

Davies's enduring interest in education is apparent in his television work, especially in his earlier programmes. Some of his first programmes were written for children, rather than adults, which reflected his contemporary experience as a new parent. He created the much loved Marmalade Atkins character, the troublesome young girl at the centre of a series of books and programmes, and a number of other children's characters, such as Alfonso Bonzo and Doctor Boox. While Davies's work for children is typically playful, celebrating childlike exuberance, he takes the issue of formal education seriously, as his contributions to the 1960s 'Look and Read' series and his educational programmes for schools reveal. A further interesting facet of his writing for children is that it crosses the boundaries between literature and television,[1] echoing his noted preoccupation with literature–screen adaptations.

During the 1960s, Davies penned several plays for radio and theatre. In 1963, he bought his first television set, and glimpsed an opportunity to work in a new medium. His career in television was launched four years later, in 1967, with the broadcast of his first television play, *Who's Going to Take Me On?*, which was based on the character of 'Steph', the protagonist of some of his radio plays. Davies continued to produce numerous programmes throughout the 1970s and 1980s. As was the case with many contemporary writers, most of his early works were in the single play format, for dedicated slots like 'The Wednesday Play', 'Play for Today', 'Screen One', 'Screen Two', and so on. In the 1980s, the trends for longer programmes and serials were reflected in Davies's oeuvre. It was in this period that he made some of his best-known works, including *To Serve Them All My Days* (1980), *Diana* (1983), *A Very Peculiar Practice* (1986, 1988) and *Mother Love* (1989).

Reluctant to give up his stimulating and secure teaching job, Davies sustained his lecturing career until the age of 50, at which point he quit his 'day job' to focus on writing full time. By that point (1987) he was already a familiar name to television viewers, and in the last decade or so he has gained celebrity status, becoming a recognisable face and voice to the general public. This is in great part attributable to his adaptations of classic novels. Davies's adapted screenplays greatly outnumber his non-adapted ones, and constitute his most celebrated work. By the 1980s, adaptations were beginning to dominate his oeuvre, and as the 1990s began, Davies's name became synonymous with 'good quality', classic-novel adaptations, such as *Middlemarch* (1994), *Pride and Prejudice* (1995), *Emma* (1996), *Moll Flanders* (1996) and *Vanity Fair* (1998).

In recent years, Davies has continued adapting, but he has often turned to other sources, moving away from adaptations of classic British novels, and taking on, for example, *Othello* (2001) and *Doctor Zhivago* (2002), though he sustains an interest in classic-novel adaptations (as with *Daniel Deronda*, produced in 2002). Davies continues to innovate and experiment, creating engaging, ambitious and stimulating television drama, and in 2001 his contribution to British television was recognised when he was awarded a BAFTA Fellowship.[2]

Davies's attitude to his work is neatly summed up in his own words, taken from his Huw Wheldon lecture to the Royal Television Society in 1994: 'drama should be all about trying to make masterpieces ... If you try for a masterpiece and you fail, you might end up with something pretty good. If you try for mediocrity and you don't achieve that, you are wasting everybody's time' (Davies, 1994). In such an immense body of work, it is only to be expected that there are a few programmes that fall short of the mark. However, Davies's extraordinary energy and enthusiasm, his love of both literature and television, and his fearless confidence in taking on new and risky projects, ensure his position as one of the pre-eminent television writers in Britain today.

Notes

1 Many of Davies's texts for children are produced as both television programmes and books. See Chapter 3 for further details.

2 The BAFTA Fellowship followed numerous awards and nominations bestowed upon Davies during his career. He has won several BAFTAs, including: Best Drama Serial, 2001, for *The Way We Live Now*; Film Award Best Screenplay – Adapted, 2001, for *Bridget Jones's Diary*; Best Single Drama, 1999, for *A Rather English Marriage*; Best Drama Serial, 1993, for *Anglo Saxon Attitudes*; and Best Drama Series/Serial, 1990, for *Mother Love*. Nominations for BAFTAs include: Best Drama Serial, 2003, for *Doctor Zhivago*; Best Single Drama, 2002, for *Othello*; Best Drama Serial, 1999, for *Wives and Daughters*; Best Drama Serial, 1998, for *Vanity Fair*; Best Comedy (Programme or Series), 1997, for *Game On!*; Best Drama Serial, 1996, for *Pride and Prejudice*; Best Drama Serial, 1995, for *Middlemarch*; Best Drama Series/Serial, 1991, for *House of Cards*; Best Drama Series, 1987, for *A Very Peculiar Practice*; and Best Children's Programme (Entertainment/Drama), 1983, for *Educating Marmalade*.

Davies also won a Primetime Emmy Award (Outstanding Writing in a Miniseries or a Special) in 1991, for *House of Cards*, and was nominated for an Emmy (Outstanding Individual Achievement in Writing for a Miniseries or a Special) in 1996, for *Pride and Prejudice*. In addition, he won the Evening Standard British Film Award for Best Screenplay, 2002, for *Bridget Jones's Diary*; won the ALFS Award British Screenwriter of the Year, 2002, for *Bridget Jones's Diary*, at the London Critics' Circle Film Awards; was nominated for the Royal Television Society Award for Best Writer, 2002, for *The Way We Live Now* (2001); was nominated for the USC Scripter Award, 2002, for *Bridget Jones's Diary*; was nominated for the Writers' Guild of America (Screen) Award for Best Screenplay Based on Material Previously Produced or Published, 2002, for *Bridget Jones's Diary*; won the Golden FIPA TV Series and Serials: Screenplay Award, 1999, for *Vanity Fair*, at the Biarritz International Festival of Audiovisual Programming; won the Writers' Guild of Great Britain Award for TV, Dramatised Serial, 1996, for *Pride and Prejudice*; won the Writers' Guild of Great Britain Award for TV, Dramatised Serial, 1994, for *Middlemarch*; won the Writers' Guild of Great Britain Award for TV, Dramatised Serial, 1992, for *Anglo Saxon Attitudes*; nominated for Writers' Guild of Great Britain Award for TV Drama Serial, 1991, for *House of Cards*; won the Broadcast Press Guild Award, in 1990 and in 1980; won a Royal Television Society Award, in 1987; and won the Pye Colour TV Award, 1981. Davies has been awarded the Guardian Children's Fiction Award, 1979, and the Boston Globe–Horn Book Award, 1980.

Davies's programmes have also been nominated for, and won, many further awards, including BAFTAs, in other categories (editing, music, lighting, acting and so on).

Questions of authorship

'The work of Andrew Davies': Davies and authorship

The scale and variety of the work of Andrew Davies affirms the importance of his individual contribution to television specifically and culture more generally. However, it simultaneously challenges conventional notions of authorship, auteurism and/or artistry. Can we identify Davies as the author or artist behind *The Signalman*, *To Serve Them All My Days*, *Vanity Fair* and *Othello*? What does it mean to make such a claim? If it can be made, does an awareness of Davies's authorial role aid our interpretation, understanding, and evaluation of those texts?

Davies is of course most famous for his literary adaptations, a fact which in itself problematises the notion of him as an individual, original author or artist, by virtue of his adapting the original work of others. And Davies's original screenplays pose a further challenge to the notion that one can define a coherent, consistent 'oeuvre': he has worked within a number of disparate television genres and forms, from single plays to ghost stories, children's television to sitcoms. Yet despite this eclecticism, Davies's work can be seen as expressing an individual authorial 'signature' that permeates the majority of his work. This book will explore the aspects of content, style and tone that constitute this signature, characterising it in terms of, variously, a 'world view', an 'authorial voice', and a specific 'sensibility'. This project therefore has two related aims. The first is to explore and evaluate Davies's work. The second is to offer some related reflections upon the critical notion of authorship, addressing notions such as the idea of 'control' over the text; intention and individual expression; contextual limitations; world view, voice and sensibility; artistic development and progression; interpretation; art; and claims for value.

In a sense, this book explores the ways in which one might justifiably and profitably talk about 'authorship' within the context of television.

The question of authorship is a contentious one, and has always been crucial within television studies. Contemporary cultural theory has attempted to render the question obsolete, as we shall see. However, this book proposes that our commonplace understanding of authorship – the one that encourages us to speak of 'the new Andrew Davies serial' or 'an Andrew Davies adaptation' – cannot be so easily put aside. The notion of authorship is one that remains pre-theoretically (i.e. instinctively) important, and which is employed in everyday speech and common language, and for this reason it demands to be taken seriously: it must be challenged, interrogated, analysed and qualified. Within the demarcated context of Davies's work, this is a task undertaken here.

Speaking plainly: authorship in common speech and in 'theory'

Currently there exists a curious, overlooked divide between the implicit acceptance and usage of broad, vague notions of 'authorship' in common speech and popular criticism, and the vehement rejection of such notions within many sectors of the academic community (or more specifically, within dominant theoretical paradigms therein). In recent years, theorists from various, disparate corners of academia – from cultural studies to gender studies, literary studies to analytical philosophy – have cast doubts upon age-old beliefs and mores surrounding 'the author'. Previously commonplace understandings of the existence of a single, definable author/artist; of the relationship between author and text, and text and audience; and of the importance of authorship and intention to interpretation and evaluation, have been genuinely challenged and troubled by these attacks. Some theorists have even gone so far as to proclaim the author 'dead'.[1]

Yet outside the academic context, most people find that it is usually easier to ignore such troubling thoughts, and to behave, talk and criticise texts as if the more commonplace acceptance of authorship were true; they find themselves discussing artists and authors with no regard to the pronouncements of continental philosophers and cultural theorists. Certainly many readers of books and viewers of films and television programmes are competent enough to recognise intertextual references, artistic influences, generic conventions and the ironic deployment of a wide range of registers. Yet despite recognising the text before them as a 'fabric of quotations' (Barthes, 1968: 53), these readers and viewers still blithely persist in talking about authors (writers, filmmakers, scriptwriters), attributing the work to those named, special individuals. Consequently, a gap arises between theories of authorship and those pre-theoretical, intuitive notions of authorship that underlie common usage.

This book does not propose that either 'theory' or 'common language' is 'right' or 'wrong'. Instead, it accepts many of the criticisms of common-sense notions of authorship, while also recognising that the endurance of such notions belies their fundamental and abiding importance. In observing the roots and shape of common perceptions of authorship, a great deal can be revealed about the ways in which we instinctively and pre-theoretically approach the criticism (interpretation and evaluation) of art and artworks.

Authorship, intention and art

What does it mean to make a claim about authorship? Why do we 'need' authors? Why do critics in newspapers and magazines, and viewers in their conversations, refer to Andrew Davies when they talk about 'his' latest work? Why do some television practitioners, like Davies, and like the others addressed in this series of books, come to be known and recognised above others? And perhaps most importantly, are we wrong to indulge in this discussion of 'authorship'; is it a conceptual red herring, based only on historical common parlance? Why does the author persist, even in a mass medium such as television?

I would tentatively propose that the persistence of such practices and their perpetuation of the notion of 'authorship' are related to fundamental and enduring preconceptions about art. Noting and emphasising Davies's authorship is part of the process by which we may recognise television as an art, as something elevated above mass-produced material, and thus justify its centrality in our lives and emotions, and, for some of us, our work. (The link between the two – authorship and art – is forged by one further concept: intention, which we shall address in a moment.)

Auteurism and the study of film

Traditionally, the notion of the author or artist has been a legitimating force in the conceptualisation of art forms. Clearly an exploration of authorship in television might usefully draw upon the comparable case of film. Within film studies, authorship has been most notably conceptualised in terms of 'auteurism'. Auteurism is an explanatory and interpretative paradigm, which posits one named originator (creator/author/artist),[2] and refers to this person in order to explain, explore and evaluate the films they make. The approach was established in the 1950s by writers like Andrew Sarris, and the editors of the French film journal *Cahiers du Cinéma*.[3]

Historically, the auteurist approach posits a set of films made by one director as an oeuvre (a body of work), seeking out recurrent thematic, generic and stylistic details within the films, and observing variations, fluctuations and developments across the works. This analytical process is undertaken with reference to a particular named auteur. Auteurism also implies almost the opposite process: looking at an oeuvre in order to discover the presence of authorship through finding consistencies across a number of works. The approach can be both analytic and evaluative, assessing the worth of an auteur's output and making claims for value about his or her films. What is most important for our purposes here is that within this paradigm, authorship is closely linked to both interpretation and evaluation (that is, the conceptual basis provides a useful methodology for the rigorous study of films); also, this approach builds upon intuitive understandings of intention, authorship and art, as we shall see.

Since its heyday in the 1950s, the auteurist approach has been subjected to considerable criticism, reassessment and revaluation; television studies was established at a time when cynicism about traditional concepts of authorship and art was reaching its height, and such notions seemed irreversibly debunked. This determined the shape of television studies, guiding scholars towards a focus on the audience as the locus of meaning, rather than the artist, author, or text. Before exploring the implications of this for the field, it is useful to outline the changing attitude to authorship: first, the reasons for its initial and fundamental importance in the study of art forms, and second, the challenges, problems, and motivations that led to the questioning, and in some cases the rejection, of the paradigm.

Although it is now quite unfashionable in some branches of film studies to speak of auteurs, the idea retains its importance in the field, and in a way, the reasons for the incipience and longevity of the auteur in film are comparable to the motivations behind the dogged per-sistence of the notion of the television 'author'. Why did the auteurist approach arise when it did? The answer is partly that critics needed a way of talking about and categorising films – and the notion of an auteur seemed responsive to actual, discernible details that distinguish different films one from another. However, the eagerness to determine the existence of the auteur in film arose also from a desire to defend the art of cinema. In the late 1940s, cinema was still regarded as a somewhat inferior medium compared with other art forms. There was an underlying apprehension that film was a mass medium, rather than an art. The group of film critics involved in *Cahiers* wanted to contest this view and to communicate the rich potential of the medium. They were determined to prove that film was indeed an art, worthy of the kind of attention and recognition afforded to literature, painting and sculpture. As Edward Buscombe puts it, these critics aimed 'to raise the cultural status of cinema. The way to do this, it seemed, was to advance the claim of the cinema to be an art form like painting, or poetry, *offering the individual the freedom of expression*' (my emphasis) (Buscombe, 1973: 75). Crucial to their argument and project, then, was the notion of the individually expressive artist or author, or, as they called it, the auteur. Without the auteur, there could be no art of film. So it was asserted that some films had authors – auteurs – and that this made them works of art and worthy of serious attention and study.[4]

Rosalind Coward astutely observes that 'it is an interesting reflection on the interdependency of the idea of art and the idea of the individual artist, that the higher the valuation of the medium as an art, the more likely you are to find the quest to establish an author for a work' (Coward, 1987: 79). Thus the auteur aided critics in claiming the status of art for film (or at least, for some films). The auteur took on the role of the Romantic artist, who had long been important in the establishment of literature and poetry. In the case of film, the director was designated the auteur, and conceived as the artist whose guiding vision shapes the film. But for what reason is the notion of the auteur (author/artist) so indispensable to film as art? It is because the notion of *intention* has always been central to both philosophical and common-sense understandings of art.

Intention and art

To define something as art, one assumes the existence of an artist. So the existence of an author, or artist, can help us to distinguish art from not-art. A simple definition of an author is offered by aesthetician Paisley Livingston: 'author = (def) the agent (or agents) who intentionally make(s) an utterance, where "utterance" refers to any action, an intended function of which is expression or communication' (Livingston, 1997: 134). Clearly, this definition is insufficient on its own, for it seems to put in the same category the creator of an artwork and the participant in a conversation. The key issue here, though, is the inclusion of the word 'intended'. It is not enough that an utterance is expressive or communicative; it must be *intended* to be. Intention appears central.

There is a well-known philosophical example that illustrates the importance of intention. Imagine that a computer programme could be devised that, without human intervention, would churn out clauses, laid out on the page in sets of fourteen lines. The clauses would be proper ones, grammatically constructed, but composed of words thrown out at random. Given an infinite amount of time, the computer would eventually put together a series of words in such a way that it would actually 'write' a sonnet; indeed, it may actually generate a sonnet identical to a pre-existing one (one of Shakespeare's, perhaps). Note that the question here is not whether or not this can be done, but 'If it *could* be done, what does that say about authorship and art'? One long-established opinion on this hypothetical example would be that the randomly generated text, though identical to a sonnet, and even if indistinguishable from a pre-existing sonnet in terms of content and form, is not art. The reason it cannot be classified as art is because it was composed by chance; it was not intended. There was no intention to communicate or express meaning, feelings or beliefs. The computer had no knowledge of or investment in what it had produced; to the computer, the text *means nothing at all*. The resulting verse cannot be art, because it is merely a randomly generated series of words, and the coherent group of words – the sonnet – was not intended. The sonnet would constitute a *text* which might appear identical to another text, but the *work* – the entity that lies behind it and is made manifest in the text – does not exist, for no work pre-existed the text to be communicated or expressed.[5]

This is not to say that the attitude expressed above is the 'correct' one. But, in its rehearsal of familiar human sentiments and responses, it does underline the extent to which we value the presence of an actual human being behind an artwork, and the central role that person's individual intentions play in our response to it. This is one reason why a pile of bricks on the floor of the Tate Modern is considered art, whereas the identical pile of bricks in my front driveway is not. One was deliberately constructed, intended to mean or express something; the other is accidental and incidental.[6] The presence of perceived intentions also impacts upon the process of interpretation. If one considers an object an artwork, one is ready to interpret it, to assume that details of its content and form are determined and meaningful. This is how the auteurist approach, with its understanding of authorial intention, facilitated a careful scrutiny of the details and achievements of particular texts (and is perhaps one of the reasons that close textual analysis is as absent from the mainstream of television studies as is serious attention to questions of authorship).

Television, authorship and art

We have seen that common presumptions about authorship are part of typical assumptions about what constitutes art. The presence of a skilful, intentional artist or author behind a work contributes to its being acknowledged as an artwork, as the auteurists in film studies recognised. It is probably becoming clear how this might impact upon the medium of television. Television faces the same problems of not being taken seriously that film faced in the 1940s. It is a disparaged medium. Therefore to talk about television authorship is not just to explore those individuals who stand behind particular texts, but also to make an implicit, but powerful, argument about television as an art. When a critic makes a claim for Davies's authorship of a television text, he or she is positing an intentional author/artist behind the text, and thus claiming the status of art for Davies's work, and the status of art form for television. Whether this can be logically justified is a moot point, but the popular notion of the author thus remains vital to common practices of interpretation and evaluation. The author in this book is in this sense a rhetorical device, a symbolic figure which helps to establish the artistic credentials of television.

Some television 'authors' appear to be acutely aware of this series of connections and inferences. Dennis Potter, for example, worked with a deliberate attentiveness to all the implications of television authorship explored above. John Cook writes about Potter's long-term intentions:

> Potter's career was a conscious attempt to create a self-consistent *oeuvre* for television, through the weaving of an intricate web of theme and cross-reference from work to work. Behind this enterprise lay a deep desire on the writer's part to demonstrate that, far from its alleged ephemerality and domestic conditions of viewing being a handicap, television and its audience could be accorded the same degree of intelligence, 'seriousness' and respect by the practitioner as other cultural forms such as the novel, cinema film or stage play. (Cook, 1995: 2)

Potter deliberately established himself as a television author/artist, and this project affected the content and form of his work – and its reception by critics. He did so in the hope of proving the status of television as art, and not as mere mass entertainment. Indeed, his artistic and creative decisions rested upon an astute awareness (and perpetuation) of commonplace perceptions regarding television 'authorship' and quality. Television that is marked out as 'authored', in contrast to the anonymous programmes that make up the bulk of the schedules, denotes 'quality' of some kind; it is special by virtue of the fact that a unique, named individual created it. It is this distinctiveness that implies value. Thus in the case of television, as indeed in many other arts, authorship is an important component of value, and, relatedly, a conceptualisation of authorship underlies the critical process of evaluation, as we shall see later.

The television screenwriter as author

Readers of this book who are trained in film studies have probably observed that Davies, like Potter, is not a director but a writer. He wrote the screenplays for all the programmes discussed in this book, but other people directed them. In film studies, the author/auteur – the person who is named as the 'owner' of the work – is ordinarily the director; hence we have Ford's *My Darling Clementine*, Tarantino's *Pulp Fiction*, Lean's *Lawrence of Arabia*. In television studies, the author of the work is the screenwriter, so we have Dennis Potter's *The Singing Detective*, Alan Bennett's *Talking Heads*, Russell T. Davies's *Queer as Folk*.[7]

Part of the reason for this difference is historical. Television, as a broadcast medium, has its roots in radio, and in some sense words have always been more important to television than to film. In the early days, the screenwriter was centrally important for both artistic and practical reasons. Primitive television offered only a small, crackly and indistinct image, so it was necessary to rely upon words, rather than complex, detailed images, to communicate meaning. Furthermore, the programmes were filmed in studios by cameras that were too heavy to move around much, limiting the opportunity for flashy camera moves or interesting camera angles, and containing the actors within a relatively small space. The writing had to be gripping enough to hold the viewers' attention, especially given the lack of other visual stimulation. Initially, dramas were broadcast live, and the action was performed in front of the cameras as if in a stage play, with no second takes; within this production context the script was the framework that held everything in place, and it had to be precisely constructed so that producers knew exact running times for each scene and programme. While screenwriting was a highly skilled task, directing involved little more than telling the actors where to move in front of static cameras. Even today, freed from all those early constraints, much television tends to foreground dialogue or speech over images and other sounds, and the screenwriter remains pre-eminent.

It is also the case that the screenwriter in television often has a higher status than his counterpart in film, whereas the opposite is true for directors. A script for a Hollywood film might go through several re-writes by different writers, and then be viciously cut at the post-production stage (Davies has seen his own contributions to feature films end up on the cutting room floor – and that is if they make it into the final shooting script). In television, where the rate of production is higher, and costs relatively lower, scriptwriters tend to be commissioned to write a specific number of episodes, in communication with a script editor assigned by the production company. Rarely is a programme heavily rewritten or passed through several writers – that is too expensive a process. In comparison, directors in television are more dispensable than those in cinema, and are periodically replaced in serials and long-running series (in the case of *EastEnders*, for example, the job of direct-ing is rotated). It is true that screenwriters are also replaced midway through runs, and that many programmes are co-written by a team of writers, but this has historically been far more common in the United States than in Britain. In Britain the writer tends to be viewed as the 'creator' and as such maintains an input throughout a run. Davies, like Potter, chose to work in television because he saw that the medium offered greater authorial control and freedom: 'I dreamed of being a writer and now I am – writing for a medium where they don't fuck with your work' (Davies, quoted in Jeffries, 2002: 7). Common televisual practice supports Davies's claim to authorship: his name has become a recognisable trademark, with programmes he has scripted tending to highlight his name (usually prioritising him above the director and producer).

Following all this, the maintenance of notions of authorship and intention seem reasonable within the context of television. They rest upon commonplace and intuitive understandings of art; they help us to respect the potential of television, and encourage us to pay close atten-tion to its texts; and they reflect the history and common practices of the medium. Furthermore, someone like Davies has a greater claim to authorship, since screenwriters have historically been considered more important than the director in television, and have played a more central role in the creation of programmes, and this has continued for economic and practical reasons. It therefore seems defensible to attribute the authorship of the programmes discussed in this book to Davies.

Problems with notions of authorship

This book therefore claims to explore 'the work of Andrew Davies'. Yet behind this deceptively simple assertion lies a host of presumptions regarding the 'ownership' or 'authorship' of television programmes as varied as *Bavarian Night, Pride and Prejudice, A Very Peculiar Practice*

and *Game On* – the central implicit claim being that the programmes
are in some important sense 'owned' and/or 'authored' by Davies. It is
assumed that Davies's intentions strongly shape the programmes,
which thus express his concerns, thoughts and preoccupations. Further,
his name above a title gives rise to certain expectations regarding the
content, style and tone of the programme. But this is to imply a number
of things about Davies's authorship. It suggests, for example, that
Davies is more than just a writer of dialogue – that in some way he has a
greater impact upon the programmes he scripts. Beyond that, it implies
that to accept Davies's authorial role brings positive benefits to us as
viewers and critics, helping us to interpret and evaluate 'his work'. But
these assumptions are by no means unproblematic. That is why the
second aim of this book is to investigate the implications of the
seemingly straightforward claim 'This is a book about the work of
Andrew Davies', and to reflect upon how authorship might help (or
hinder) the interpretation and evaluation of particular television texts.

'Real world' considerations: television authorship, control and collaboration

There are significant problems inherent in applying a notion of
authorship in the case of television, and claiming Davies as an author,
even if we conceptualise 'author' in the broad and ambiguous way we
have done above, where the author is the 'originator' of a work.

In terms of 'real world', practical considerations, the nature of
television production highlights the issue of 'control' that is vital to a
conventional understanding of authorship (or artistry). While idiosyn-
cracies, continuities and qualities in the dialogue of the programmes
discussed herein can be reasonably attributed to Davies,[8] to talk of 'the
work of Andrew Davies' (or indeed any other famous screenwriter, such
as the others included in the Television Series) implies an influence
beyond the preparation of the script. We may see – or feel that we see –
traces of Davies permeating the programmes he scripted, as if his
handprints were all over them, not only in terms of the recurrence and
development of certain themes and concerns, but also in terms of an
apparently idiosyncratic style and tone. It is as if we perceive his
authorial signature on the work. Yet Davies, unlike a painter, a writer of
books or poetry, or a sculptor, does not have overall control over his
work; it is manipulated and completed by others: the director who
stages his scenes, the actors who perform his characters and their lines,
the composer whose music accompanies the action, and the editor who
integrates the images and sounds. In film and television, the processes
of production are collaborative. When the scale of collaboration involved

in making a television programme is considered, Davies's part in the process seems to shrink in significance, constituting as it does only a tiny part of the final product.

Such collaboration, and lack of overall authorial control, flies in the face of our usual understanding of what an author is and does. We value individual expression and actualised intentions within a work of art. Would we call Jane Austen the author of *Persuasion* if she had devised the initial idea, but then drafted in other people to write different chapters? Consider the hand-painted pictures that are mass produced in factories, with each element of the painting being contributed by a different person: the canvas travels along on a conveyor belt system, and one person fills in the sky, another the trees, another the people, and so on. We would baulk at naming any one of those painters the 'author' or artist of the painting. Collaborative work muddies the waters with regard to attributing the 'ownership' of a piece. Given the links highlighted previously between authorship, art and evaluation, the collaborative nature of television production implies that there are no proper authors or artists behind television programmes, and that the medium's artistic merits are therefore dubious.

In what sense, then, can I make the claim that this is a book about the work of Andrew Davies? In what way might *Othello* or *Pride and Prejudice* 'belong' to Davies rather than to his collaborators? How might one justify singling out one cog within the larger machine? What is it that makes us feel able to assert Davies's ownership over the programmes for which he wrote the screenplay? Are we right or wrong to do so? It seems we must adapt our long-standing ideas about authorship to a new medium.[9]

In this book I shall reveal, through close analyses of selected texts, that as Davies's career has progressed, he has worked more closely with the crews who have participated in his projects, engaging particularly in dialogues with the respective directors, and expressing his thoughts regarding the way in which his script ought to be 'visualised'. This has led to a productive and coherent synthesis between Davies's 'words' and ideas, and the visual and aural elements that the crew create. Davies's ideas, intentions and voice have come to be expressed by those working with him, and he has thus been able to establish and sustain a discernible 'authorial signature' across his oeuvre; such an observation tallies with viewers' and critics' suggestions that his work exhibits particular, recurrent features. Davies speaks warmly of the cooperative context of television production; notably, he emphasises its contribution to his own development as an artist, rather than regarding collaboration as a threat to his authorial autonomy: '[In television] you don't get treated like a piece of shit, which is what generally happens in the movies – and you don't get treated like a god, either. You get challenged all the time, and you learn all the time from [those around you: producers, editors, directors, actors, etc.]' (Davies, 1994). Further, Davies's talent for self-deprecating yet vigorous self-promotion has also helped to establish him as the dominant personality in the projects he undertakes, so that he is commonly perceived to 'author' the programmes he writes.

Earlier, I drew attention to a second concern: how does the imputation of authorship to a named individual impact upon interpretation and evaluation? This has been of great interest to theorists, especially since the 1970s, with understandable concerns that 'auteurism' or 'authorship' limits our reading and appreciation of texts. Given that the primary objective of this book is to offer a critical overview (and reading/ appreciation) of Davies's work, it is vital to question whether my emphasis on authorship might stifle and undermine this aim.

Theoretical challenges: authorship, intention and criticism

In commonplace conversation, there seems to be a natural link implied between intention and interpretation.[10] It is revealed when one finds oneself discussing Aaron Sorkin's concerns in *The West Wing*, or the development of Martin Scorsese's filmic style. In everyday speech, we frequently refer to the author behind something, assuming that where there is a text, there is an author. In the cases of film and television, viewers tend to overlook the problem of collaboration and the complexities of authorship, and insist upon seeking recurrent thematic concerns and stylistic motifs, and tracing links between the films 'belonging to' one individual. They may even come to a generalised conclusion, such as that they do, or do not, like 'Scorsese'. Similar behaviour arises in relation to television 'authors' like Potter, Bennett and Davies. Each new programme by a named author is considered in relation to others created by the same author, and interpreted and evaluated accordingly. This is the common-sense use of 'authorship' referred to earlier.

There are many reasons why people persist with this notion of authorship in the face of complicating knowledge and contradictory arguments. However, one of the most fundamental is that we are always aware that films and television programmes are constructed and contrived. Someone made them happen. There is a sense, then, that if we can discover the intentions of the author, or learn something of their concerns, beliefs, experience or personality, we shall be able to enhance our understanding of the programme. But this assumption is by no means proven; questions remain unanswered. What impact does (and should) our knowledge of an author have upon our interpretations of individual texts? What is the importance of 'authorship' to interpretation and evaluation? And what is the role of the author's 'intentions'?

Against the Author 1: challenges to intentionalist or author-based interpretation
There have been many paradigms within literary criticism that have regarded the conceptualisation of a text as intended by a particular author as foundational; some have conceived of this notion as underlying the task of criticism (which incorporates interpretation and evaluation). Wimsatt and Beardsley cite Goethe's 'three questions for "constructive criticism"': 'What did the author set out to do? Was his plan reasonable and sensible, and how far did he succeed in carrying it out?' (Wimsatt and Beardsley, 1954: 93). Notice that two of Goethe's questions explicitly refer to the author's intentions, and that all three assume, and are underpinned by, the existence of an actual, specific author behind the text being studied.

This approach to criticism and its basis in a notion of clear, determining authorship has come under attack during different periods, but especially since the 1970s, as I mentioned above.[11] The implications of the authorship paradigm for the tasks of interpretation and evaluation have been repeatedly raised. There are myriad reasons for this heavy assault on authorship, and a comprehensive outline of these falls outside the scope of this study. In short, however, a challenge was made to the autonomy of the author and his or her authority in fixing the meanings of his/her text and its meanings, in the hope of opening up and extending the process of critical practice.

Literary theorist Stephen Bonnycastle highlights the key aspects of author-centred criticism succinctly:

> Author-centered criticism is largely concerned with works of literature as expressions of the author's state of mind. Above all, this kind of criticism places emphasis on understanding what was going on in the author's mind, and what her intention was in writing the work. The meaning of the work is what it meant to the author … In this approach, there is a certain disregard for both the text and the reader. (Bonnycastle, 1996: 35–6)

In order to correct this imbalance in which the author seems to have a disproportionately large influence in fixing the meaning of a work, Bonnycastle proposes that critics should focus on the reader, not the author nor even the text. He advocates this to be a more egalitarian and open-minded approach that favours no one particular reading, and no one particular interpretation of any text as the 'right' one, approved by the author. Bonnycastle proposes a pluralistic and, on the whole, relativistic criticism, recognising the many and varied interpretations that readers of texts may choose to produce.

It is clear that Bonnycastle, representing the views of dominant literary theory, perceives that the choice between author-based, text-based or reader-response-based approaches is not so much a 'theoretical' or 'logical' one but a political one; he himself asserts that 'a state of ideological conflict exists between these [three types of criticism]' (Bonnycastle, 1996: 37). His views echo those of the wider group of literary theorists who have been inspired by continental philosophers and cultural theorists. Terry Eagleton, although he couches some of his arguments in pseudo-logical or philosophical registers, is nevertheless strongly politically motivated, and his Marxism is the motivation that drives his theorising about literature. He rejects author-centred criticism because he believes that it is extremely important to acknowledge that no work is created in a vacuum by an autonomous author, and received in a similar vacuum by an independent, objective, free reader. Instead, he asserts that we must move beyond an understanding of self-determined individuals such as those epitomised in the Romantic notion of the author, and instead regard authors and readers as 'speakers and listeners in a whole field of social values and purposes' (Eagleton, 1996: 99). In his commitment to stressing the social nature of language and communication, he nails his ideological colours to the mast, opposing 'old-fashioned' notions of authorship and interpretation. There is a strong polemic note to such literature.

Roland Barthes, in his famous piece 'The death of the Author', argued that if one disposes of 'the Author' in criticism, and interprets a text as if it were not 'authored', but rather constituted by a wealth of references to previous works, the result is a liberation of both the text and the reader:

> Once the Author is removed, the claim to decipher a text becomes quite futile. To give a text an Author is to impose a limit on that text, to furnish it with a final signified, to close the writing. Such a conception suits criticism very well, the latter then allotting itself the important task of discovering the Author (or its hypostases: society, history, psyche, liberty) beneath the work: when the Author has been found, the text is 'explained' – victory to the critic. Hence there is no surprise in the fact that, historically, the reign of the Author has also been that of the Critic, nor again in the fact that criticism (be it new) is today undermined along with the Author. In the multiplicity of writing, everything is to be *disentangled*, nothing *deciphered* ... (Barthes, 1977: 147; italic in original)

Barthes claims to be descriptive, observing the downfall of 'author-ship' within the realm of criticism and the consequences of this for interpretation. However, his egalitarian vision arises not so much from a desire to describe accurately and explain contemporary trends in criticism, but primarily from an ideological investment that compels him to challenge the foundations of criticism in the same way as other 'continental theorists' mentioned above. Barthes hopes to persuade the reader that potential freedom lies in the rejection of the 'Author' (with a capital A), whom he regards as a restrictive, repressive figure (he refers to him as the Author-God). The Author places limitations upon the reader's freedom in interpreting the text, and constrains potential alternative readings, thus closing down the text to multiple and disparate interpretations. In removing the Author, one simultaneously discards the overriding salience of the author's intentions, and both we (readers) and the text are then liberated from the limitations of what we believe the author to have meant; instead, we are free to interpret the work as we feel appropriate, with no reference to the author's existence or intentions. Interpretation becomes not a 'deciphering' of the author's intended and expressed meanings, but a 'disentangling' of the various references and meanings that are present in the text: these arise from the cultural environment in which the text was created[12] and include generic and intertextual references. The text itself is therefore opened up, treated as if it is endlessly available for meaningful (re)interpre-tation, for interpretation does not 'stop' when the author's project has been wholly illuminated, but continues as more and more meanings, references and 'quotations' are drawn out by the reader. This core argument has been influential in literary and cultural studies, and has held sway for many years.

Barthes's invective is attractive and subtle, and it has influenced many theorists based in cultural and literary studies. But his work repre-sents only one paradigm. Other theorists, based in Anglo-American analytical philosophy and aesthetics, have similarly argued against an interpretative approach that depends upon authorship. However, they have constructed their arguments very differently, as one would expect. They have sought for the *logical* flaws in such an approach. It is from these quarters that the most troubling, and most potentially damaging, challenge to 'authorship' in interpretation has come.

Analytical philosopher George Dickie narrows his target to the kind of criticism that refers to the author's intentions (rather than to the author's life and experiences): 'intentionalist criticism'. He argues that 'intentionalist criticism is fundamentally misguided' (Dickie, 1997b: 97), for to refer to the author's or artist's intentions is to refer to something outside the work one is dealing with, and indeed something that is often ultimately inaccessible. Dickie asserts that if we wish to interpret a work, we need only look at the work itself and what is expressed within it; whether its meanings were intended or not is irrelevant to the act of criticism, and if the author intended meanings that are not present in the work (through some failure of execution), then those meanings do not form part of an analysis of that work. Only that which is there, wholly present within the painting, the novel, the film or the television programme, matters for our interpretation.[13]

Colin Lyas deftly reiterates this simple but potentially devastating allegation made against intentionalist/authorial criticism in his summary of anti-intentionalist arguments:

> The upshot of this line of argument is that inferences from work to artist are irrelevant to criticism because they take us away from the study of the work to the study of some other thing. And inferences from what we know about the artist to what we can know about the work are unnecessary. If we want to know what properties the work has, we need only look at *it*. So references to the artist are either irrelevant or unnecessary. (Lyas, 1992: 383; italic in original)

The argument against intentionalist criticism offered here is both simple and sound, and Lyas is correct to imply that we must be sure of our motives and purposes in selecting our methodologies. If we intend to study a work, then we should guard against being distracted into studying something else, such as the author of that work. I shall return to the question of purposes later in this chapter.

Criticism involves both interpretation and evaluation, and analytical philosophers and aestheticians have also challenged the intentionalist evaluation of works.

Against the Author 2: problems with intentionalist or author-based evaluation
Further problems arise when the *evaluation* of artworks is carried out with reference to the 'author' and his intentions. The danger is that author-based evaluation ultimately judges the author rather than his or her work, so that intentionalist evaluation tends to assess the author's intentions rather than the final manifestation of those intentions – the work. There is a similar distracted movement away from the critic's proper and appropriate focus.

Lyas also observes that evaluative criticism founded on a clear vision of the individual author behind his or her texts is often 'back to front' in its procedure: 'we normally undertake genetic studies [that is, the study of the background and creation of a work] because we have already, and independently of such studies, recognized the merit of the text whose genesis we seek to explain. We study the genesis of, say, Wordsworth's poetry because we already know that it is great poetry. So it looks as if critical judgements of value precede and give a point to genetic studies of works of art' (Lyas, 1992: 383). Lyas thus exposes a curiosity in the methodology of intentionalist evaluation: it seems to reverse the usual order of critical judgement, in which an evaluation regarding the quality or value of a work is reached only after thoughtful attention to its composition and achievements.

What is valid criticism? The author, the work and critical practice

What status should the author have in the processes of interpretation and evaluation, then? What roles should author and work play in the act of criticism? Many of the arguments both for 'the author' and against him/her are rather black and white, offering an all-or-nothing choice between the author or the work (however the latter is defined). Since the 1970s, study of the work within its various contexts, and the response of the reader to it, has dominated literary and cultural studies, at the expense of author-based or intentionalist criticism.[14] Despite Barthes's jubilant declaration that this 'frees' the text and the reader, there have been some detrimental effects upon critical practice, as E. D. Hirsch elucidates. He explores the motives and intentions behind the 'heavy and largely victorious assault on the sensible belief that a text means what its author meant' (Hirsch, 1967: 108). Hirsch applauds the resulting shift of focus from the author to his work, which benefited critical practice and encouraged closer attention to the text,[15] but also offers a note of caution:

> That this shift towards exegesis has been desirable most critics would agree ... But the theory accompanied the exegetical movement for historical not logical reasons, since no logical necessity compels a critic to banish an author in order to analyze his text. Nevertheless, through its historical association with close exegesis, the theory has liberated much subtlety and intelligence. Unfortunately, it has also frequently encouraged wilful arbitrariness and extravagance in academic criticism and has been one very important cause of the prevailing scepticism which calls into doubt the possibility of objectively valid interpretation. (Hirsch, 1967: 109)

Thus while recognising the positive consequences of 'banishing' the author from criticism, Hirsch also observes that the action led to the prevailing contemporary state of pluralist relativism, which endows all interpretations with equal weight and significance and disallows the idea that there are valid and invalid interpretations. At its most extreme, such a position proclaims that a text can mean anything one would like it to mean. So the move away from authorial authority over a text's meanings opened up alternative interpretation, but offset against this benefit was the disadvantage that 'once the author had been ruthlessly banished as the determiner of his text's meaning, it very gradually appeared that no adequate principle existed for judging the validity of an interpretation' (Hirsch, 1967: 109–10), and that the balance of power shifted towards the critic or 'reader',[16] with each person's response, interpretation and evaluation being accepted as equally valid.

In practice, this degree of pluralist relativism often disintegrates into a free-for-all that prevents the individual from exercising his or her capacity for discrimination and judgement (and is thus, ironically, disempowering). Why should you, the reader, accept my interpretations of Davies's work, especially if they happen to contradict your own feelings and responses? Surely that would be to undermine your freedom to exercise your own critical judgement? Some method for determining the validity and viability of different interpretations is vital; below, I propose three features that might allow one to distinguish a reasonable and justifiable interpretation.

Determinacy and detail

It is more likely that an interpretative claim will be accepted as valid if the reader is able to return to the text in question and seek out the details referred to for him- or herself. In acknowledging that this 'checking procedure' is possible, one is accepting that there is some determinacy within the text. The concrete details of the text may be interpreted and reinterpreted in disparate ways, but those details remain the same, and place necessary limitations upon alternative readings. An interpretative claim that seems to contradict the evidence before one's eyes is less valid than another one that seems to comply with those details.[17] E. D. Hirsch defines determinacy as 'self-identity of meaning'; for now, we may regard it more loosely as being that aspect of its being that places limitations upon what a signifier (a word, an image, a sound, a gesture) might mean. This certainly does not mean that a signifier is precise or univocal; it is likely to be ambiguous and potentially rich in alternative possible meanings. However, there are boundaries to its conceivable meanings. Interpretation is a process by which one reasonable, justifiable determinate verbal meaning is proffered. A convincing, legitimate 'reading' of a text contains references to concrete details in the text, which is why close textual analyses of particular aspects of Davies's programmes are central to this book.

Awareness of form and context

A valid interpretation also exhibits an awareness of the locus of a signifier within a particular formal context (this might include genre and register). In Chapter 6, I offer an interpretation of the opening lines of Boris Pasternak's novel *Doctor Zhivago*. I do not claim that this meaning is the 'correct' one, but I do claim that it tallies with concrete details of the sentence and, further, it is also offered with an awareness of 'form'. *Doctor Zhivago* is a work of literature, and it is therefore fair to assume that some of the sentences within it will make both literal and metaphorical references; it is reasonable to read it figuratively. Pasternak was aware that the form he chose permitted, and was likely to elicit, certain kinds of responses and particular kinds of reading. Through its specific formal characteristics, the text sustains a level of determinacy, and governs the validity of my reading. One is free to wilfully 'misinterpret' a text, choosing to see irony when all evidence suggests sincerity, for example, but in this case one must acknowledge that the interpretation is deliberately ignoring (or disputing) the determinacy of the text.

Context is similarly vital to the delimitation of reasonable interpretations. While driving, I may choose to read a road sign metaphorically (e.g. 'Dead End'), but that would be to wilfully ignore or deny its form, context and purpose. It would also be to ignore the intentions of the person who placed the sign there, for in its present context he or she intended me to take it literally, as describing a particular road feature.[18] A valid interpretation displays sensitivity to a work's 'formal context', attributing to it reasonable or probable meanings, given the creator's awareness of this formal context and of how the audience is likely to respond. An awareness of form must also underlie valid evaluation, for a critical judgement must be sensitive to the framework and limitations of a work, and the expectations that both creator and audience bring to it. In this book, then, texts are considered within their artistic and cultural contexts, taking into account their formal and generic situations.

Embodied intentions

Interpretations are valid if they respect the determinacy of text, and its form, context and purpose, as described above. This moves us away from the tricky matter of validating interpretations with reference to the author and his intentions. However, we were necessarily drawn back to authorial intentions to a limited extent, above, when referring to the author's awareness of the formal context of his work and the audience's potential expectations/responses, so some clarification is necessary on this point. This book does not assume, especially given the collaborative nature of television production, that Davies's intentions are *necessary components* in the interpretation of his work, nor that his intentions were fully realised in it; similarly, the book recognises that meanings are present in 'Davies's work' that were intended by others, or not at all intended. As Jeremy Hawthorn notes, 'when we move from single-author texts [such as books] to texts with multiple authors, or to the performance arts, then the issue of authorial intention becomes even more complex' (Hawthorn, 1987: 80). What this book explores, then, is only the *embodied intentions*[19] – the ideas, thoughts, beliefs, images that actually made it onto the screen and into the final cut. In this way, the work, not its author, is our starting point and our primary focus.

An awareness of a text's determinacy, its formal context, purpose(s) and embodied intentions helps us to offer valid interpretations and evaluations, and to sustain the correct balance between author and work. These principles underlie the criticism offered in this book.

Davies and his work: finding a balance

It is clear that some of the material contained within this chapter might pose considerable challenges for the kind of project undertaken in this book, with its dual focus: it attempts to offer both a critical overview of the work of Davies and an insight into Davies as 'author' of his work. Yet even in simpler cases of authorship (the authorship of a novel, the artist of a painting), the theoretical challenges to author-based and intentionalist criticism pose a problem for the kind of criticism contained herein. The latter project problematises the former. If this book is to pursue its twin emphases (a critical review of Davies's work and an exploration of (his) authorship), it is vital that the right emphases are placed upon the 'author', Davies on the one hand, and his work on the other.

M. H. Abrams outlines three potential 'levels' of an author-based approach to criticism:

> We may profitably distinguish the level at which a critic pursues the con-nection between art and temperament, whether his aim is explanatory, biographical, or appreciative. First, a literary product may be taken to reflect the powers, faculties, and skill of its producer ... On the next level, there is held to be a particularity in the style, or general cast of language, which serves as an index to the particularity of its author's cast of mind. But on the third level, the style structure, and subject matter of literature are said to incorporate the most persistent, dynamic elements of an individual mind; the basic dispositions, interests, desires, preferences, and aversions which give continuity and coherence to a personality. (Abrams, 1953: 20)

This book explores Davies's relationship with his work at the first and second levels, but it originates wholly from an interest in and appreciation of the work, not the man. This is why it does not extend to Abram's third level, which seems to illuminate the personality of an author as much as his work, and which regards the artist and his work as indivisible. I make references to Davies in order to understand his oeuvre better, not the other way around. With regards to interpretation, this book does not propose Davies as the means of deciphering his texts, but it does suggest that to give a full account of his work involves considering his authorship alongside other influences. As Lyas states, 'aspects of the artist's character and intelligence may be visible in a work ... consequently, we cannot have given a full account of that work if we do not include references to those of its aspects' (Lyas, 1992: 388–9).[20] Davies's work is understood here not as entirely or simply an encapsulation of his individual expression, but as individually inflected and expressive.

This book explores individual texts and the continuities and connections in an oeuvre, recognising Davies as one, vital cause of these, though not the only one. The purpose of this is to position each programme within the oeuvre, given the importance of this context to its genesis, and to assess each text's significance and achievements. In the chapters to follow, 'theory' is rarely employed, with the programmes themselves taking centre stage. In a sense, the criticism undertaken herein is more text-centred than author-centred, to use Bonnycastle's terms, but this excludes neither a consideration of Davies's perceptible impact upon the text, nor an awareness of other factors influencing the work.

In attempting to discover authorial traits in Davies's work, I begin by seeking aspects of his 'world view': the ideas, thoughts, beliefs, and affiliations that determine his choice of subject matter and his presentation of the material.[21] I then move on to consider the more diffuse notion of 'voice', considering authorial voice amongst other kinds. Finally, I proceed to propose a 'sensibility' – a more obscure and subtle conceptualisation of authorial influence within a text. All three elements can be regarded as constituting an authorial signature that appears in all Davies's work, whether it be original or adapted. The movement from world view to voice to sensibility responds to developments in Davies's work, and thus implies a progression within his oeuvre and the development of a stronger, yet more subtly defined, authorial voice.

These authorial elements will be sought by close attention to details of particular texts, and in this sense at least, this book draws upon auteurist principles – as John Caughie puts it, a consistent personality behind the work must 'be sought out, discovered by a process of analysis and attention to a number of films [or programmes]' (Caughie, 1981a: 11). In the auteurist paradigm, themes and particularly style were very important, because many directors working within a studio system had little control over the story they were provided with, so it was reasonable to focus upon those aspects over which they had clearer authority (Caughie, 1981a: 11–12). In the case of a television writer like Davies, elements of content and story, including characterisation, are the most clearly relevant features, yet I shall also pay attention to theme and style, especially when I consider voice and sensibility, as the increasing expressiveness of the style of his programmes reveal a concerted effort on the part of both Davies and his directors to create a strong authorial voice for the former. I will not gloss over the problems inherent in regarding stylistic (directorial) elements of the programmes as part of Davies's authorial signature, though; instead I shall consider how the challenges and difficulties of collaboration are addressed by, and indeed have proved stimulating to, Davies. Similarly, my attention to Davies's authorship will not preclude or override references to other factors that influence the texts, such as institutional, artistic and cultural (including generic and televisual) contexts, and indeed the programmes' adaptive contexts, where applicable.

Purposes and aims of this study

Why pursue the authorship connection in relation to Davies's work here? Why undertake a study that requires such sensitive balances and emphases to be sustained within it?

First, a consideration of 'authorship' brings some benefits to the process of critical practice. Classifying the programmes discussed herein as 'Davies's work' is, at one level, merely a convenient way of delimiting a group of texts in order to explore a range of much loved and admired television programmes. Additionally, though, by exploring the limitations of Davies's authorial role, the book highlights details of television production and television history, and reveals the construction and 'promotion' of 'authorship' within television. And in seeking out traces of Davies's authorship, this project pays close attention to the composition and achievement of particular television texts, thus promoting critical appreciation and evaluation.

Second, this book offers an implicit but critically engaged reflection upon concepts and theories of authorship, exploring how authorship has been constituted and understood within the televisual context, and examining how one famous writer has developed an authorial signature within the medium.

A note about authorship and adaptation

The nature of Davies's work challenges pre-theoretical notions of authorship, not just through its eclecticism but also through its heavy reliance upon adaptation. Brian McFarlane, stressing the vital importance of the screenwriter in the process of literature–screen adaptation, writes:

> The issue of *authorship*, always complex in film, is especially so in relation to the film version of a literary work. Not only will the directorial signature inscribe itself with varying degrees of forcefulness on adapted material; not only will the spectre of the novel's author, especially in the case of the classic or best-selling novel, hover over the spectator and critic's reading of the film; also, the status of the author(s) of the screenplay will intervene between the former two. (Brian McFarlane, 1996: 35; italic in original)

As we will see, a huge proportion of Davies's work is adapted from other sources (from classic and popular novels, short stories, plays, and so on). Adaptation challenges the traditional image of a unique individual author whose work is original and innovative, for adaptation, by definition, is the re-presentation of someone else's work, in another medium.

Further problems for critical evaluation are posed by adaptation. In a previous work,[22] I proposed that adaptations are frequently judged on the basis of 'fidelity to intention twice removed': that is, the adapter's intentions are regarded as limited to his/her intention to faithfully adapt, and the source novel's author is posited as the intentional author behind the adaptation. Dickie astutely summarises the intentionalist's problems when evaluating performed and visual arts, especially 'performances' of pre-existing texts such as playscripts and musical scores. His comments are readily applicable to the case of a screen adaptation of a literary source and the typical responses of critics who are concerned with 'fidelity' to the original: 'if something is omitted [from the performance], then the intention of the [source's] artist is knowingly flouted by the performer (director, composer, arranger, i.e., whoever has the responsibility for the performance). In this case, the intentionalist critic feels that violence has been done to the work of art' (Dickie, 1997b: 104). Dickie's description accurately captures the sense of 'violation' that intentionalist critics feel when they watch an adaptation of *Emma* that appears to transgress Jane Austen's intentions. Yet the intentionalist approach is logically flawed in this instance, as Dickie persuasively argues:

But what of it? If a critic is concerned with the description, interpretation, or evaluation of the performance of a work, what difference does
it make that the performance the critic experiences and talks about is
derived by altering an existing work? The critic can still explain and
evaluate the performance he or she has experienced ... The point is that
the critic must talk about and evaluate the performance work. (Dickie,
1997b: 104)

This book similarly perceives that the source text author's intentions
have no reasonable bearing upon the analysis and evaluation of an adaptation, for the adaptation is an independent and 'original' work of art (a
performance work)[23] which must be judged according to its own criteria.

Powerful, instinctive notions about art and authorship are evoked by
adaptation, which explains why critical reception of Davies's adaptations is sometimes heated and intense, with fidelity to a much loved
source text and its author being regarded as more important than the
artistic innovation and creativity of Davies and the director. This book
puts aside the 'fidelity' paradigm and assesses Davies's adaptations on
the same terms as his original work, seeking profound, subtle, coherent, innovative and engaging television drama. However, it also
includes some references to the source novels, and given my previous
rejection of the comparative approach (in which adaptations are compared with and judged in relation to their source novels) this requires a
little clarification.

This book does not evaluate or interpret Davies's adaptations in
comparison with the source texts. When *Vanity Fair* is discussed, some
time is spent on determining key features of the source novel, before the
adaptation is explored. The aim is not to see whether the adaptation has
'succeeded' in faithfully representing the source novel. In fact, the
analysis of the adaptation could feasibly stand alone, without the
analysis of the source novel. However, the references to the source text
are useful for highlighting and elucidating conceptual and stylistic
issues that will be explored in the adaptation.

Indeed, underlying this book is a belief that studying television
adaptations can enrich our understanding of television as an art form.
When we make tentative but detailed comparisons between texts in
different media, we are moved to notice features of each medium that
distinguish them from one another. This is to exploit the particularity of
adaptations, which by their very existence draw attention to the unique
features of two media – those features that distinguish them from one
another and constitute their artistic potential. Thus the study of
adaptation(s) may be employed as a tool in the exploration of the
medium specificity of television.

Notes

1 This refers to Roland Barthes's famous essay 'The death of the Author', quoted later in the chapter (Barthes, 1968).

2 The French term 'auteur' usefully combines these meanings. In this book, I have chosen to use the term 'author', but I intend this word also to imply 'artist'. Broadly, I mean the originator – the person who has the clearest artistic authority over the text and the greatest claim over its material.

3 John Caughie's reader *Theories of Authorship* (1981) includes a number of the most important essays in the auteurist paradigm. A recent succinct and straightforward analysis of authorship and film is offered ·in Peter Lehman and William Luhr's *Thinking about Movies* (2003: 77–88).

4 The auteurists did not wish to argue that all films were good and worthy of the status of art, but rather that some films were good and that film was an art. There is some lack of clarity over how these two claims interrelate: it is either being claimed that all films are art (whether good or bad art) or, less logically (but more likely), that only films with auteurs can be classified as art.

5 Here, I make a vital distinction between 'work' and 'text', in keeping with my definition of these in my previous work (Cardwell, 2002: 26). Elsewhere in this book, I use the term 'work' in a much more imprecise and colloquial sense, frequently referring to 'Davies's work'; conceptually speaking, I really mean to refer to 'Davies's texts', but have chosen to make use of the more informal sense of the word 'work', given that the work/text distinction is not crucial to this particular project (beyond this specific instance).

6 Another reason why the pile of bricks in the Tate is considered art is, broadly speaking, because it is recognised to be art by art critics and the gallery-attending public – i.e. by the 'art world' or 'art circle' (the latter is Dickie's term – see his discussion of 'The institutional theory of art' (1997a)). Again, this definition of art implies nothing about its value, for it need not mean that a work is good – it may be poor art. The institutional theory simply illustrates that one of the ways that a work is recognised as art is that the 'art world' recognises behind it an individual artist with intentions that are related to the finished product (i.e. the work displays embodied traces of that person's intentions).

7 Some television authors are even more clearly 'in control' of their texts and take on the roles of both writer and director. Stephen Poliakoff is a good example of such an artist.

8 On most of Davies's projects, there is ordinarily a 'script editor', assigned by the production company, who offers comments and suggestions on the script as Davies develops it. However, the level of input from this individual is ultimately Davies's choice, as he expressed to me in an interview (21 February 2003).

9 This is not the place for the considerable conceptual work that needs to be done on the question of collaboration, control and authorship. However, other writers working within the analytical philosophy of film have begun this project; see e.g. Paisley Livingston (1997) and Berys Gaut (1997).

10 This intuitive connection is reinforced and explored in the work of some literary theorists. For a good overview of the subject, see Stein Haugom Olsen (1987).

11 For examples of attacks upon authorship from other paradigms, see Hirsch (1967: 108).

12 Viable meanings and interpretations are also considered to arise from the context in which the text is read and reread. This is implied in the following sentence in the text, in which it is stated that meaning continues to be available to successive readers.

13 I have necessarily had to abbreviate Dickie's argument here, and would refer

interested readers to the original essay (Dickie, 1997b).

14 In fact, more accurately, the response of the *reader* has dominated, so that even though the work might be thought to have gained its autonomy from its author, it still warrants less close attention than one might hope. The key point for us here, though, is the downgrading of the *author* within criticism.

15 Though as I have noted, in many cases the shift away from the author failed to have the beneficial effect of enhancing close analysis; instead, the focus shifted to the work's context and to ideological concerns.

16 This altered the hierarchy noted (hoped for) by Barthes, in which the author and critic were equally powerful.

17 A claim that proffers as evidence for its validity textual details that are *indeterminate* is not necessarily invalid; it simply requires additional proof of some form in order to persuade the reader. It is clear that the criterion proposed here does not help the critic in proffering other kinds of claims about the work, for example claims about the subconscious motives of the author.

18 I refer to a road sign under normal circumstances here. Of course, the situation is changed if the sign is part of an artwork, such as the road signs in Davies's *A Very Peculiar Practice*, which harbour metaphorical as well as literal significance, and are intended to be read on a second, figurative level.

19 In referring to embodied intentions, I am drawing upon Gregory Currie's ideas (Currie, 1995a). Currie concurs with intentional explanations that recognise the fundamental importance of intention to the constitution of an artwork. His elucidation of embodied intentions clarifies the relationship of authorial intentions to the finished artwork and subsequent interpretation. Currie insists that we understand a story as 'told' (1995: 248), and we recognise that what is present on the screen is there primarily because it was intended; hence a notion of 'intention' has some explanatory power. Those meanings that are commonly referred to as 'implicit' are actually meanings that we perceive as being intended by the author; they are placed there for us to discover and unravel. Interpretation is thus intentional explanation (1995a: 226, 249, 258). Currie insists that his is not a version of auteur theory (1995a: 258), but is instead a version of 'Implied Author Intentionalism' (245).

20 Lyas argues, furthermore, that we cannot simply separate out the artist from his or her work, for when we cite qualities like 'perceptiveness' in a work, 'the best answer is that we are referring to a quality displayed by the artist in the work' (Lyas, 1992: 387). He confirms that to make such an observation is not to be distracted into a commentary about the author, but is still to be concerned with the work: if we claim a work is 'witty', we are not saying the person is witty, but that he or she displayed 'wittiness' then and there (1992: 388).

21 The term 'world view' is taken from Helen Stoddart (1995: 40). However, the world view to which Stoddart refers is typically to be found in a director's visual style – his or her way of 'looking at' the world. Thus the meaning is slightly different and broader here, moving beyond visual perception to incorporate Davies's attitude towards the world, his ideas, affiliations and prejudices.

22 See Cardwell, 2002.

23 I am strongly implying that Davies ought to be considered as the (an) author of the 'performance work' – that is, the finished television programme – and not just of the screenplay. Part of the reason for such an assertion is that the screenplay cannot straightforwardly be regarded as a completed artwork in its own right, for it serves an ancillary function, preceding the actual work (the programme). Davies himself concurs in this view; indeed his belief in the television text as the finished work, and the screenplay as only a stage in the process of the work's creation, is highlighted by his practice of disposing of each of his screenplays once the programme has been made.

Making his mark: Davies's non-adapted ('original') television work

Davies has written a large number of 'original',[1] non-adapted television screenplays, particularly during the earlier years of his career. These programmes form the focus of this chapter, which simultaneously draws upon some of the basic, commonplace and pre-theoretical (intuitive) notions of authorship introduced previously. It explores the conceit that there are particular features that denote authorship and that constitute a kind of authorial signature. These include: an appropriate level of authorial control over the finished text or artwork, so that the essential content of the final text, and its subtleties, are determined by a singular 'author'; the presence of perceptible elements of individual expression; and some kind of discernible continuity (and possibly progression) across an oeuvre, which indicates the existence of an enduring personality behind the work. This chapter investigates whether such fundamental notions of authorship are indeed relevant to Davies's television oeuvre. Bearing in mind the importance of continuity to the idea of authorial 'signature', this chapter seeks recurrences, movements and cycles within the works, isolating motifs of theme, characterisation and style. Implicitly drawing upon a notion of artistic/authorial progression, it also considers whether the development of a keener and more accomplished artistic sensibility might be found across Davies's oeuvre (this project is necessarily continued in Chapters 4, 5 and 6).

Davies's writing is conceived of as establishing the framework for each programme, determining fundamental aspects such as story, plot and character, and suggesting boundaries for more complex elements such as pace, style and tone (these will be influenced by Davies's ordering of scenes, the register and style of his dialogue, his placement of characters within particular settings, and so on). Given that this chapter deals with the aspects of Davies's work that may be most straightforwardly and unproblematically attributed to him, the focus is primarily upon the 'content' of the programmes, including dialogue, story and characterisation (particularly characterisation through dialogue, rather than performance). There is some discussion of aspects of style, but this is limited; later chapters are much more concerned with matters such as style, genre, voice and tone, and will emphasise how Davies's vision is conveyed and enhanced by directing, camerawork, design, performance and so on.

In Davies's earlier, non-adapted work we see him establishing his concerns as a writer, presenting to the television audience his 'world view', and expressing his ideas, values, beliefs and personality. In his work for adults, these things are communicated almost entirely through the revelation and development of characters. Davies's work is primarily melodramatic in the sense of focusing upon individual characters and their interpersonal relationships, rather than upon social or historical problems. His work is not strongly politically motivated and does not claim to elucidate larger truths about society. However, Davies proffers a coherent and engaging liberal world view, which seeks to question accepted social norms and conventions, and which is keenly concerned with issues such as education, the role and status of the individual within the group or institution, and the impact of families and other groups upon the development and fulfilment of the individual. These concerns can be discerned even in his work for children.

Davies's television work for children: education, absurdity and excess

Davies has created much work for children, from television programmes to books to educational videos, and he has sustained his interest in children's work across his career. In a sense, his work for children creates a potential problem for the critic, especially in terms of evaluation. Children's television does not fit readily into accepted artistic categories; the perception is that it is designed either to entertain or to educate, and in serving these larger purposes it seems to fall outside the category of 'art'. Few auteurs specialise in work for children. Davies's long-standing commitment to children's television may imply to the critic that he is more entertainer than artist; it simultaneously broadens his oeuvre, suggesting a craftsman who will turn his hand to anything (a jack of all trades, and master of none). I would oppose such a view.

It may not seem vital to include a consideration of Davies's programmes for children in this book, but it is intriguing to see the connections that exist between this work and his writing for adults. In creating programmes for children, Davies was able to hone his skills as a storyteller; beyond that, his children's programmes establish the bare bones of his world view, and present thematic and stylistic concerns that are more fully developed in his work for adults.

Most of Davies's work for children relates closely in terms of content and theme to their everyday experiences, with many programmes being based around school and education. However, this goes beyond a desire to represent a familiar situation to his viewers, for Davies's work for both adults and children reveals a recurring concern with the issue of education. He repeatedly asks what constitutes a good education, and why it is important; in short, he challenges us to consider what education is (should be) for.

Educating Marmalade (1982)

Davies's popular Marmalade Atkins character first appeared in the 1980s, and evolved through a number of books, television series and subsequent novelisations.[2] The two longest running series were *Educating Marmalade* (1982) and *Marmalade at Work* (1984). The programmes starred Charlotte Coleman as the rebellious troublemaker, Marmalade. In *Educating Marmalade*, each episode relayed a doomed attempt to educate this obnoxious character within varied schools and systems; each time, Marmalade fought the system and won, and was expelled or 'freed' from the respective institution.

The narrative structure and characterisation of the programmes are designed with young viewers in mind. The episodes are only approximately fifteen minutes long, and are divided into short, engaging scenes, creating fragmented but simple storylines that attract and sustain the viewer's attention. Characterisation is exaggerated and stereotyped for comic effect, incorporating clear and demarcated 'types' of people: the first episode, 'Cringe Hill', includes a soft social worker; a snobby, posh family; vicious and stupid school bullies; and Marmalade's own dysfunctional family.

However, the humorous critique of educational methods within *Marmalade* is also of interest to adult viewers, so that both children and adults can engage with the programmes (as is the case with many of the most successful children's programmes). The range of diverse educational strategies that are experimented with in an attempt to curb Marmalade's anti-social behaviour are exaggerated and embellished to the point of absurd excess, but nevertheless engage with a number of conventional views regarding the roles of discipline and creativity in children's education, and the ideal content of that education.

It is not unusual to find children's programmes that defend and celebrate the freedom and creativity of the child against the apparently tyrannical discipline of adults, and Davies draws upon this tradition. In 'Marmalade at St. Cecilia's', a St Trinian's-style tale, our heroine manages to undermine the routine of a strict boarding school and frees its young residents from the Cinderella-like conditions they are kept in. Similarly, in 'Walkies', Marmalade is trained like a dog, rewarded for good behaviour and punished for bad, in a parody of behaviourist methods. Again, Marmalade subverts the system and wrests control from her trainer.

More unusually, though, the emphasis is reversed in 'The Convent of the Blessed Limit', in which Marmalade finds herself the subject of a new educational 'project', when the nuns return from a trendy teaching course full of new, progressive ideas. The threats of being locked in a cupboard or suffering violence from the baseball-bat-wielding nuns are abandoned as the sisters try out 'modern educational methods' and 'child-centred projects'. The result of course is a complete failure of discipline and Marmalade's expulsion.

The questions of what ought to be taught, and what education should prepare a child for, are also raised in an oblique way. In 'Marmalade at Eton', she is permitted to study 'boys' subjects', and learns practical and vocational skills of the kind advocated by some educational theorists as more 'useful' than 'book learning'. Using her new skills, Marmalade causes chaos, and is eventually expelled when she 'adapts' the school longboat so that it sinks during a race. Old-fashioned 'female' education is similarly lampooned in 'Marmalade in Venice', when some brave souls attempt, in vain, to communicate to the wayward girl the finer details of manners, deportment and etiquette.

Interestingly, none of the programmes ends in resolution, and Marmalade remains uneducable and uneducated. Davies raises the questions but does not suggest he is able to advocate any solutions. A similar ambivalence and open-endedness is combined with much greater complexity in his work for adults that touches upon similar topics (such as *Inappropriate Behaviour*, *A Very Peculiar Practice* and *To Serve Them All My Days*).

The Boot Street Band (1993)

In 1993, approximately one decade after *Marmalade*, Andrew Davies (and Steve Attridge) wrote *The Boot Street Band*, a serial for BBC2, which ran for two six-part series. This serial was aimed at slightly older children than those who watched *Marmalade*, and this was reflected in a more complex narrative structure and longer episodes (around twenty-five minutes each). Again, the serial offered pleasures for both adult and child viewers, combining a defence of children's autonomy and intelligence with a sharp critique of contemporary educational practice.

The children in the programme are depicted as superior to the adults who attempt to contain them, but unlike Marmalade they are not rebellious and destructive but capable, intelligent and mature. They are shown applying skills learned in their formal education to real-world problems in an enterprising way. When the protagonist, Mikala (Nadia Williams) arrives at Boot Street School for her first day, she is welcomed not by the teachers but by the schoolchildren, who refer to themselves as the 'management' and appear to be running the school. Mikala's observation that it 'must be a funny sort of school' is met with the response that 'It *is* a funny sort of school, but then again most schools are'. It transpires that the staff have disintegrated into confusion and madness, and that the children have taken over the asylum. They keep the school open, outwitting the system, faking classes and activity clubs to pass the School Inspection (and when that does not work, successfully bribing the School Inspector with threats to release photographs of him guzzling chocolate cream éclairs). Instead of attending ordinary classes, the children adeptly use their knowledge of mathematics, geography and foreign languages to run an international, environmentally friendly business.

As is clear, a level of absurdity is important to the programme's appeal. Davies has said, 'I still really like writing for children ... I like fantasy in children's stories and I tend to not like it as much in adult stories. I just think it goes so naturally and easily into kids' fiction' (Davies, quoted in O'Brien, 1996: 29). Fantastical elements are indeed more apparent in his work for young viewers. The excessive, cartoon qualities seen in *Marmalade*[3] are similarly present in *Boot Street*. One teacher is a life-size dog (a man in a dog costume); another teacher, Mikala is informed, left a class to get a rubber from the stationery cupboard six months ago, and ended up in Fiji.

Absurd elements are not employed simply in the service of humour; they also offer a critique, for both child and adult viewers, of contemporary government initiatives in education. The nominal Head, Mr Lear (Roland MacLeod), is discovered by Mikala in his office, surrounded by huge cardboard boxes stacked ceiling-high, containing copies of the National Curriculum. According to Mr Lear, they almost crushed his secretary, and she quit with a nervous breakdown: 'It's called the National Curriculum, and I think it will be the undoing of us all. Nobody can understand a word of it. The piles grow higher and higher every day. I think it is a plot, Mikala – a plot to turn all the trees of the world into textbooks. Poor innocent trees! What have they done to deserve it?' The children save the day, removing all the boxes and files to their 'National Curriculum recycling plant' and turning them into useful products: toilet rolls and comics. The commentary on the National Curriculum was timely: this was the year in which Ron Dearing was asked to review the curriculum after complaints from schools about its detrimental impact upon workloads, and in which teachers boycotted the first NC tests.[4] Contemporary educational jargon is also mocked: Deputy Head Mrs Springit (Linda Polan) fails in her attempt to go 'back to basics', and three bullies are re-classified by the teachers as having 'special needs' but otherwise remain a problem. (The other children deal with them more bluntly and successfully, making no allowances, manipulating them into playing a positive role within the school, and forcing them to comply with their 'rules'.)

Davies's concern with the subject of education and the values that it ought to convey to children continues into his work for adults. He addressed the issue in single plays including *Is That Your Body, Boy?* (1970), *A Martyr to the System* (1976), *Bavarian Night* (1981), and *Inappropriate Behaviour* (1986), and serials including *A Very Peculiar Practice* (1986, 1988) and the adaptation *To Serve Them All My Days* (1980).

Although a dominant theme, education is not the primary focus of all Davies's work for children. Nor has he written only 'entertainment' for that audience; he has also made educational and informative programmes that explore particular social and cultural issues. *Bill's New Frock* (1997), made for Channel Four Schools, is a half-hour programme that provokes school-based discussion about gendered behaviour and identity.[5] Strictly an adaptation (but included in this chapter because of its target audience of schoolchildren), this programme was based on a book by Anne Fine. Bill (Daniel Lee) wakes one morning to find that he has changed gender (though he looks the same to the viewers), and he experiences a day in the life of a girl. His mother dresses him in a hideous frilly pink dress, and entreats him to get involved in the household and caring tasks he usually avoids; his teacher is appalled by the messy, slapdash presentation of his work, when these flaws are ordinarily overlooked; and he is not allowed to take part in his beloved football. Children are encouraged to question why those around Bill treat him differently when he feels exactly the same as he did, and has the same fundamental identity, as when he was a boy. The 'what if?' scenario is not preachy or proselytising, but engages children's interest through humour and absurdity, as well as eliciting imaginative, sympathetic engagement for the protagonist's predicament. This technique for provoking discussion about larger social and cultural issues without moralising respects children's ability to consider arguments that pertain to their lives in a reflective way, and echoes Davies's tongue-in-cheek jibe to Mary Whitehouse supporters at the start of each *Marmalade* episode: there is a 'Bad Girl Warning', complete with flashing lights and siren, notifying children that they ought not to mimic the behaviour they see in the programme. Episode three takes this further, with the additional, mocking voice-over, chiding young viewers, 'We've been getting reports from all over the country that girls have been watching this programme and going Bad.'

Bill's New Frock also intimates Davies's interest in playing roles, and the limitations of the roles which we are forced to play in social situations, and which are determined by factors such as age, gender and class. This is a concern that is fully developed in his other work, such as in the adaptations *To Serve Them All My Days* (1980), *Moll Flanders* (1996), *Vanity Fair* (1998) and *Othello* (2000), all of which explore role-playing and performance, and the effect of situation(s) upon characters' behaviour.

Single plays and short serials: characters and situations

Like many other screenwriters who began writing in the 1960s, Davies was able to create a number of works for dedicated single-play slots on the BBC, such as 'The Wednesday Play', 'BBC Playhouse', and later 'Screen One' and 'Screen Two'.[6] Some of these plays, such as his first, *Who's Going to Take Me On?* (1967), a 'Wednesday Play' about a young girl seeking work in a factory, have since been wiped and are unavailable for viewing (even Davies himself does not hold copies of them all), which makes an exploration of this early work rather more difficult.[7] However, the texts that are available to researchers[8] convey a strong sense of Davies's early artistic experimentation and development.

The institutional framework that allowed for the single play to flourish was invaluable to young writers like Davies, especially because the single play placed a huge emphasis upon the authorship of the screenwriter, unproblematically attributing all of Davies's plays to him.[9] There was also an expectation, relatedly, of formal innovation as a marker of the individual expression of the author. All this was to the advantage of the writer.

The revelation of character and situation

In his Huw Wheldon lecture to the Royal Television Society in 1994, Davies quoted Arthur Miller on the subject of 'tragic heroes': 'What moves us most about the tragic hero is not so much his greatness but that he allows himself to be *wholly known*' (Davies, 1994; his emphasis). Indeed, it is the careful revelation of character – the process by which each character becomes 'wholly known' – that is perhaps the most noticeable feature of Davies's early non-adapted work, and it is this that distinguishes his work for adults from that produced for children. Davies is clear that his characters are the driving emotional force within his dramas, and that they form his most obvious and powerful connection to his work: 'You just have to love and identify with your central characters and inhabit them completely. That's really all I can say' (Davies, quoted in Ransome, 2000: 19). As a result, Davies's work is 'personal' rather than socio-political in emphasis; he is primarily concerned with individuals and their interpersonal, intimate relationships. In later non-adapted work, a greater interest in the effect of situation and environment upon characters is evident, broadening the scope of his work to consider the impact of social mores and expectations upon individuals' behaviour and relationships.

In early programmes, it is Davies's dialogue that achieves the revelation of character, gradually exposing the workings of an individual's mind, and giving the viewers an insight into his behaviour. A classic example of this can be found in the character of PE teacher Carstairs (Ron Moody) in *Is That Your Body, Boy?* (1970), Davies's earliest surviving single play, produced for 'Thirty Minute Theatre'. Carstairs, 59 years old, is a PE teacher on the verge of involuntary retirement, who seems obsessed with controlling himself and those around him. He is harsh and unyielding, even sadistic, in his punishment of four young pupils caught scrawling graffiti on the ceiling of the gym. Davies, exploiting the temporal characteristics of television, uses his half-hour slot to present the boys' half-hour detention in real time. Carstairs forces the boys to stand on tiptoes for the full thirty minutes, with the threat of 'the stick' if they fail: three of them, including the fat Penrose (Robert Yetzes) to whom the title refers, founder; one boy, Miller (Keith Skinner), succeeds and earns Carstairs' respect.[10] Alone with this last solitary pupil, Carstairs begins to talk about his life and situation, and reveals his character, his hopes and fears, and his subconscious motivations (figure 1). We learn that he does not want to retire, that he lives in a rented furnished room, not the house he once inhabited, and that his old dog, Prince, recently died. He is a man who has lost almost everything, despite his attempts to control the direction and details of his life. He detests 'soft bodies and soft minds', and values control as an old-fashioned and reliable virtue. Speaking of trendy new PE lessons, he sneers derisively at the new buzzwords 'flexibility and movement',

1 *Is That Your Body, Boy?* (1970): Carstairs opens up to Miller

spitting them out as if they leave a sour taste in his mouth. The things he dislikes he dismisses as 'immaterial' or 'insignificant'; it seems he wishes to exclude any uncontrolled or uncontrollable experience from his world.

Above all, Carstairs fears letting go, and represses his instinctive desire to do so. Most moving is his tale of running on the moors as a child. Having taken up running to improve his strength and fitness, he set himself the goal of jumping a stream at the end of his long cross-country route. The first time he attempted this feat, he slipped and fell backwards, and lay in the stream, with the cold water washing over him. At that moment that he realised he did not want to get up, and he lay there, feeling the water move around him, and staring at the sky. The powerful, overwhelming feelings of tranquillity and release, of letting go, that this experience aroused in him led him, he claims, to realise the dangers of being distracted from the goals of control, strength and resilience. Carstairs feared his own desire to give up, give in, and enjoy such moments, terming them 'a surrender of the will'. The next time he ran, he jumped the stream; he proudly boasts that he has done so every time since. The symbolic poignancy of this tale offers a careful and engaging revelation of a fearful and unfulfilled character.

Davies's dialogue carries almost all the weight in this programme, with little action or 'plot' to distract us from the revelation of character. It is not only the content of Carstairs' speech that is expressive, but also its style. His vocabulary is simple, his diction precise and clipped, and his speech stylised and non-naturalistic, employing excessive repetition (he repeats many words, phrases, and sentences more than once). This is expressive of the character, who wishes to assert his views categorically, with no room for argument, in order to convince not just those around him but also himself. Beyond this, repetition heightens the viewer's awareness of what is being said, increasing his/her level of attention to particular words, phrases and sentences, so that he/she is encouraged to 'read' the dialogue more carefully, at a figurative level.[11]

A *Martyr to the System* (1976) traces a similar trajectory to that utilised in *Is That Your Body, Boy?*: the protagonist, a radical student on teaching practice in a comprehensive school, is gradually revealed to be not so much a martyr but 'a dangerous user of people'.[12] In these early programmes, Davies tends to focus upon a singular protagonist, whose inner life is exposed piece by piece. This is true, for example, of *Grace* (1975), which presents a middle-aged man who takes up tap dancing and falls in love with his dance teacher, and of *No Good Unless It Hurts* (1973), which focuses on a female university student described by Davies as an 'Amazon', and her exploits on the basketball court. Interestingly, these programmes arose directly out of Davies's own experiences: *Grace* was written because Davies 'had a little craze on tap myself around that time'; *No Good* was based upon a student he taught at Warwick; the protagonist in *Martyr* professes ideas that Davies contemporarily 'identified with'.[13] This might suggest that a 'biographical approach' to the work is justified – that knowledge of Davies's life and experiences can contribute to our interpretations of the programmes. This issue is considered in the discussion of *Bavarian Night* that follows later in this chapter.

Davies's interest in the revelation of character is also evident in the biographical programmes he created, based on 'real people', actual historical figures whom we think we already know or who have been overlooked by history. His short serial *Eleanor Marx* (1977) was inspired by the book *The Life of Eleanor Marx 1855–1898*, by C. Tsuzuki.[14] The serial traces the life of Karl Marx's daughter Eleanor (Jennie Stoller), who was deeply involved in her father's work, committed to his cause, and overwhelmed (and overshadowed) by his great presence. The first episode is titled 'Tussy', the family name bestowed upon Eleanor, implying an intimate portrait of the woman within the context of her family. Indeed, although this episode covers her youth in her family home, and thus includes depictions of Marx (Lee Montague), his work, his tribulations, and his friendship with Engels (Nigel Hawthorne), it also examines the relationship between father and daughter, and exposes the sacrifices Eleanor made for the sake of her father's project. The programme views Marx through the eyes of his daughter. Eleanor, a person generally (and understandably) overlooked by history in favour of her father, is revealed here, and is given a voice[15] in a programme which offers a fresh reflection upon her life and that of Marx. Davies's later single play *Renoir, My Father* (1978), a 'Play of the Week', a text that has unfortunately been wiped, was based upon Claude Renoir's memoir of his father, Auguste Renoir, offering an affectionate and intimate portrait of the artist. Other biographical programmes by Davies include *Prizewinner Cowboy in the White House* (1977), which explored the political career of Ted Roosevelt; *Happy in War* (1977), based on the life of Edith Cavell; the experimental *Fearless Frank* (1978), about popular novelist and bon viveur Frank Harris; and the recent *Boudicca* (2003), which was inspired by a small excerpt from Tacitus's account.

While Davies's characters are always necessarily located within and affected by particular situations, the situations themselves (the historical, social and political contexts) are rarely the direct focus of his work. In *A Private Life* (1988), he was loyal to his customary emphasis upon characters, but placed them within a very particular, loaded environment, and developed a revelation of their situation through his exploration of their interpersonal relationships. In this case, then, Davies reveals a situation that we think we know, through his characters.

A Private Life is based on a true story. Set in South Africa during the time of apartheid, it explores the relationship of white policeman Jack Dupont (Bill Flynn) and his partner, Stella Kleurley (Jan Cilliers), who, being of mixed race, is designated 'coloured' shortly after they meet. Her attempts to get re-classified fail, and the programme investigates the implications of this within a society that condemns miscegenation and outlaws mixed marriages. Interestingly, while the problems of (re-)classification and prohibition of mixed relationships affect Jack and Stella, the programme focuses primarily upon the effect of the situation upon their son, Paul (Kevin Smith). While Jack and Stella manage to get by, living in a mixed neighbourhood in relative anonymity and safety, Paul's life choices are profoundly limited due to his mother's classification. He is unable to marry his girlfriend, Andrea (Joanna Weinberg), who is white, and he resents his mother for her involuntary role in keeping them apart. Eventually Paul is driven into despair by his insoluble situation and commits suicide; his girlfriend is compelled to abort their child because its father is 'coloured'. After Paul's death, Stella is finally re-classified, and is able to marry Jack, but this comes too late to save her son's life.

The details of life under apartheid are made significant in terms of their effect upon individuals and their relationships, so that broader political critique is rejected in favour of an intimate, persuasive appeal to the liberal values Davies holds dear. Impressively, the programme avoids presenting a simple tale of repression by the state, and instead shows how apartheid and its prejudices insinuate themselves into the most intimate relationships, such as that between parent and child. Stella is forced into a situation in which she unwillingly hinders her son's chances for happiness; Paul feels compelled to reject his racially blurred origins and seek a wholly white identity, but is prevented from doing so. The effect is not to downplay the larger socio-political framework but to reveal its enormous, profound, and enduring impact upon the everyday lives of ordinary people. The opening titles present this larger framework in legal terms, listing the pertinent Acts passed in the 1950s (Population Registration Act, Group Areas Act, Prohibition of Mixed Marriage Act, Immorality Amendment Act), but the sudden and sustained shift of focus to 'melodrama' emphasises that this framework does not exist in isolation from the lives of individuals.

In his early work, then, Davies presents the revelation of characters within specific situations, exploring the impact of the situations upon the characters, but maintaining a focus on the individuals and their relationships (the emphasis is upon a revelation of character, or of situation through character, rather than of situation more broadly). Most of this work is centred upon one or a small number of protagonists, and expresses the subjectivity and psychology of these protagonists primarily through dialogue.

The revelation of self: Davies's world view

Through his choice of subjects and material, one can infer something about Davies's world view, and so one can regard his work as expressive of him in this basic sense. He is clearly concerned with individuals, their subjectivities, psychology and interpersonal relationships. Although not a political animal, Davies is committed to a liberal world view that questions restrictive ideological tenets and simplistic notions of identity, social roles and mores. Davies's world view is also a humanist one. He prioritises the needs and objectives of the individual over those of the state: he values people over institutions and systems, lauding the iconoclast and the rebel, and rejecting the unthinking conformist. However, he is keenly aware of the impact of a person's situation upon his or her behaviour, and he also conceives of the importance of communality, of shaping and perpetuating those institutions that manifest shared, liberal values, such as the education system. Central to Davies's perspective is an awareness of the importance of education as a vital engine of progress; relatedly, he promotes an interrogatory attitude to its purposes, content and ideals.

Most of the key elements of this world view are encapsulated in his single play *Bavarian Night* (1981), in which Davies also expresses his experiences and beliefs more directly, through the characters' dialogue, and through his protagonist in particular.

Bavarian Night *(1981): character, situation and self-expression*
This single play examines familiar themes of the function of education;
the role and status of the individual within a group or institution; the
impact of situation and environment upon character; the importance of
interpersonal (especially sexual) relationships; and the value of non-
conformism and individuality. It also offers an insight into Davies's
more specific personal experiences, as it reflects upon the task of writing
as a creative and parasitic endeavour. There is thus a higher level of
introspection present within the text than we have seen in previous
examples.

Bavarian Night was produced for the 'Play for Today' slot, and
typically credits Davies as the 'author' (only his name and the title
appear in the opening credits). Joe Pike (Bob Peck), a writer, is married
to Alice Pike (Sarah Badel), and they have two young children, Carl and
Florence. Joe and Alice are invited to attend a school fund-raising
evening – a themed 'Bavarian night' at which there is to be traditional
Bavarian dancing, food and beer, and at which the new school uniform
will be on display. The two attend with their friends Jim (Malcolm
Terris) and Arlene (Arwen Holm); over the course of the evening it is
revealed that Joe is having an affair with Arlene, and that underneath
the veneer of politeness the relationships between these four friends are
strained and difficult.

The programme proffers a strong critique of conformism, advocating in its place anti-authoritarianism and a version of rebellious anarchy.
The new school uniform, displayed on mannequins, is regarded by the
protagonists as a symbol of enforced and unnecessary conformity that
will compel children to comply with an externally established norm.
Davies's dialogue extends the significance of the uniform beyond its
sartorial implications. The Headmaster, Mr Fosil, gazes upon the
mannequins and sighs, 'Wouldn't life be simple if they were all like
that?' Both his question and the reply offered by a passing colleague,
'They will be', refer explicitly to the uniform and implicitly to the
dummies/children. Later, in an apparently radical, libertarian gesture,
the mannequins are destroyed, as the drunken, rowdy parents rebel and
revolt, creating chaos out of the imposed order of the school.

Yet the protagonists fail to realise that their participation in extreme
forms of group behaviour such as this is a version of the conformism
they condemn.[16] In particular, the programme displays the insidious,
sinister capacity for the hoard to overwhelm and crush the individual.
Alice, who is a reluctant participant in the evening's events, seems
surprised at her own behaviour as she finds herself joining in with yet
another chorus of the inane drinking song that the parents tonelessly

holler, and banging her knife and fork on the table, joining in the demand for the promised sausages. Her individuality is eroded as her resistance to mob rule is reduced. The exclusive nature of the group is underscored when the occasional, dejected lone dissenter is spotted, sitting silently amidst the boisterous rabble; similarly, Mr Chin, who runs the local Chinese takeaway, and who takes the children's education seriously, displays only bemused detachment from the rowdy proceedings, and is repeatedly excluded from conversation and activities.[17] A striking image of a drunken, comatose man being held up by his partner, as she 'dances' around the room with him, highlights the willingness of those who ought to respect our individuality to impose upon us roles and behaviour we would not choose for ourselves. The power of the group and its threat to the individual, and to individuality, are made clear.

The setting of the school also impinges upon the parents' identities and behaviour, turning them into children and stripping away their guise of mature, responsible adulthood. Attending a parents' meeting in one of the classrooms, Joe finds himself seated at a child's desk, being lectured by a more dominant parent who has taken up an authoritative stance at the front of the class. Reacting to his situation, Joe instinctively raises his hand before speaking, as if to mimic a pupil seeking a teacher's approbation (figure 2). The impact of a hierarchical structure, although temporary, is to turn him into a child, incapable of asserting himself in the face of others' views. Typically, then, Davies is concerned with the interrelation of character and situation. Both the physical environment and the group dynamics that together constitute a social situation are revealed as influences upon the demeanour and states of mind of the characters.

As I mentioned previously, *Bavarian Night* also offers more personal reflections on Davies's part, through the character of writer Joe. In

2, 3 *Bavarian Night* (1981): Joe seeks permission to speak; and the writer at work

creating Joe, Davies acted upon his previously noted desire to 'inhabit' his characters 'completely': 'You have to bring all of yourself to it, all of your hopes and dreams and resentment and fury, all the stuff that's been boiling up inside you and distribute it amongst your characters' (Davies, quoted in Ransome, 2000: 19). Not only does the story of *Bavarian Night* reflect Davies's recent life experiences as a parent and teacher, but Joe's vocation as a writer is also foregrounded. The programme opens with a shot taken from outside his house; the camera moves slowly to a window, and Joe sits framed within it, at his desk, lit by a bright desktop lamp. Almost unmoving, and framed thus, he appears as if in a painting, and the shot is held so that the image of the writer at work is captured, frozen (figure 3). Moreover, Joe is explicitly connected with Davies as author of the television text, for in the opening moments he appears to have appropriated Davies's control over the text in which he appears. Joe types, 'Di [the protagonist of his novel] comes in and stops', and as he does so, his wife Alice performs the same action, standing unspeaking until he initiates a dialogue with her. It is as if he has control over her actions.[18]

The process of writing is depicted as being a balancing act between self-expression and a more mechanical act of 'going through the motions', which implies that Joe's character is not entirely confident in himself, and not wholly sincere. Joe composes and types slowly, but his word processor prints each line out very quickly when it is completed, contrasting the laborious investment of the writer in his creation with the simple task of churning out words on a page (writing versus typing). Indeed, his daughter Florence entreats him at one point, 'Go on, type', downgrading his creative activity to a physical, mechanical one. Moreover, Joe himself resorts to this kind of attitude, when he ruminates on the plot of his novel and decides that 'Di is due more tears', as if there were a formula for the perfect structure – a recipe he can follow. This possibly echoes Davies's own process of writing within the context of television production and its institutional, formal and generic constraints. More introspective concerns about the process of writing are also expressed – Joe's family accuses him of appropriating their lives and experiences as 'material', sometimes leaving them bereft of untainted memories.

Joe reflects upon his own character more continually than any other character does. Alongside his reflections upon his vocation, he bemoans the onset of middle age and its concomitants: the distance that grows between him and his children, the breakdown of once fresh relationships, and his uncertainty regarding his ability to recollect accurately the rosy days of his youth. His T-shirt proclaims 'I cheat but I can't win', which potentially refers to several aspects of his life: his extra-marital affair, his appropriation of others' lives in his writing, and his failure to think and behave truly individually. If Joe stands for Davies in some sense, one could infer that he personifies various dilemmas facing Davies at that moment.

However, to make such an assumption, even if warranted by details of the text, is not necessarily constructive in terms of interpretation, for our aim is not to uncover the man (Davies) behind the text but to tease out the details and implications of the text itself. At times, *Bavarian Night* seems to refer outside the text, gesturing to its author, Davies, and in those moments we are made aware of the constructedness and authorship of the programme. Unfortunately, this is rather clumsily executed. Joe is not a convincing, fully rounded, independent character, for he appears to stand in for Davies, speaking Davies's words and expressing Davies's world view rather than his own. This has potentially detrimental consequences for the viewer's engagement. The viewer is encouraged to refer outwards from the text towards the 'real' author, Davies (and away from the character, Joe), which may impact upon Joe's individuality as a coherent character, and may encourage a feeling of detachment from him on the part of the viewer. Additionally, the presence of Davies within Joe might prevent the viewer from seeing something of him- or herself, or his or her peers, within him. Thus the drama's ability to make 'universal' or at least broadly applicable references is undermined; so, too, are the pleasures of engaging with a psychologically complex character. This undercuts Davies's humanist and pluralist world view, for a character like Joe does not appear to be self-determined and self-expressive, but is instead revealed as a marionette, created only to serve the ends of another person (the author, Davies). It is as if there is too much of Davies's 'self' within the text.

This claim may sound a little strange, given the importance of self-expression to artistry and authorship, but T. S. Eliot noted the same issue, couching it in terms of seeking a positive separation between the actual author behind a work (the real person) and the 'author' as constituted within his work. He argued that a level of 'impersonality' is a virtue in an artwork. Peter Barry summarises Eliot's notion of 'impersonality':

> whereby there is a distinction between (as we might call it) the author (who is the person behind the work) and the writer (who is, so to speak, the 'person' *in* the work). In Eliot's view, the greater the separation between the two, the better, since 'the more perfect the artist, the more completely separate in him will be the man who suffers and the mind which creates', so that poetry is not simply the conscious rendering of personal experience into words. (Barry, 1995: 24)

Interestingly, Davies himself echoes this idea when he speaks about how important it is for young writers to have other jobs and other interests besides their creative work: 'Otherwise they've got nothing to write about except their own hang ups or things they've stolen from other writers, or "the meaning of life"' (Davies, 1994).

Although *Bavarian Night* is an intriguing experiment, it is not entirely successful, for Davies does not achieve a sufficient distance between himself as author and his text. There is a sense that the programme is over-authored. This does not just apply to Joe's character – other aspects also reveal too blatantly Davies's desire to imprint his authorship/authority upon the programme, and control the viewer's response to it. When the mannequins are destroyed by the unruly parents, the symbolic nature of the action is clear to the attentive viewer, but Davies gives Joe, who is observing, the line 'It's emblematic'. The point is overstated.

Deepening and extending characterisation

In *Bavarian Night*, for the reasons cited above, Joe's character is revealed almost as if he is frozen in time, expressing as he does a particular moment in Davies's life and experience. However, in other work, Davies does not limit himself to revealing characters as they are constituted at one moment, but moves to display them in a state of development and change. He is aided in this by an extension in the duration of programmes beyond thirty minutes, allowing for a fuller exploration of characters. Davies's characterisation deepens, as he explores how an individual has come to this moment in his life and how he or she has been shaped and affected by past experiences. Characterisation is also expanded in terms of the number of protagonists, with Davies moving to ensemble dramas that focus on a breadth of characters, rather than allowing one or a couple to dominate. In these ways, complexity of characterisation is developed.

Memory: the influence of the past upon a character
Several works in Davies's oeuvre offer depictions of and reflections upon memory, its importance in constituting characters' present selves, and its capacity to change those selves. *Pythons on the Mountain* (1984), a single play for the 'Playhouse' slot, follows John Prothero (Richard Pasco), a successful writer and academic, as he returns to his childhood home following his father's death. Past scenes from John's life are presented in flashback: these scenes open with black and white shots into which the colour bleeds back, until the images regain their liveliness. It is places and objects – those tangible elements that persist

into the present – that inspire John's memories and the flashbacks: standing in his usual pew in the local church, he relives his childhood services; as he touches the freshly painted date of his father's death on the list of preachers, an image of his father is brought to his mind. Through his memories of his past, John is able to revisit and reflect upon his actions, admit his mistakes and find peace with himself. Importantly, this process is aided by the contributions of others, such as his sister Marion (Rhoda Lewis), who are able to fill in missing details in his memories, correct his faulty assumptions, and reshape his views of past events.

A significant number of Davies's adaptations, explored in Chapter 4, picked up this theme, offering reflections upon the power of memories to change characters, and valuing the access to the past that can be gained and sustained through tangible objects such as buildings and mementoes, and through a character's contemporaries. These include *To Serve Them All My Days* (1980), *Time after Time* (1985), *The Old Devils* (1992) and *A Rather English Marriage* (1998).

Inter-personal relationships: the influence of others upon a character
As implied above, Davies's later non-adapted screenplays (and indeed much of his adapted work) included a wider range of characters who were revealed in more depth, such as in his entertaining ensemble drama for 'Screen One', *Filipina Dreamgirls* (1991). In particular, Davies often focuses upon family groups, exploring the effect of parents upon their children, siblings upon one another, and so on. This focus on family does not mean that Davies's work is insular or that it depends solely upon the close interrelationships or melodramatic mode central to television soap opera. Frequently, his work moves beyond the depiction of a singular family group and reveals the connections that are forged between the family and other groups in the outside world. This is the case in his single play *Ball-Trap on the Côte Sauvage* (1989), for instance, in which a couple who are experiencing some problems in their relationship take their children away to a holiday camp; the couple learn to address their problems through coming into contact with other families, each flawed and troubled in its own way. Unlike in Davies's earlier non-adapted work, characters are not simply revealed – they are explored: they address and work through problems, rather than just expressing them. Characters undergo a process of adaptation and change, and in turn they affect and alter those around them. This is clear, for example, in the effect of Arthur Prothero on his son John, in *Pythons*, and in the mutual effect of all the siblings upon one another in *Time after Time*.

The interweaving of Davies's thematic concerns and his development of more complex aspects of characterisation can be found in his
'Screen Two' play *Inappropriate Behaviour* (1986).

Inappropriate Behaviour *(1986)*
This play focuses upon a strangely matched central pairing of characters: Helen Bardsley (Charlotte Coleman), a disruptive and troubled
teenager, and Jo McLoughlin (Jenifer Landor), a self-assured educational
psychologist and behaviourist from the USA, who is asked to take on
Helen's case during her brief secondment to her school (figure 4).
Charlotte Coleman's performance as Helen interestingly echoes her
role as Marmalade Atkins, that other troubled and difficult school pupil
created by Davies, a connection which might at first mislead the viewer
into assuming no complex causes for Helen's 'inappropriate behaviour'
(an assumption later undermined). Befriending Helen, Jo comes into
contact with her strange and isolated farming family: her tired and
distant mother, overbearing and bitter father, and silent sister, Shirley
(Rudi Davies), who closely watches those around her but does not
participate and rarely speaks.

Here again Davies displays a concern about the limitations of educational institutions. Helen is at the point of being rejected by her school
when Jo pleads with the Head to give her another chance. Jo recognises
that it is likely that Helen's problems have a deeper cause, one that lies
outside the school; she asserts that through behaving badly Helen 'is
asking the school for something'. Jo is correct. A long history of familial
problems is gradually exposed; this includes the sexual abuse of Shirley
by her father.

This storyline thus reveals a set of hidden motivations and complications behind Jo's behaviour, and in this it is fairly typical of television

4, 5 *Inappropriate Behaviour* (1986): Helen and Jo; and Helen and Shirley at the window

drama, which frequently offers a 'cause' or 'reason' for a character's current state. However, Davies builds a more intricate diegesis by adding an intriguing complication in his treatment of Jo, who undergoes a transformation through her relationship with Helen. Jo's initial confidence in her behaviourist methods is undermined: she states at first that 'Changes in behaviour are the only real changes people can make', but soon realises that without tackling the underlying causes of Helen's behaviour, and without those around Helen (for example, her father) changing their behaviour, such changes are superficial and destined to fail. It is not as simple as she thought; her technique works superficially, improving Helen's behaviour at school, but it does not help Helen to deal with any of her problems, nor does it prevent the calamity that concludes the serial.

Jo finds herself unable to take a scientific approach, for she cannot sustain the appropriate critical distance; she gets too closely involved in Helen's case and her deep affections for the teenager undermine her in her task. Helen succeeds in breaking down Jo's professional air, entreating her to 'talk like a person' to her, not like a 'quack'. (Later, Jo echoes Helen's views in a scene with her lover Alex (Brian Deacon): he realises that something is wrong and observes that Jo wants to 'renegotiate the terms of the relationship'; impatiently, Jo snaps back 'I'm ending it, you prat'.) Jo, realising that her jargon and her fancy terms cannot help someone in such dire straits as Helen, loses faith in her behaviourist training and her work, and when Max (John Cording), a teacher in the school, confesses to her that he is 'in despair' and cannot go on, and pleads for her help, she rejects him, saying she is not able to do anything. In a reversal of roles, Max asks, in desperate hope, whether his despair may not be the overwhelming depression that he feels it is, but only a 'cluster of behaviours', 'small and neat', that she can help him to change, and thereby solve his problems. By that point, Jo knows better, and rather callously sends Max away.

A synergy between the writer Davies and the director, Paul Seed, is evident in the programme. Stylistic devices complement Davies's script and express the isolation and claustrophobia of the family's situation. In the internal shots in the farmhouse, and in those of the farm's outbuildings, the mise-en-scène is cluttered and crowded. Repeated point of view shots reveal that the whole family watches one another, conveying a secret and ominous complicity within the group, which binds them together. In particular, Shirley is filmed observing others' actions, caught behind objects (the window of her bedroom, the farm gate, fences).

Stylistic devices also present characters' subjectivities. Helen's alienation from normal, everyday life is emphasised through the use of a recurrent window motif. A shot outside the family house, initially from Helen's point of view, lingers upon the downstairs window as Helen enters the room; then, as she leaves the room to climb the stairs, the camera elevates slowly to reach the window of her bedroom, just as she arrives and greets her sister. It then holds the two characters within the frame, caught in separate panes of the window (figure 5). The effect is first that the family are imprisoned within the house, and second that Helen is depicted as the only force of movement and potential progression, sustaining an important connection with the outside world and between her parents and her sister. When Helen lingers outside the classes at school, peering through the windows, she can hear the voices of the children inside, but remains outside their childish activities, and her sense of exclusion from her 'ordinary' peers is reasserted. In this way, setting and space are expressive of the characters' situations and of the observer's (Helen's) state of mind.

The programme presents other aspects of subjectivity by bleeding between 'real' scenes (actually happening in the story) and dream or thought sequences. The scraping of Shirley's fork across her plate at the uncomfortable meal Jo shares with the family is a sound carried across and exaggerated into the next scene – a surreal dream sequence in which Jo dreams of the huge pigs on the farm as menacing creatures having noisy sex with one another. Later, the boundary between 'real' and fantasy is blurred, as we cut between Jo dismissing Max from her office, and the farm, where we see a shocking image of the family – the mother and two sisters shot dead, and the father just about to shoot himself. Jo, sensing that something is wrong, hurries to the farm to find that the mother and father have been shot by Helen. Their bodies lie in different locations from those she imagined, and Shirley and Helen are safe, so it is clear that the preceding images were a premonition on Jo's part and not a depiction of reality. This troubles the reliability of the programme's images (what is real, and what is imagined?), while simultaneously enforcing a close relation between Jo's thoughts and fears, and Helen's intentions and situation. Their subjectivities are intricately intertwined.

Some recurrent stylistic motifs: style, subjectivity, voice

As we have seen, in these earlier non-adapted works, stylistic motifs are more often linked to the expression of character rather than to the expression of Davies's authorial presence or signature. However, the repetition of particular motifs *across* different works has the effect of asserting a more consistent artistic influence behind the disparate texts.

For example, the window motif used in *Inappropriate Behaviour* is employed elsewhere. In *Bavarian Night*, the opening shot shows Joe captured within a window frame within his house; later, a similar shot reveals the gathered parents within the school. In both cases, there is a sense that the characters are trapped within the frame, and their insularity is reasserted through the motif. The emphasis and meaning of such shots are variable, of course. When the shot is not a point of view shot, what is 'inside' the window becomes our key focus, as it is picked out for our attention; in *Inappropriate Behaviour*, the fact that such shots are at least initially from Helen's point of view causes us to reflect upon the scenes' relevance and importance to that character in particular. The window motif is picked up in later work, including *The Old Devils*, *Getting Hurt* and several of Davies's classic-novel adaptations.

Another discernible trait of Davies's oeuvre is that, although he is primarily a realist, his work is not straightforwardly naturalistic, and indeed Davies has claimed that 'all the best television drama transcends or subverts tele-naturalism' (Davies, 1994). Davies's programmes contain elements of the absurd, which frequently communicate reflections upon the central characters. Moments of absurdity and strangeness of characterisation occur in much of his non-adapted work, from *Is That Your Body, Boy?*, to *Bavarian Night*, to *Ball-Trap* (as well as in adapted programmes such as *The Imp of the Perverse*). In these cases, absurdity is often included for humour or satire, though bizarre moments in *Inappropriate Behaviour* are employed for pathos, to express the twisted situation in which the characters find themselves. Other examples bend the relationship between reality and fantasy. In *Heartattack Hotel* (1983), a nervous young doctor, Stephen Daker (who later reappears in *A Very Peculiar Practice*), visits a strange hotel, only to find that the other guests start dying suddenly and mysteriously. In this case it is the plot that contains absurdity, and that blurs the boundary between what is realistic and what is not; in *The Water Maiden* (1974) it is the protagonist, Colin (Jeff Rawle), a vulnerable and imaginative young man, who appears to reshape the world around him into a fantastical one that suits his purposes, and whose attempts to coerce the woman who is the object of his affections into fulfilling the role he has chosen for her end miserably.[19]

Fearless Frank (1978), a 'Play of the Week', exhibits a level of bizarre anti-naturalism that is relatively rare in Davies's work. Again however, this is in the service of expressing and critiquing character and subjectivity. The programme's ironic title refers to its protagonist, Frank Harris (Leonard Rossiter), an old and impotent figure who relates (or, more accurately, invents) his life story, attempting to compensate for the lack of excitement in his current situation.[20] Davies's script was based loosely upon the life of the real author Frank Harris, whose books Davies enjoyed when he was a teenager 'looking for filth', and upon Philippa Pullar's biography of Harris. The programme is clearly fantastical, exposing the falsity of Frank's claims. It exploits the limitations of contemporary television technology, using obviously fake studio shots to present Frank unconvincingly in exotic places, with famous figures. Scenes from his childhood are amusingly constructed – the fully grown, adult Frank plays himself, shuffling around on his knees amidst piles of oversized books. The same actors are reused to play the many roles, undermining any sense of deep engagement with the characters. Thus we are asked to engage with the character of Frank who is *not* shown – the real, unhappy, disillusioned, and not at all fearless Frank who has constructed such a fanciful tale. The exaggeratedly stylised presentation is *implicitly* expressive of his character, which is not straightforwardly revealed but which must be inferred by the viewer.

Within *Fearless Frank*, then, there is a critique of the constructedness of characters, which can be regarded as an attempt to encourage the audience to recognise characters' fictionality and potential unreliability. Davies returns to this idea and develops it very successfully, much later in his career (see Chapter 5). A similar notion is discernible in his first long serial, *The Legend of King Arthur* (1979), in which Morgan le Fay (Maureen O'Brien), Arthur's half-sister, is given a major role, and is permitted a curious level of self-reflection. Morgan alone is permitted a direct glance to camera (after Uther chokes to death, in part 1), and although this device is not repeated, she underlines the performative aspect of character at other moments, when she reflects upon the diegetic world – the story in which she finds herself. In the final battle between Morgan and Arthur (Andrew Burt), Arthur is overwhelmed by her long-standing, long-concealed malevolence, exclaiming 'So much evil!' Morgan's reply is that 'You [Arthur] chose good ... In a game of chess one player has to take the black pieces. And now the game is over.' The intriguing chess analogy implies that she has been given no choice in her role – that a story, a television serial, depends, like a game of chess, upon the presence of protagonist and antagonist, and that she drew the short straw and was condemned to fill the role of the latter. It is as if she was forced to take the part and fulfil the (stereo)type. The reflexive nature of this comment and the way it highlights role-playing are developed in Davies's later work, especially in his classic-novel adaptations.

The Water Maiden, similarly, explores the potential conflict between a character and the role they are coerced into playing. The voice-over recreates the discourse of the fairy tale, and overlays realistic actions and events with a mythic, fantastic story; other features of the programme sustain the fairy-tale analogy – such as the presence of a 'wise woman' as sage/witch (one of Colin's workmates, Linda, played by Cheryl Hall). The bare plot of the programme follows Colin (Jeff Rawle), who becomes besotted with a young woman, Marianne (Lisa Harrow). She is reluctant to accept his advances, but eventually his persistence pays off and she agrees to go out with him. They move in together, marry, and have a son, but Marianne remains dissatisfied, and finally leaves Colin.

The fairy-tale discourse corresponds with Colin's world view: he is an egotistical idealist who desires a fairy-tale romance, and he stubbornly refuses to ignore the challenges and difficulties that face a real-life relationship and to accept Marianne's own individual subjectivity. He idealises and idolises Marianne, who is compelled to take on the role of the 'water maiden' of the title. Colin's first glimpse of her is accompanied by the voice-over, which explains that he was destined to be a lonely young man 'until the day that he would see a magical sea maiden, more beautiful than any on earth, and then he would fall head over heels in love with her'. While Colin is entranced by this ordinarily attractive woman, re-visioning her in fantastical and romantic terms, Marianne is less impressed with Colin, and rebuffs his initial expressions of interest. Moreover, she is a real, flawed human being, and she feels uncomfortable with the way in which he expects her to play the role he has chosen for her (as the perfect, transcendent water maiden): she argues that 'I can't stand your expectations of me'. Gradually, though, she begins to be drawn into Colin's world view, and persuades herself to comply with his intentions. Colin beseeches her to look into his eyes and seek her own reflection, and recognise that it is indeed beautiful. Seeing herself in (through) Colin's eyes, Marianne is moved to agree to initiate a relationship with him.

The voice-over continues to offer a re-description of the action, the use of language establishing an ironic commentary upon the story. Marianne's pregnancy is described in terms of her being 'big with child', consciously invoking an archaic, pseudo-biblical discourse that contrasts sharply with the contemporary Marianne. At this point the voice-over is divorced from contemporary reality in terms of both its register and its ignorance of the 'true' meaning of the representations on screen. Marianne suffers from post-natal depression, triggered partly because of the old-fashioned expectations that Colin imposes upon her (he demands that she behave in an appropriately feminine and maternal manner, which does not come naturally to her). However, the voice-over seems unaware of, and uninterested in, the real reason for Marianne's change of behaviour after the birth of their son, commenting that 'she bore him a lovely child. A boy, as perfect as herself. But from that day onward, she never spoke another word to him [Colin]'. Her behaviour is presented as having inexplicable, magical roots, as if a witch had placed a curse upon her, which undoubtedly reflects Colin's failure to recognise the real source of her unhappiness and take some responsibility for it himself. The correspondence between the world view of the voice-over and that of Colin, and the roots of Colin's idealism within his fundamental egotism, is revealed in the words 'she bore him a lovely child', which emphasise her use value only for Colin; her role is to serve him rather than herself. Marianne loses her individual subjectivity.

The discourse of the fairy tale is ordinarily regarded as positive, romantic and appealing (thus we have 'fairy-tale' endings, 'fairy-tale' weddings, and so on). Here, though, that discourse is interrogated and critiqued through its superimposition over images of real-life relationships. The programme criticises its restrictive implications for gender roles and the expression of individual personality. Further, the programme establishes a dialogue, or argument, between a number of voices: the fairytale voice-over (which is related to Colin's point of view), and those of Colin, Marianne, Linda, and Colin's friend Bob, who responds to Colin's complaints that Marianne has 'changed' and is cold towards him with the astute words 'Maybe you made it all up. Never really happened'. The voices comment upon one another, disputing the veracity and integrity of each individual point of view, and no one point of view is shown to be flawless (Marianne is not a meek, innocent victim of Colin's egotism – she is self-centred, vain and fickle). This kind of interplay between fallible but persuasive voices is something that Davies develops in his later, adapted work, and I shall return to the question of 'voice' in more detail, in Chapter 5.

Finally, and relatedly, Davies's early work for adults contains a number of experiments with points of view, subjectivities and character. Characters are interrelated not just at a narrative level but also in terms of their subjectivites, such as when Jo's daydream at the end of *Inappropriate Behaviour* is momentarily confused with, and is ultimately prescient of, reality. As in this case, the depiction of a particular character's subjectivity, through the presentation of his or her thoughts, feelings, imaginings or dreams, is a vital way in which the programmes convey a character's imbrication in a situation – his or her often unwilling inextricable involvement. Interesting instances of this can be seen in Davies's later work, such as *The Signalman* (Chapter 4) and *Emma* (Chapter 5).

Longer serials

John Caughie notes that

> If there is a classical form of television narrative, it may be the dramatic serial. While the television film emulates, to a greater or lesser extent, the form of the cinema feature film, and the single play derives its form from the theatre play, the drama serial, having failed to establish itself as a continuing tradition in cinema, now seems specific to television and radio. (Caughie, 2000: 205)

Davies, who wholeheartedly embraces the medium of television, has increasingly worked within this most televisual of forms, especially in recent years. However, this is not simply a matter of artistic preference; institutional influences determined his move away from the single play and towards the serial form. Serials have existed on British television since the 1950s, but the longer serial form really flourished from around the 1970s, and during the 1980s and 1990s serials dominated the schedules, overtaking the 'older' format of the single play. This was primarily for economic reasons: serials are more cost effective than one-off dramas, as sets, props, costumes and personnel can be reused, with the relative price per hour of drama decreasing with each additional episode. Serials are also effective in holding on to audience share, as they are able to develop a loyal following among regular viewers, something that appeals to both broadcasters and advertisers.

Davies has written two non-adapted, long serials: the thirteen-part serial *The Legend of King Arthur* (1979) and *A Very Peculiar Practice* (1986, 1988), comprising two series which ran for seven fifty-minute episodes each. These series were followed by a ninety-minute sequel, *A Very Polish Practice* (1992), for 'Screen One'.[21] He also devised, with Bernadette Davis, one of the best examples of British situation comedy: *Game On!*, which exploited the conventional spatial and narrative claustrophobia of the genre particularly successfully: the show was restricted almost entirely to the space of the flat shared by three friends, Matthew, Martin and Mandy, and gradually disclosed a sharp, intriguing and comic insight into the confused personality of Matthew, an agoraphobic who refuses to accept his condition. Perhaps the best-known example, though, is *Peculiar Practice*.

A Very Peculiar Practice (1986, 1988)[22]

This successful serial was directed by David Tucker and produced by Ken Riddington for the BBC. Set on the campus of a redbrick university, Lowlands, it centred upon the campus medical centre, and offered an entertaining, engaging, wry view of contemporary academic life, and a study of an ensemble of eclectic characters.

'Education, education, education'

Peculiar Practice condemned the undermining of the principles, values and traditions of higher education by the Thatcherite government of the day, and constituted a timely intervention in contemporary education policy (it is perhaps overdue for revival!). Davies's interest in exploring the value(s) and purposes of education is central to the programme. The opening shots show a post-apocalyptic ground, blue-black, cracked and barren, overcast by dark, menacing clouds in an inky sky; at the centre of the frame stands an indeterminate pile of rubble on the horizon. People materialise on the ground, facing away from us, their shadows stretching out towards us, as they gaze into the distance. A heart-shaped sun, with visible rays, rises above the pile and reveals it to be a derelict-looking building (a crumbling 1960s university). The impact of the sun is like a neutron bomb, and everything is bleached white; then the people disappear. The sequence could not be clearer in its depiction of the state of academia.

The traditional principles of a liberal, humanist education, central to Davies's world view, are here depicted as under attack by those who would turn higher education into a competition-led business; interestingly, there is also a threat from the growth of non-traditional subjects such as cultural studies, interdisciplinary studies and so on – or rather, from the over-reliance upon jargon, obscure vocabulary, slapdash thought, excessive theorisation and political correctness that these subjects dangerously indulge in. The serial resists proffering any clear-cut answers, though, and a balance is struck between a cool-headed critique of these new subjects and a generous recognition of their potentially progressive and stimulating influence. A conversation between protagonist Stephen Daker (Peter Davison), a keen doctor who is new to the university, and Megan Phillips (Kate Eaton), a young fresher, exposes the difficulty in finding a reasonable route between a blinkered, reactionary resistance to change and an indulgence in trendy, muddled irrelevance:

> Megan: I'm doing Education and Religious Studies for my main subjects. You'd think that would be about schools and religions, wouldn't you? Well it's not. Education's about Freud and Marx, and religion's about curry and marijuana, as far as I can make out ...
> Stephen: I think you might give some consideration to the idea that coming to University is about opening your mind to new ideas. You don't have to swallow them whole – just allow for the possibility of change. Otherwise what's the point in being here?

Megan: I came here to be a teacher, not to get brainwashed.

Megan's acid criticisms touch upon a nerve, and expose the problem of over-theorisation in contemporary education; while Stephen makes a valid and persuasive point about 'opening one's mind', the weight of his argument is undercut by the fact that the words he uses here are not strictly his own, for he is paraphrasing an earlier speech by his feminist colleague, Rose Marie (Barbara Flynn). Therefore, although Stephen's words resonate with genuine sentiment, they also betray his lack of resoluteness and the insidious attraction of pleasing platitudes to those with impressionable minds. Stephen participates in the very activity that Megan wishes to condemn – speaking with another person's voice and expressing another's ideas and beliefs as if they were his own, reached by rational deliberation.

The theme of words and language is a central one, and it contributes to the programme's criticism of contemporary academia: both the jargon of the new, business-led higher education and the absurd non-sense of the fashionable, novel humanities subjects are exposed as facile and meaningless. Language is twisted, distorted, perverted and made to mean what it does not.[23] Its capacity to state even the most limited and conditional of truths is undermined. When the vice chancellor, Ernest Hemmingway (John Bird), refers to 'loyalty' (the commitment of his staff to his institution), the word takes on new and ominous connotations, and sounds like a threat. Academics in the serial openly argue about what language means, and it is noted that language is used as a plaything, something to be fooled with, a tool for entertainment (Stephen asks a colleague at one point, 'Do you mean anything you say?'). A bold attempt to use a literary reference in order to express something about the current condition of the university's inhabitants is found in a graffito: 'Abandon hop' is scrawled on a wall – the writer was clearly interrupted in the act of writing, leaving us with an absurdity rather than an expressive truth.

If academics are shown to be losing their way partly through their own fault – through lassitude and an eagerness to abandon language and the pursuit of truth(s) – they are also revealed to be lost because of the broader political context. As Stephen enters the university, a montage of road signs confuses him, and he loses direction. This sequence is repeated as a dream sequence later in the serial. On one level, this is expressive of the character's state of mind – his own confusion. However, given the extended nature of the montage, and its later repetition, we are encouraged to extend its referentiality; the reason for Stephen's loss of direction is that he is being over-directed, just as academia is being over-directed by the government.

The combination of fashionable subjects and theories, and the pressures upon universities to meet targets, compete, and behave in a business-like manner, work to crush the central activities that define academia, and which have historically bestowed upon it its unique value. This is presented symbolically through the impact of government initiatives upon the staff of the medical centre. Ordered to 'produce research output', they are distracted from their more vital duties (healing the sick, preventing illness and promoting health). Jock narrates his book even while patients are sitting in front of him, paying far greater attention to the expression and analysis of his own thoughts than to the human being who seeks his professional help. He is eager not to 'do' but to talk about doing. Practicality, action and genuinely original or creative thought are thus subordinated to empty words and meaningless gestures. This contrasts with the inspiring character of Chen Sung Yau (Takashi Kawahara), an outstanding PhD student in Maths, with whom Stephen shares a room. Chen's constant active involvement with his subject – the blackboards mounted around his room on which he scribbles endless formulae, his all-night sessions with only a box of board chalk for company – and with his related music, are presented as the epitome of real academic work. This is true work of the mind: a constant search for discovery, the refinement of ideas, the communication of truths. Chen states with pride that his most recent work is 'Beautiful, original, elegant, and it's never been said before'. He thus calls upon attributes (beauty, originality, elegance) that are frequently disparaged in contemporary academic criticism and theory. Chen is fully engaged in academic life and thought in a way that current conditions attempt to undermine.

Stephen manages to avoid being sucked too far into the abyss; although he is not an academic like Chen, he is true to his vocation as a doctor, mostly undeterred by government targets, business initiatives, or woolly ideas that lead him away from his real work. He retains contact with the 'real world' and practicality. Entreated to gaze into the drama teacher's eyes in order to make a profound spiritual connection, Stephen makes a more mundane but more valuable discovery, spotting the growth of glaucoma quickly enough to prevent it. He sees something that is tangibly present; his down-to-earth gaze sees truth.

Parts 5 and 6 of *Peculiar Practice* are particularly caustic about trends in contemporary higher education, yet they are simultaneously positive about the potential value and power of academia. The central storyline of part 5, 'Contact Tracer', is the spread of non-specific urethritis (NSU) across the campus, through sexual activity. This storyline is presented to be read both literally and metaphorically, as is overtly stated by Jock

McCannon (Graham Cowden), Stephen's colleague: 'Consider how a new intellectual concept spreads and garners strength within the academic community – it's very much the same with non-specific urethritis.' This echoes the vague, jargon-filled speech delivered by the vice chancellor as he announces a new appointment that has been made to establish the subject of 'interdisciplinary studies': 'Daniela Theodoulou [Madlena Nedeva] is opening up some new lines of investigation along the interfaces between subject disciplines.' Thus an analogy is drawn between NSU and the kinds of ideas (and abuse of language) that one might find in such Frankenstein's monsters as interdisciplinary studies.

The medical staff gather evidence and work to stem the spread of NSU. It is found that the 'contacts' are concentrated within certain areas on campus: in the Arts there is by far the biggest epidemic, then among the secretaries, porters and catering staff, and within communication studies. Sociologists only seem to 'make contact' with each other, and there appears to be barely any 'contact' at all in Engineering and Physical Sciences. The medical team struggle to find a link between these disparate cases, but eventually it becomes clear – it is their new Reader in interdisciplinary studies. Thus this new subject, introduced to 'bring people together' and create 'productive interfaces', merely results in the spread of disease across academia (as do the intellectual concepts and their concomitant jargon that Jock mentioned).

Details of Theodoulou's characterisation forge further links between her and 'new' (late 1970s to mid 1980s) subject areas. She is presented as a charming and rather sexy woman, appealing to many, though somehow clichéd in her good looks, with exaggerated shiny lips, tinted glasses, gold jewellery – it is a recycled image, copied from various sources. She is ruthless and unprincipled in creating bizarre 'connections' out of nothing, between disparate subjects, and in seeing potential areas for 'business' where there are no natural crossovers: 'I'm a kind of catalyst. I see a possibility – make something happen ... I have to go and talk about cell cultures to the law department.'

Of course, Theodoulou is the vice chancellor's pet project, and is foisted upon the sceptical academics. The VC is presented almost entirely negatively. He is a mouthpiece for the Thatcherite administration, and has little sympathy with the traditional aims and values of education. Instead, he is determined to make the university financially successful. He approves Bob Buzzard's (David Troughton) plans to market a floppy disk for the treatment of seventeen minor ailments, complimenting him on this 'hard-nosed research, packageable product'. In part 6, 'The Hit List', the VC attempts to convince a group of

Japanese investors to set up a science park, but while initially they are enthusiastic, believing that they are being promised a state-of-the-art wildlife park, complete with crocodiles in the lake, they overcome the double language barrier, of English and of jargon, to perceive the truth of his plans:

> VC: No, no, gentlemen, a science park is a dense concentration of high-technology research and development labs. Not crocodiles, gentlemen. Portakabins.
> Japanese interpreter (Eiji Kusuhara): Oh, I see. In Japan we call that 'industrial estate' or 'row of factories'.
> VC: No, no, not the same thing at all. Well, not quite.

In trying to cross a language barrier, the VC's rephrasing/translation of his words exposes their real meaning, and he is forced to concede the uncomfortable truth, when he is more accustomed to shielding behind euphemisms – his 'high-technology research and development labs' are amended to the more honest 'Portakabins'.

The Japanese pull out of the deal when a further problem with the building of the science park arises. The VC plans to build the park on a regenerated site, having demolished an old teaching building in which are housed several lecturers specialising in 'old-fashioned' subjects. One of those lecturers is historian Lillian Hubbard (Jean Haywood), whom the VC regards as a troublemaker and whom he intends to oust. Again, the storyline has metaphorical significance, with the VC's attempt to overpower Hubbard speaking symbolically about the disrespectful and unwise abandonment of traditional established and reflective subjects like History in favour of the dominance of media, communication, cultural and interdisciplinary studies. Peter reflects that the university needs people like Hubbard, Chen, his girlfriend and committed student Lyn Turtle (Amanda Hillwood), and even the unreliable but decent Jock; each of these people is committed to their subjects (whether traditional or more modern) because they believe in the importance of their vocation. Set against the mental image of a high-tech, concrete science park is the real and rather romantic image of Hubbard lecturing from her second-floor window to the students assembled on the lawn (for she refuses to leave her room and concede to the VC). Her words make History relevant to the students, who listen with attentive interest to her heartfelt and expert views.

Lowlands University campus is a microcosm of contemporary academia – a world in which nothing is quite as it seems, or as it should be. Davies's familiar moments of absurdity are used here not so much to express characters' states of being or mind, but for satirical purposes, pinpointing the problems that bedevilled universities in the 1980s (and still do). In this context, the infamous, destructive, devious, ultimately murderous nuns, who engage in vindictive fun at the expense of the campus residents, are no more bizarre than the state of affairs affecting actual academia at the time.

The presence of Davies

Davies writes into the screenplay an explicit reference to himself, in the form of a cameo character, Mr Rust (Joe Melia), a new Arts Council Fellow in Creative Writing. Mr Rust is in the process of writing a 'Sharp, satirical black comedy with a bit of Chekhovian understated pathos. Heaven on wheels, right' (reflecting the very programme that contains him). He is writing it in order to discharge the debt of £17,000 that he 'somehow' owes the BBC; this was Davies's own position at the time and his reason for creating *Peculiar Practice*. Rust complains that as soon as he writes a new plot twist, reality 'tops it', implying the ludicrous conditions contemporary universities are labouring under. Finally, Rust meets his demise: he is run over by the nuns. However, although this character constitutes a knowing wink from Davies to the audience, he does not really symbolise Davies's presence within the serial. That presence is found within the central character of Stephen Daker.

Stephen stands, beleaguered but resolute, in the chaos that surrounds him, forming an epicentre of rationality amidst the extremes represented by other characters (figure 6). In a sense, he is the voice of reason, but he is not a sturdy authority figure, for he has no particular view of his own. In attempting to find a balance between the sharply divided individuals and the ideas and beliefs they epitomise, Stephen finds himself a little confused and somewhat lost at times, for he is able to see some value in everyone's point of view, while he rejects their more strident declamations. Perhaps the only key character that he can find no agreement with is Bob, for Bob is selfishly ambitious and lacks

6 *A Very Peculiar Practice* (1985–86): the beleaguered Stephen Daker

sincerity, while others may be disillusioned, misinformed or plain wrong, but they do have some integrity and principles. One might regard Stephen as embodying Davies within the programme. Stephen, like Davies, attempts to weigh up the arguments, and seeks value in every view, but he resists sitting on the fence when it is necessary, and stands for the core principles of liberal humanism as they are manifested in traditional, liberal education. To regard his character thus is to emphasise the notion of self-expression over other aspects of authorship.

Unlike Joe in *Bavarian Night*, Davies is careful to place some distance between himself as author and Stephen as protagonist – both through including himself in the guise of another character, Mr Rust, and by allowing Stephen to be unsure in his views, indecisive and weak at times, unclear of what it is that he wishes to say. There is no sense that Stephen speaks for Davies rather than speaking for himself, for his has no air of authorised superiority over other characters, no sense that he presents an overview. Instead he is fully imbricated within his situation and his relationships with other characters. For this reason, while it is valid to note the connection, the consequences of approaching Stephen's character as a personification of Davies's authorial voice are ultimately limiting, for the text does not suggest such an approach. To regard Stephen in such narrow terms leads us away from the broad dialogue of voices within the text towards the viewpoint of a singular speaker, and undermines the validity and vital importance of other voices (such as Chen's and Lyn's). Perhaps it is more constructive to regard the text *as a whole* as an expression and exploration of liberal, humanist, secular values, which obviously reflect Davies's own experiences as an academic, and his views on education, but which also mirror the experiences and views of many others. This potential for universality is, after all, the very reason for the enduring popularity of *Peculiar Practice*, particularly amongst those who work in or care about (higher) education. As Stephen Daker states, 'I'm not a hero'; he thus downplays his individuality and places himself firmly within the academic milieu of which he is a part. What is prized here is the team effort, a like-minded community, collective dialogue and debate over the words and actions of one individual. This entreats us not to seek Davies within Daker, but to recognise ourselves alongside Davies, within the text that he has brought into being.

The elements of content and style that have been drawn out in this chapter form a world view that can be attributed to Davies and that connect these disparate programmes in some loose but discernible sense. Chapter 4 extends this focus, considering how Davies sustains this world view when dealing with adapted texts.

Notes

1 I have placed the word 'original' within inverted commas because although this is the most obvious, colloquial term for non-adapted work (we are accustomed to referring to an 'original screenplay'), I do not wish to imply that adapted work is, in contrast, 'unoriginal'; adaptations can be equally innovative, unique and 'original' in their own right. Henceforth, therefore, the term 'non-adapted' will be used to refer to Davies's 'original' screenplays.

2 Davies wrote the first Marmalade book, *Marmalade and Rufus*, in 1980; it was reissued in 1995 as *Marmalade's Dreadful Deeds*. Following this, he wrote the television series *Marmalade Atkins in Space* (1981), *Educating Marmalade* (1982), and *Danger: Marmalade at Work* (1984); each of these was followed by a novelisation (1986, 1995 and 1984, respectively). Davies wrote a new Marmalade book, *Marmalade Hits the Big Time*, in 1995, which was subsequently released on audio tape (1997).

3 Cartoon elements are employed in the credits, so that we are introduced to Marmalade first as an animated figure and then as a 'real' person (performed by Charlotte Coleman). This comic mixing and disjuncture of formats is also used within the main diegeses, such as when Marmalade sinks Eton's longboat, and real news footage of a sinking boat is intercut into the scene.

4 The National Curriculum was introduced in 1988, under the Education Reform Act. In 1993, teachers boycotted the first national tests in protest against the increase in their workloads created by the NC. Ron Dearing's report of that year recommended several changes to the curriculum, and the national tests were run in 1994. The curriculum was further revised and became statutory in 1995.

5 Another example of Davies's educational videos is *Baby, I Love You* (1985), a teen drama about teenage pregnancy.

6 Readers who are interested in finding out more about the single play, especially 'Play for Today' and 'The Wednesday Play', will find an insightful, knowledgeable and engaging record and defence of these strands in Shubik, 2000.

7 The problem of missing texts is an enduring and frustrating one for television scholars and researchers. The undervaluing of television, particularly television drama, meant that in the earlier days of television many dramas were wiped so that the tapes could be reused to save sporting events and news. Those that were preserved are rarely released commercially. It can only be hoped that with the range of new digital channels, older dramas that are still available will be shown as part of 'retrospectives' and so on. BBC4 might prove to be particularly useful in this respect: they broadcast a limited number of Davies's programmes during a 'Davies season', over Christmas 2003; and also ran a Poliakoff season earlier in 2003, broadcasting much of his television and film work.

8 I made use of various sources to get hold of copies of Davies's work, but especially the British Film Institute viewing services, who can arrange viewings of any tapes that are available to them; I also managed to locate some programmes through Davies, and through libraries and colleagues across Britain. I try to focus in this book on the programmes that the reader might feasibly be able to view for him- or herself (that is, those accessible through the BFI or, especially in later chapters, those available to buy on video and DVD).

9 For example, the opening credits of these plays often simply state that the text is 'by Andrew Davies'.

10 Significantly, though, Miller chooses to 'lose' at the end of the programme, deliberately dropping down onto his heels (which intriguingly echoes the ending of the British New Wave film *The Loneliness of the Long Distance Runner* (1962)). Miller disappoints Carstairs, who felt he had perhaps found a kindred spirit, and

thus forces Carstairs to question what the point of this punishment, with its emphasis on resilience, self-control and strength, really is.

11 This use of repetition, patterning, and rhythm is characteristically present in Stephen Poliakoff's dialogue. It is interesting to see how Davies experimented with these non-naturalistic tendencies in his early programmes, but moved away from them later, whereas Poliakoff intensified them as his work developed.

12 Quoted from one of Davies's e-mail communications to me, sent in February 2004.

13 Quotations are from previously cited e-mail from Davies to me, February 2004.

14 *Eleanor Marx*, like *Renoir, My Father*, is not a literary adaptation (it is not adapted from fictional literature, but from biography). For this reason, although it is adapted from a written source, we tend not to classify it as an adaptation. This is one of the curiosities in the way in which adaptations are defined; interested readers should see my previous discussion of this issue (2002: 10–20).

15 The notion of voice becomes increasingly important within Davies's oeuvre; see later in this chapter and Chapter 5.

16 The protagonists are similarly shortsighted in their inability to see the effects that their actions have upon others (for example, the effect of Jo's infidelity upon those involved). They are in no sense the 'heroes' of the piece; instead, far more sympathetic and upstanding minor characters (like Mr Chin) offer a critical view upon their actions.

17 Mr Chin is found by a teacher as he quietly rummages through the children's desks, seeking to find out what his daughter is learning, and how she is getting on; the teacher is pleased and touched by Chin's genuine and deep-felt concern about his daughter's education. This behaviour is contrasted favourably with the immature silliness of the protagonists.

18 This anti-naturalistic moment was perhaps inspired by the work of Dennis Potter, whom Davies regards very highly: he was inspired to write for television by his viewing of, among others, Potter's *Stand Up, Nigel Barton* (1965) and *Vote, Vote, Vote for Nigel Barton* (1965). The moment here in *Bavarian Night* is comparable with the more sustained play with 'authorial control', and consequent reflections upon authorship and autobiography, found in much of Potter's work, especially the *The Singing Detective* (1986).

19 *The Water Maiden* is discussed a little later in the chapter, with particular reference to its use of role-playing and voice.

20 There are clear echoes here of the character of Colin in *Water Maiden*, and indeed of the over-imaginative protagonists Emma, in Davies's adaptation of Jane Austen's novel, and Becky, in his version of *Vanity Fair*.

21 *A Very Polish Practice* retained the ironic and surreal elements of *Peculiar Practice*, but was a much darker, more serious piece. Shot on a bigger budget, it had a glossiness and visual complexity beyond that of the earlier series, but in moving away from the context of British higher education, the series was less intensely related to the British political scene, and did not speak to contemporary viewers' everyday experiences in the same way. *Polish Practice* has never attracted such affectionate acclaim as its predecessor did.

22 I deal only with the first series of *Peculiar Practice*, partly because the second is not easily available, and partly because of space limitations.

23 A recent powerful indictment of contemporary British university education focuses similarly on the language (jargon) that is destroying the most valuable central tenets of traditional liberal education (see Maskell and Robinson, 2001). Its analysis of the Dearing report's (ab)use of language makes for fascinating reading, and echoes *Peculiar Practice*'s critique.

Authorship and adaptation: Davies's adaptations from 'non-classic' literature

4

While Davies is best known for his adaptations of classic novels (discussed in the next chapter), it is notable that most of the programmes he scripted in the mid years of his writing career, from the late 1970s to the mid 1990s, are adaptations from non-classic literary sources.[1] The adaptive status of these programmes is perhaps less obvious, for in many cases the source novels are not as widely known and recognised as *Pride and Prejudice, Middlemarch* or *Vanity Fair* – nor are the authors as esteemed as Austen, Eliot or Thackeray. Instead, these are adaptations of more contemporary popular or middlebrow literature, and they frequently fit more easily into generic categories such as the thriller, the romance or the ghost story.

Therefore this chapter and the next, although both dealing with Davies's adapted work, will address diverse issues, responding to the differences in material upon which they focus.[2] Some of the most hotly debated issues in adaptation studies tend to focus upon adaptations of respected classic texts, and recurrent concerns about fidelity, integrity and voice are more easily sidestepped when dealing with adaptations of 'lesser' works, for the latter do not hold such cherished places in the canon and in the hearts of their readers. An adaptation that is seen to denigrate Jane Austen's work is often seen as an attack upon English literature more generally, and upon related values that are held dear. In comparison, an adaptation that takes licence with a less well-known potboiler, sentimental novelette or short story is less likely to raise viewers' hackles, and more likely to be judged on its own merits (or flaws), as questions of fidelity and the source-text author's voice are deemed less important and become less central. This chapter, then, will avoid such contentious matters as those that bedevil the study of classic-novel adaptations, and instead offer an introduction to the work of Davies as an adapter, considering the challenges that adaptation from literature to television pose for a screenwriter, and revealing the different ways in which he has negotiated such challenges to make his own mark upon the final texts. In discussing several of Davies's key adaptations, I shall refer back to his authorial presence and world view, outlined in Chapter 3, for despite the restrictions of another writer's story, characters and themes, Davies succeeds in further perpetuating his own concerns and motifs in these programmes.

Extensive theoretical work on the process of adaptation already exists, and the purpose of this book is not to engage with this topic on a general level, but to deal only with those aspects that arise directly and pertinently from Davies's work.[3] Underlying Chapters 4 and 5, then, is a consideration of how adaptation complicates and problematises questions of his authorship. Specific features that have already been linked with authorship, such as world view, traits of content and theme, voice, and genre, will form our focus here.

Contextual influences: technological, institutional and artistic/ cultural (generic)

There are several contextual frameworks within which Davies must work, besides that imposed by the source text: these include technological and institutional constraints, and prevailing artistic and cultural (including generic) expectations. These contextual influences will be borne in mind throughout the ensuing analysis of Davies's adapted work.

Technological and institutional contexts are fairly self-explanatory. At any particular time, Davies can use only the technology and resources available to him – and it is clear that as the technology of television has developed, allowing mobile cameras, better image quality (through film and digital technology), better sound quality, and so on, Davies's work has become correspondingly more polished and accomplished. This is not just limited to good craftsmanship and a smooth finish; Davies is adept at exploiting new possibilities to their fullest, and his later adaptations in particular exhibit greater complexity, not just through the subtleties of dialogue and characterisation but also through a more intricate manipulation of sounds, music and images.

Institutional constraints include the personnel appointed to work with him, the limitations of their abilities and experience, and the budget assigned to a project. Davies must contend with the potential challenges to his authorial vision that such a context implies, and he couches his views on this in terms of a struggle for control: 'Part of what I'm trying to do is control the director to some extent – to write it in such a way that he's going to have to shoot it the way I want.'[4] As Davies's reputation has grown, he has gained a much bigger say over the directors and editors of his programmes, and considerably more money has been made available to support the projects; these changes have enhanced the concordant relationship between Davies as the writer, and the crew who must interpret his screenplay. In later adaptations, there is a strengthening creative integration (productive synthesis) between his approach, voice and style and those of the directors of his work. Davies' prolific output and characteristic thematic concerns has meant that while he has practised and honed his art, his directors, directors of photography, composers and other crew have begun to develop a sense of the 'Davies style', and to work synergistically with his scripts to create a more integrated, complex and polished visual style that complements and enhances his writing. This intensifies both the sense of Davies's authorship of the work and the quality of it. Thus in this and the next chapter, considerable emphasis will be placed upon exploring the relationship between Davies's script (and its characterisation, plotting and structuring, explicit and implicit themes, and tone/style) and the visual style of the adaptations.

The limitations imposed upon Davies's work by the prevailing artistic/cultural context are harder to pinpoint, and too numerous to cover in full. I shall refer to just one aspect of this context: genre. Davies's relationship with generic frameworks is an intriguing one. The adaptations in Chapter 5 sit fairly comfortably together within a single genre – that of classic-novel adaptations. The amount of work that Davies has created in that genre is such that he must be regarded as a key figure in consolidating, manipulating and perpetuating it; for reasons I suggest in the next chapter, he appears entirely at home in the genre, to the extent that he is able to challenge and reshape its conventions from within. The programmes dealt with in this chapter fall within different genres, most usually corresponding to the genre of the original source novel (e.g. the ghost story remains a ghost story, the romance remains a romance, and so on). There are two consequences of such generic variation for this study: first, Davies must work harder to sustain a sense of continuity of authorship across a set of eclectic programmes and genres; second, certain genres seem to constrain Davies negatively, and limit the possibilities for meaningful, complex and intricate work. That is, this eclecticism in genre, alongside the limitations created by other contextual factors, potentially disrupts the quality of Davies's writing, and undermines claims for his accomplishments.

'Quality' and evaluation

The question of 'quality' is inescapable in both this chapter and the next, and neither chapter shies away from evaluation. Broadly, these chapters propose that Davies's work problematises some commonly held presumptions regarding adaptation. Common parlance often declares that a great adaptation can be made only from a mediocre novel, for a great novel will overshadow an adaptation of it, whereas a good adapter might be able to improve upon a second-rate novel. If this were true, Davies's adaptations of 'lesser' books would generally display greater creativity, boldness and achievement than those of great classics and, conversely, Davies's classic-novel adaptations would appear adversely constrained – stymied, even – by the power of the original sources and their stalwart and vociferous defenders. One might expect tamer classic-novel adaptations, with Davies exhibiting less courage in meddling with the sources.

However, this is not the case. There are some fine examples in both chapters of Davies's output. Yet at the end of this chapter I shall touch upon a number of Davies's adaptations of popular literature that seem to be rather more limited in scope and ambition compared with other examples of his work, and especially in comparison with his classic-novel adaptations. It is interesting to note that the limitations in these programmes seem to arise not really from Davies's writing but from the interpretation and presentation of his work by the crew (director, composer, editor, actors). The defining feature of this process of interpretation is that *genre* becomes central in shaping the final product. The directors and actors made an attempt to preserve the genre or type of the source material, and they thus sustained the perceived attributes of that genre or type – its qualities, limitations and flaws. In short, the artistic and cultural contexts – especially the production teams' assumptions about genre, authorship and theme – deeply affect the form and the achievements of the programmes considered herein. Davies is usually able to turn this to his advantage in the case of his later adaptations, but he has less control over this process in the case of his earlier adaptations, and some of them are consequently disadvantaged, as we shall see.

Despite these exceptions, Davies's adaptations generally constitute the strongest works in his oeuvre, and it is interesting to consider why this is the case. In Chapter 3, I suggested that Davies sometimes revealed himself and his introspective concerns rather clumsily in his early, non-adapted work (e.g. *Bavarian Night*). I proposed that while self-expression is a vital aspect of authorship and of art, the very literal inclusion of his direct experiences and thoughts into his scripts gave rise to the feeling that characters were puppets who voiced Davies's views and enacted his personal conflicts and confusions. In adapting the work of others, he excels precisely because he is compelled to regard the diegetic world and its characters in a more detached manner. He is not in the position of originator or creator, but in the position of interpreter or adapter. He appears less tempted to manipulate characters' words and actions in order to express personal beliefs and dilemmas. Instead, he manages to work within a framework laid down by the novel's author and yet simultaneously express something of his own world view; this is often achieved by more subtle means than in his earlier, non-adapted work – through style, tone, voice, gesture and implication, rather than simply through words or blatant actions. In this way, one could regard the process of adaptation in comparison with a poet using the sonnet form: Davies must work within the structures of the novel and any generic or other contextual context, but it is the way in which he manipulates significant details within that formal structure that reveals his talent as a writer and adapter. The interrelation between Davies's creativity and the framework of the source novels is thus another aspect explored in this chapter.

Introducing adaptation

Growing out of the concerns outlined above, this chapter offers an overview of Davies's non-classic novel adaptations. A brief introduction to the process and concept of adaptation is necessary in this chapter, and an analysis of Davies's gripping adaptation of the ghost story *The Signalman*,[5] will open up this subject. Following this, I shall reintroduce the notion of Davies's authorship and world view, and consider in particular his adaptation of R. F. Delderfield's *To Serve Them All My Days* in terms of a meeting of minds between the two writers. Turning then to Davies's 1990s adaptations, and with special consideration of *The Old Devils* (from Kingsley Amis's novel), I shall investigate how his work in this period builds upon technological, institutional and artistic advances, and exhibits a stronger sense of thematic and stylistic integration, resulting in more complex and emotive work. Finally, I shall briefly consider the limitations of genre, looking at Davies's adaptations of a selection of 'middlebrow' novelists' work, and considering how the generic expectations of directors, performers and viewers undermined the potential for the irony, subtlety and stylistic achievement seen in some of Davies's other programmes during this period.

Within the above structure, there are three case studies explored in detail: *The Signalman* (1976), *To Serve Them All My Days* (1980), and *The Old Devils* (1992). These examples were chosen because they are interesting, accomplished and engaging programmes that offer very different points of view upon our central topics of authorship and adaptation. Across the three, from the late 1970s to the early 1990s, Davies appropriates the source material and reshapes it to reflect his own concerns. Whilst the first example is a successful, faithful adaptation, the second displays an intriguing mixture of agreement and tension between Delderfield's vision and Davies's (re)vision, and the third sees Davies appropriating Amis's work to offer a personal view of his own. These observations are not evaluative: *The Signalman* is not better for being 'faithful', nor is *The Old Devils* better for being more distinctively authored by Davies; simply, the changing nature of Davies's authorial presence within the programmes, and the ways in which this is achieved, clearly pertain to our concerns here.

The Signalman (1976)

The Signalman is technically impressive and beautifully paced and structured; in this programme we can already see Davies's flair for adapting great novelists. This was his second adaptation, following *The Imp of the Perverse* (1975), which was adapted from Poe's short story, and is now unavailable. *The Signalman* was more widely acclaimed than the Poe adaptation, and has recently been re-released on video and DVD. It is included in this chapter, which focuses primarily on Davies's early adaptations, although it is clearly somewhat different in that the source text is by a 'classic' author (Dickens). However, the source text is not a novel but a short story, and the text is strongly generic: a ghost story. The adaptation's generic identity is made clear by the title that opens the programme: 'A Ghost Story'; the work then becomes subsumed within another group of texts – 'classic Christmas programmes'.[6] Thus the adaptation is not announced as a classic-novel adaptation, for its status as a ghost story and a classic television text is foregrounded.

The Signalman provides a useful case study to introduce key aspects of the process of adaptation, as it highlights the changes required to adapt a literary text to an audio-visual medium. In particular, it exposes the challenges that an adapter faces in re-presenting literary elements, and reveals how a text might be successfully adapted, using details of colour, sound, music to convey characters, themes, atmosphere and specifically 'literary' features found in the source text. I do not presuppose that the adaptation ought faithfully to 'reproduce' the source text; however, it is clear that there are many continuities and equivalences to be found between these two texts, and I shall focus on these to illuminate the challenges and possibilities of adaptation.

The source text

Dickens's short story relates the tale of a signalman who is haunted by a ghostly figure that appears by the train tunnel he oversees. The figure seems to be trying to warn him of impending danger, and indeed after each appearance some sort of accident or tragedy occurs on the line near or in the tunnel. The narrator is a traveller who meets and befriends the troubled signalman, only to be drawn into and implicated within his fateful situation.

The story features many elements that aid its adaptation to the screen. Its short length is helpful to the adapter: the piece is only approximately 5,000 words long, and the adaptation runs for forty minutes; this allows Davies to avoid the severe compression ordinarily required in adaptation. The writing creates vivid images in the reader's mind. Places and people are descriptively drawn, and the story has a relatively clear time structure: these elements of precision and specificity allow the adapter to replicate them in his screenplay. Above all, the story is punchy, gripping and unusual. One can see why Davies was drawn to adapt it.

However, many elements in the story are trickier to re-present on television, especially those that are closely tied to the literary medium. These include the interweaving of the dominant themes of communication, time and the supernatural; aspects of atmosphere and mood; the interrelation of character and situation; features arising from the symbolic nature of written language, such as abstractions, ambiguity and temporal aspects; and the deployment of varied subjectivities and voices.

Themes, atmosphere/mood, character and situation

The centrality of communication as a theme is conveyed in the story's short opening line – the call of the narrator to the signalman: 'Halloa! Below there!' The story is about the attempt to communicate and the consequences of miscommunication, about speaking and listening, and about the limitations of the spoken word. The signalman is shaken by the attempts of a supernatural presence to speak to him; he is unable to understand its non-verbal communications, with dire consequences. Verbal communication is depicted as ambiguous, laden with meaning of which the speaker is often unaware – thus the signalman is terrified by the narrator's innocent greeting; interpretation is equally difficult, and the narrator must unravel the signalman's confused conversation, assessing the significance of both what is said and what remains unsaid, in the silences.

Relatedly, the story conveys a strong sense of the vital importance of time: time presses upon the signalman, who spends his days waiting for another sign, and who fears, correctly, that a moment of great consequence is bearing down upon him. He is a man trapped by time rather than by circumstance. Of the signalman's regrets about his past life, the narrator notes, 'He had made his bed, and he lay upon it. It was far too late to make another.' The second sentence implies an air of finality, of inevitability, of fate, echoing his broader situation.

Finally, there is the theme of the supernatural, which is presented as integrally connected with the real, physical world, and with the sensations and feelings of the characters. Take this moment from early in the text: 'Just then there came a vague vibration in the earth and air, quickly changing into a violent pulsation, and an oncoming rush that caused me to start back, as though it had force to draw me down.' The language used here implies a supernatural presence, building upon the sense of obscure foreboding already established. Yet the narrator continues, 'When such vapour as rose to my height from this rapid train had passed me, and was skimming away over the landscape, I looked down again ...' Suddenly it is made clear that the narrator was feeling sensations caused by a material object – a speeding train – and we are made to feel a little shamefaced in attributing the previous sentence to a greater metaphysical presence. Yet the story plays with this dynamic so frequently that we come to see that it is unwise to be certain either way: things are not what they seem, and sometimes the simplest, most tangible explanation is the wrong one.

The piece conveys an extraordinarily powerful atmosphere or mood, primarily through the cumulative effect of pertinent adjectives and adverbs: the train tunnel is described as having 'a barbarous, depressing, and forbidding air. So little sunlight ever found its way to this spot, that it had an earthy, deadly smell; and so much cold wind rushed through it, that it struck chill to me, as if I had left the natural world.' Here, the narrator offers a perfectly reasonable explanation for the tunnel's eerie effect upon him (lack of sunlight, a windy spot), but his response to its atmosphere goes beyond his reasoning, and he is compelled to suggest the existence of some malevolent being beyond the 'natural world'. Throughout the story, the narrator battles with his fears, applying his rational and scientific mind to the curious and frightening phenomena he and the signalman experience. Writing about the signalman's tale, he says, 'Resisting the slow touch of a frozen finger tracing out my spine, I showed him how that this figure must be a deception of his sense of sight ...', and then continues for several lines with a plausible medical explanation. Yet his opening words linger in our minds, and undermine the persuasiveness of his subsequent argument. Finally the narrator must accept the existence of the supernatural, for the story ends with the revelation of his own undeniable, though involuntary, part in the tale: 'Without prolonging the narrative to dwell on any one of its curious circumstances more than on any other, I may, in closing it, point out the coincidence that the warning of the Engine-Driver included, not only the words which the unfortunate Signal-man had repeated to me as haunting him, but also the words which I myself – not he – had attached, and that only in my own mind, to the gesticulation [the arm waving] he had imitated.'

The narrator is thus fully implicated within the story. A similarly intimate relationship between character and situation is emphasised implicitly throughout, such as when the signalman's appearance is described: 'a dark sallow man, with a dark beard and rather heavy eyebrows'. Coming immediately before a description of his location, a strong connection is forged between the man and his environment: both are dark and heavy. This enhances a sense of foreshadowing – as if the man was predestined to be there, fated to remain there.

Modes of expression: abstractions, ambiguity, temporal aspects
As many adaptation theorists have noted, written language is capable of particular modes of expression that are deemed inaccessible to audio-visual media like film and television: abstraction and ambiguity are two of these.[7]

Abstractions are present in *The Signalman* in its statements about non-material matters that are not in themselves perceptible to the senses; this includes aspects like atmosphere and mood, thoughts, sensations and feelings, ideas and theories, and so on. The capacity of language to present non-material things directly is the reason that literary themes can potentially be presented relatively directly (although Dickens is much more subtle here). Writing is also metaphorical, implying meaningfulness beyond the overtly presented events in the story. This aspect of literature rests to some degree upon writers' implicit awareness that readers are capable of discerning the concepts and dichotomies behind the particularities of a story, and reading a story on both literal and figurative levels. Here, Dickens suggests a number of dichotomies, which inform our reading of *The Signalman* and which endow the story with a referentiality beyond its particular contents. These include light/dark and confinement/freedom, and most importantly the dichotomy between reason, science and philosophy on the one hand, and superstition, intuition and the inexplicable (and supernatural) on the other.

Relatedly, ambiguity arises from the flexibility of written language, which is precise yet also symbolic and mutable. While words are relatively precise, sentences can be ambiguous, creating double meanings, implied meanings, irony, and so on. That is, a sentence need not mean precisely and only what it appears to say; it is open to alternative interpretations. In contrast, the visual image is relatively distinct and precise, and an adapter must work hard to replicate the ambiguity and broad referential range of language. Dickens can write, 'The monstrous thought came into my mind ... that this [the signalman] was a spirit, not a man.' The precision of language means that Dickens can temporarily allow us to consider the possibility that this man might be a spirit – not a ghoul, or a ghost, or a zombie, but precisely a 'spirit', and the particular word brings particular, intended connotations. In addition, the symbolic nature of language – the fact that there is no intrinsic relation between the way a word looks and what it signifies – means that our imagining the man as a spirit is not hindered by the material concreteness of a real, manly presence before us. Dickens is able manipulate the images in our minds because although the words are precise, their connections with particular referents are not concrete and definite but mutable and vague – this arises from language's symbolic quality. Consider the problems such a sentence might pose for a filmmaker wishing to adapt it: he does not have the precision that can specify 'spirit' over 'ghost', and he is hampered by the material presence of a particular actor, who cannot change form in order to imply a different perception of him (from man to spirit and back again, or the two entities existing simultaneously within the same space and time). Finally, Dickens's sentence represents the subjectivity – not just the perception – of a particular onlooker, and abstractions of subjectivity such as thoughts, feelings and ideas cannot be directly presented on the screen.

Temporal features like rhythm and pace can be created in language through the placement of words and sentences, the length of these, and the sounds of the words that are chosen by the writer. In the adaptation of *The Signalman*, rhythm is used to great effect; this element is less prominent in the source text. Repetition, another temporal feature, is also exploited in the adaptation, and indeed is evident within Dickens's text (e.g. the word 'figure' is echoed in the piece and conflates the narrator with the 'ghost', for both are referred to thus on different occasions).[8]

Subjectivities and voice(s)

As this is a topic to which I shall return in greater detail later (in Chapter 5), I shall offer only a few comments here – sufficient to inform my analysis of the adaptation. The story is written in the first person, by a narrator who is, as we have seen, uncertain about his own responses to events, and eager to deny his fears and quandaries, and to present himself as a rational and detached observer. We gain easy access to his subjective thoughts and feelings, though this is tempered by his desire to present a particular image of himself to the reader. Access to the subjectivity of the signalman is more tricky, and is implied through what is said of him; the narrator dominates the presentation of this character, often presenting his dialogue through indirect speech, and naming him in the third person (i.e. 'he').

Despite the consistent narrator, there are frequent changes in person and in voice in the story, especially through movements from direct to indirect speech, and from the narrator's passionate and acutely remembered account of events to his more detached attempts to commentate upon them in retrospect.

The adaptation

Themes, atmosphere/mood, character and situation

The themes of communication, time and the supernatural are fore-grounded in the adaptation, and their interrelation gives rise to an eerie and tense atmosphere. The themes are communicated through a combination of expressive elements that are carefully deployed and integrated, with stylistic decisions by director Lawrence Gordon Clark complementing Davies's script. The programme does not resort to ghost story clichés. The lighting, for example, is typically atmospheric, with the signalman often being presented in half-light and half-darkness (figure 7). Yet this is not merely creepy chiaroscuro, for it also importantly implies that the man is bound to his dark situation and his environment, and indeed to his fate, which gradually consumes him.

As in Dickens's story, the vital yet fragile nature of communication is central. The limitations and ambiguity of words and language are explored,[9] in particular through the obsessive recurrence of the cry 'Halloa! Below there!' There are repeated shots of the bell lines that run across the countryside to the signalman's box, which emphasise his connection with the outside world while also exposing the tenuousness of that connection and the man's relative remoteness. The signalman's dependency upon these lines is thus foregrounded, which presages the crucial moment at the end of the programme when he misses the Morse

7 *The Signalman* (1976): a man half consumed by the darkness

message from his head office. The signalman is ultimately undone, however, not by a lack of communication but by his inability to respond to a diversity of it: here is where the true danger lies. The man is confused and overwhelmed: what or whom should he listen to? How should he respond? In the end his indecision in these matters proves fatal.

Davies introduces the theme of time into his dialogue rather skilfully, by leaving the word unsaid, so that we supply it ourselves. The signalman explains why he does maths: 'It serves to pass the ...'; he breaks off, gets up from his chair and looks fearfully at the bell. The missing word – 'time' – is connected with the signalman's fears and his fate. Time, both the word and the concept, hangs heavy in the air, unarticulated yet felt. (It shares this quality of indeterminacy with other abstractions central to the story.) A loudly ticking clock in the signalman's box sustains our awareness of the pressing nature of time throughout the programme.

There is some sense of compression of the source text within the programme, and the performances of Denholm Elliot as the signalman and Bernard Lloyd as the traveller (the narrator in the source text) exude anticipatory apprehension. As the signalman relates previous forewarnings and their subsequent outcomes, and declares that the most recent premonition occurred only one week ago, we hear for the first time a ghostly ring (a vague hum) coming from his warning bell, which accentuates the sense of dread as we await the event it foreshadows.[10] The timing of this sound is crucial in creating tension, which is further enhanced by the timing of repeated images through the programme. In this way, fundamentally temporal features such as rhythm and repetition (explored in the next section) are employed so that they shape and structure the whole text, enhancing the viewer's awareness of temporal constraints, and creating an omnipresent feeling of unease.

The key dichotomy that underlay Dickens's story (reason, science and philosophy versus superstition, intuition and the inexplicable/supernatural) is introduced in the adaptation primarily through dialogue; it is then sustained in a more diffuse manner. Davies alters the signalman's motives for giving up his studies in natural philosophy; in the source text, the man claims he tired of studying, but in the adaptation he proclaims 'But what's it [philosophy] tell us? Nothing. No motion without cause, a reason for everything ... I found myself dissatisfied with it, I ...' (he breaks off, as the real warning bell rings). It is implied that the signalman's faith in scientific and philosophical reason has been shaken by (other-) worldly experience – and the timing of the interruption by his warning bell suggests that the bell is somehow the cause of his dissatisfaction (which in some sense it is).

Interestingly, the close relationship between this world and the supernatural, or at least the potential difficulty we may experience in distinguishing the two, is presented primarily through an inventive use of sound that vivifies the noises described within the written source text. The ringing of the bell, its ghostly vibrations, the whistling of the wind, the humming of the signalman, and the use of music that echoes these, create an overall sense of ambiguity, so that one is unable to distinguish diegetic from non-diegetic sounds, or to delineate natural from man-made from other-worldly ones. This is used most successfully at the climax of the programme, when a medley of such sounds implies the traveller's fundamental implication in the signalman's situation and fate. The traveller strides across the fields, merrily whistling; there is a cut to the signalman's box, where the signalman, busying himself, begins to whistle too, suggesting a synergy between himself and the traveller; in a separate shot, a train can be seen travelling at speed along the train track; suddenly, the signalman pauses in his work and stares at the bell – simultaneously, a faint hum can be discerned on the soundtrack; the traveller stops in his tracks, freezes, and touches his ear, as if he can hear the eerie sound too, and then, as if he has understood all these signals for the first time, and has interpreted their meaning, he runs to the train track in the hope of preventing calamity.

We saw above how the use of silence – an unspoken word – was highly effective in drawing attention to what is not said and what is not heard (the word 'time'). Similarly, Davies uses silence and those things that are imperceptible to suggest the presence of something supernatural. When the signalman's bell rings for real, he happily jumps up to perform his duties; the noise of the bell in this world is reassuringly present. It is when the bell appears silent that the signalman fears it, and gazes upon it. Later, when we discover the reason for his fearful glances – that at those times, he heard its ghostly vibration – we experience an uneasy sense that we had been present without observing, that we had watched without really seeing, hearing, perceiving. The existence of things we cannot straightforwardly perceive is thus confirmed.

Character and situation are, as in the source text, closely interrelated, particularly through Davies's dialogue, which weaves together the threads of Dickens's story. The signalman says of his situation, 'I'm accustomed to it. Why, in the early days I'd sometimes find a slack time to climb up into the sunlight, but my ... the work was always here to draw me down. I'd listen for the bell you see – my face would be in the sun, but my mind would be down here in the dark and the shadows. I think the mind makes its own places, Sir.' The signalman's psyche is presented here as fundamentally connected to his environment; the 'place' that his mind makes is precisely the dark, shadowy situation in which he finds himself. Davies endows this speech with metaphorical as well as literal meanings, making it potentially ambiguous and symbolically rich.

Modes of expression: abstractions, ambiguity, temporal aspects
We have seen how a combination of dialogue and visual details is used to present various abstractions (themes, atmosphere, mood). The adaptation must also deal with the challenge of conveying ambiguity, given the concreteness of the visual image; this problem is overcome by the careful placement of details within the frame, and by the use of temporal features such as the repetition and juxtaposition of images and scenes.

At times, framing is used to highlight particular objects – as with the close-ups of the warning bell, for example. At other times, though, significant details are not placed centrally in the frame, but are deployed almost subliminally. There is a rope hook (a noose) that hangs upon the wall of the signalman's box, next to the coat hook upon which the traveller hangs his coat. It is not a point of focus, and might be missed by a first-time viewer, but in its similarity to a hangman's noose it subtly enhances the sense of foreboding in the scene.

The use of carefully timed juxtaposition and repetition support the viewer's sense of the fusion of the physical world with a supernatural one. At one point, the signalman stands outside the train tunnel and, shifting his gaze from the traveller to the red light, utters the words 'I am simply a man'. A sudden and immediate cut shows a bird flying up and away, as if scared by something on the ground; the flutter of its wings is heightened on the soundtrack, so that the viewer involuntarily jumps. It is as if the bird's response denies the signalman's words, for the quick juxtaposition implies that the bird reacts to his statement by

8 *The Signalman* (1976): rictus

taking flight. The relationship between statement and bird is ambiguous, which leads the viewer to attempt to resolve its ambiguity: this is achieved by regarding the bird as an augury of some kind.

There are several repeated and near-repeated images and scenes in the adaptation. Perhaps one of the most striking of these is the open-mouthed scream, reminiscent of Edvard Munch's painting,[11] and conveying a similar horrific aura; we see this on the face of the spirit, the signalman, and the traveller (both as he awakes from his nightmare and in shock, after the final, fatal accident) (figure 8). The repetition of this same rictus by different characters underlines the inescapable, predestined connections between them and strengthens the cohesive nature of the story.

Near-repetition is also used to reinforce the themes of the programme, such as when a graphic match cuts from the glowing coals in the signalman's fireplace to the red light outside the tunnel. This suggests a potentially dangerous link between the two locations, and the signalman's claustrophobic entrapment within his situation, as if the invisible connections holding his world together are like a web in which he is caught and cannot escape. This is intensified later in the programme when two other similar shots depict the hot coals in the train's engine and then the most striking image: the terrible, fatal furnace in the tunnel.

Subjectivities and voice(s)
As might be expected, given its medium, subjectivity is less marked in the adaptation, and many moments that are internal to the narrator in the source text (his thoughts and feelings) are externalised in the programme. The moment in which the narrator suddenly fears that the signalman is a spirit, for example, is not presented directly, but the juxtaposition of the fleeing bird after the signalman's assertion that he is 'just a man' implies a similar doubt about that statement.

However, in staying with the traveller, and by including his dream sequences, the adaptation implies that we have access to his subjectivity, and through this the programme manages to convey the most psychologically salient aspect of the source text: the traveller's absolute imbrication within the story. The traveller dreams of a train tunnel collision. The following day, he discovers from the signalman that there was indeed a collision, and as the signalman relates his story, we see the dream images replayed, implying the subjectivity of the traveller (we are 'seeing into his mind') and a kind of prescience on the traveller's part. The active role that the traveller unwittingly (and unwillingly) plays within the story is also implied at its denouement, through the significant series of connected sounds described earlier.

Using television

The achievement of Davies's *The Signalman* is that it fully exploits its medium, drawing upon the source text for inspiration, but integrating sound and image in a way that seems utterly televisual. Details are foregrounded and layered within shots, and juxtaposition and repetition across shots and scenes enhance the meaningfulness and cohesion of the programme. In adapting such a successful ghost story to the screen, there is a risk of over-visualising, allowing shock effects to destroy the haunting, imaginative power of its source. Yet this adaptation carefully controls and restricts its visual capacity, offering only small, significant visual details and ambiguous aural titbits, so that when total visual access is promised, and the traveller strides over to the window to look directly at the haunted red light, the viewer is reluctant to look, for fear of what he or she might see. Paradoxically, the television audience begins to fear the act of seeing, and dread the event of hearing.

Kindred spirits? Davies and Delderfield

Following *The Signalman*, Davies directed two BBC adaptations of R. F. Delderfield's work: *To Serve Them All My Days* (1980), directed by Ronald Wilson, and *Diana* (1983), directed by Richard Stroud and David Tucker. Davies's adaptations followed a BBC adaptation of Delderfield's *A Horseman Riding By* (1977),[12] adapted by Arden Winch, John Wiles and Alexander Baron, directed by Paul Ciappessoni, Philip Dudley and Alan Grint, and produced by Ken Riddington, who went on to produce Davies's two Delderfield adaptations.

R. F. Delderfield's popular novels and sagas chronicle the lives, experiences and memories of ordinary people. In this, and in his focus upon interpersonal relationships against a broader social, political and historical background, he is comparable with Davies, although, as we shall see, there exist some points of disagreement and differing emphases.

To Serve Them All My Days (1980)

I shall focus on To Serve, which I believe is the richer and more success-ful of Davies's two adaptations, partly because the themes of the source novel allowed him to present aspects of his own world view within the adaptation. As implied above, there is a sympathy between Delderfield and Davies, epitomised in their fundamentally liberal, realistic and optimistic views of the world, and the first part of my analysis will explore this concord. However, Davies also marks his authorship within To Serve by extending and highlighting tensions present in the novel, and by introducing his own productive complication into the text. This vivifies what might otherwise have been a rather restrained nostalgic piece.

To Serve was an extended serial of thirteen parts. David Powlett-Jones (John Duttine), the protagonist, has been released from the army with shell shock, and takes up a job at a private school in the Devonshire countryside; his rehabilitation and adaptation to this new environment are the focus of the story. In a sense, life begins afresh for David, though memories of his experiences in the war still occasionally haunt him. This tale of communal school life, its absurdities but also its ability to inspire and encourage, echoes Davies's ongoing reflection upon the value(s) of education (as seen, for example, in A Very Peculiar Practice, and in his series Marmalade and The Boot Street Band for children).

The credits of the adaptation tell us something of the institutional and cultural context in which it was made. They depict the authorship of the programme thus: 'To Serve ...', 'by R. F. Delderfield', 'Dramatised by Andrew Davies'. The use of the term 'dramatised' (rather than 'adapted'), was a BBC convention at the time, and its connotations are interesting. While 'adaptation' implies a determined attempt to reshape source material to fit a new medium, 'dramatisation' implies that the source material is more readily re-presented – that it merely needs to be performed, acted out (mimesis), made more 'dramatic' (in the sense of being staged). The first implies amendment of plot, theme and character, the second that the source is being brought to life almost unaltered. Consequently, the notion of authorship implied in each case is different. With 'dramatisation', authorship is reduced to the necessary stage in-between, the groundwork for the subsequent performance of the original text; 'adaptation' suggests a process of working upon, rebuilding and reshaping the text. The contemporary BBC notion of dramatisation suggests that the role of a screenwriter-adapter like Davies was regarded as primarily functional or skilful, rather than artistic or creative.[13]

A meeting of minds: the essence of To Serve in Delderfield and Davies

> Howarth's words came back to him – 'Here you've got something to hold on to, to live for, to make something of. It won't make much difference for a month or a year, but it will in the end, I promise.'
>
> Was there anything in that beyond conventional words of comfort? Howarth's astringent way of saying that time would heal, or something equally banal? Winterbourne's [a boy at the school] private battle seemed to insist that there was, that by submerging body and soul into the ethos of Bamfylde, or some other school with an identical function, he could, in the years left to him, find shape and cohesion in the way he had when he had emerged, equally battered, from an earlier ordeal. (Delderfield, 1972: 191)

David's recovery (from the war and then from his bereavement) at Bamfylde is vital – it is the essence of the school and its community, and it forms the backbone of the narrative; Davies's adaptation aims to re-present these central aspects. Yet the kind of writing above, which is essentially an internal dialogue, full of ideas, thoughts, memories and questions, is a challenge for the adapter. As in *The Signalman*, the adaptation of *To Serve* often externalises such passages, and images and sounds are interwoven to create a layering effect particular to audio-visual media. In this way the central themes are sustained.

The credit sequence, repeated at the start of every one of the thirteen episodes of *To Serve* allows the interaction of a song with salient images of the school and its environment. The choice of music is crucial for setting the mood, style and pace of the serial – and in choosing lyrical music, the words also becomes influential. The sequence begins with a shot of the school gathered for morning assembly; the boys stand and sing the school hymn; their singing continues on the soundtrack as images of the school are presented in a montage sequence, edited through dissolves:

> Look ahead to a life worth living,
> Full of hope, full of play, full of cheer,
> To a life that is made for giving,
> Without sin, without shame, without fear.

Look ahead to the one who leads us,
To the hope who lights our way,
We shall follow, follow, follow,
We shall follow him all our days.

Immediately, the words of the song establish the central themes of the serial. Looking forward, being hopeful, and giving to others – these notions are vital, for in these lie David's salvation and recovery, and the same for those at the school (and outside it) who must face the future after losing so many of their number to the First World War (just ending as the novel begins). Although one can obviously understand 'the one ... the hope' as the Christian God, it is significant that God is not explicitly named. 'The one ... the hope' allows for a broader interpretation, and indeed it is not so much Christian faith that lights the way for David and the others at Bamfylde, as a sense of shared purpose, shared values, and a recognition of members' individual goals and vocations. Indeed, both the book and the programme trace David's discovery of a sense of purpose and consolation, and these are found in his vocation, his work in the broadest sense: in his teaching of History (and English), his study and research in the subject, and his communications with others about it. It is not God who 'lights [his] way', when David's wife and children are killed in a car crash[14] – it is his work, and the community at Bamfylde that supports it.

The editing of this sequence, through slow dissolves rather than cuts, does not just slow the pace to reflect the rather elegiac hymn; it simultaneously connects images more strongly, as one image fleetingly exists simultaneously with another. As images of the old school buildings (devoid of humans) are mixed with images of present pupils of the school, there is a strong sense of the place's reassuring permanence and continuity through the generations – a sense that the school stands, and stands *for* things, long beyond the era of particular members of its community. The song stresses the importance of looking ahead, not backwards, but the images affirm the value of the past and of history, and the lingering of the past within the present.

David and his peers must learn, then, to balance their attachment to the past, present and future, and this can be done only by forging and sustaining the links between them. When David considers quitting the school, after his bereavement, one of the boys notes that he 'belongs here', because he 'gets through' to the boys: 'Particularly in your subject. I never gave a damn about history before you taught it. I mean, it was no more than a string of dates, and dead mutton to me and to most of the other chaps. But you made it ... well, *mean* something. You showed us how it fits in with today, if you see what I mean?' David is a natural teacher of History, and 'fits into' the school's ideal community, because he is able to make learning meaningful – and he does so by emphasising how history connects with the present. Again, Delderfield's concerns tally with those of Davies; this moment is picked up *A Very Peculiar Practice*, when Lillian Hubbard, a much respected Professor of History, finds herself forced to stand up for the values of her subject against the undermining of higher education by those who would turn it into a business.[15]

The credits end with the image of a clean blackboard: a clean slate, a space waiting to be filled, a story waiting to be written. It reminds the viewer how important it is to be sure about what should be written on that board, what should be taught, and with what consequences. The answer proffered by the programme is not simplistic (not black and white), but it is sincere and heartfelt. The values of a traditional, broad, liberal education are defended, with particular emphasis placed on History, English and (to some extent) Science and Drama. The characters explicitly debate the nature and purpose of education; the topic is also implicitly addressed by scenes of successful teaching, which combine an emphasis on traditional subjects and high academic standards with participatory, question-led teaching techniques. Threats to this positive vision of education are represented, as in *A Very Peculiar Practice*, by careerist teachers more interested in their own success than the boys', and by invidious ideologies and bureaucracies.[16]

In the choice of *To Serve*, then, Davies found a way to express his belief in the central importance of education within his liberal world view, and it is intriguing to note how his later screenplay *A Very Peculiar Practice* recalled particular themes and moments from this serial.

Notes of tension

While the synergy between Delderfield's and Davies's preoccupations is strong, there are two key notes of tension within the serial that constitute a minor but troubling undertone to the utopia presented above. The first, arising from the novel, and retained and heightened by Davies, is an ideological or political tension around the notion of the individual within the institution, community or group. This is explored within the adaptation as various characters, including David, must come to terms with familial, class and political affiliations that are sometimes in conflict. The adaptation gives relatively more time to these issues than does the novel.[17]

The second key tension is introduced by Davies, but it relates to and grows out of the first, in that both are concerned with the question of identity and the placing of the individual within a particular role. This complication of the source text highlights Davies's authorial role and voice within the adaptation.

Passion and women

Davies is often accused of adding sex and passion to his adaptations with blatant disregard for the nature and tone of the source texts. At the same time, he is praised for his powerful, witty, cunning female characters. What many critics fail to notice is that the two features are frequently positively linked. In *To Serve*, it is such additions that create an intriguing, unresolved undercurrent, a sense that all that is on the surface is not all that there is. The adaptation introduces passion and its repression, partly through its presentation of the women in the serial and their role within this 'ideal community', but particularly through Julia (Kim Braden), a shortlived teacher of English, who enlivens the programme and brings to the school a sense of reckless endangerment, disturbing its dear but somewhat staid inhabitants. She is a threat, or at least a provocation, to the cherished status quo at Bamfylde, which headmaster Algie Harries (Frank Middlemass) describes as 'our refuge from womankind'; however, her influence is an appealing and welcome one to the viewers. In dramatic terms, Julia brings not open conflict but unexpressed tension – she asks questions that the ethos of Bamfylde, and the 'perfect' housewife Beth (Belinda Lang), David's wife, cannot answer. There is something ultimately unrestrained about her, as she struggles against the limitations of the roles open to her. Unlike in the novel, Julia is presented in direct contrast to Beth; later, Chris Forster (Susan Jameson) also troubles simple notions of feminine domesticity and docility. Through its depiction of Julia and Chris, the adaptation offers a wider range of female roles and subjectivities with which viewers may engage.[18]

Part 4 is the key episode in which these tensions are established and explored, for it focuses upon Julia's story at Bamfylde. In this episode, Julia's meaningfulness seems in excess of the actual duration of her presence; thus, the values and ideas that are encapsulated by her are given greater prominence than in the novel. Davies gives Julia a stronger voice than does Delderfield. Julia's powerful significance is conveyed directly through dialogue, but is enhanced by sympathetic direction from Ronald Wilson, which complements Davies's script and subtly emphasises his concerns. In particular, a visual motif of windows is used throughout this episode in connection with Julia. This motif comments upon Julia's sense of containment at Bamfylde, and also, further, it links her with passion, especially sexual passion, which is related to freedom – she is potentially a breath of fresh air. Julia evokes and then personifies potential unrestrained passion within the warm but dry atmosphere of the school; David's response to this is intriguingly ambiguous.

In an original scene by Davies, Julia is shown setting her English class a composition entitled 'My dream'; she encourages them to be as bold and imaginative as they can in their essays. Proclaiming that 'if I were writing this, I wouldn't know where to stop', she reveals a passionate soul, and gazes from the window as if yearning for escape, or at least a different horizon. Later, after her departure, we see Howarth teaching his English class, this scene rhyming with the first. Howarth (Alan MacNaughton) reads aloud Shakespeare's Sonnet 129, 'The expense of spirit in a waste of shame', to the three sixth-formers, one of whom is Blades (Philip Franks) (with whom Julia had her relatively innocent dalliance). Julia's connection with poetry has been emphasised throughout, and is implied as the catalyst for her relationship with Blades. The connection between Julia, love poetry, and the outside world as glimpsed through a window is reinforced, as Blades gazes towards the window just as Julia did earlier. The camera cuts to a shot from the vantage point of that window, looking down on Julia as she leaves the school for the last time. Back in the class, the noise of her car leaving disturbs the poetry, and Howarth closes the window. He offers his summary of the poem: 'The subject of course is sexual passion. Hmmm ... And Shakespeare spares us none of the unpleasant truth.' Howarth rejects a heartfelt, emotional response to the poem; instead he attempts to classify and contain its sentiments, and indeed to turn the verse to his own ends and use it as a moral example. 'Sexual passion' is a dry descriptor of the more subtle longing expressed in Julia's character and actions. Furthermore, Howarth's resolute closing of the window expresses a desire to shut such things out, to deny them to himself and the boys. The noise that Julia makes – her interruption of his re-reading of the poem – is suppressed, her interjection denied.

Most interesting of all are the connotations of the final instance of this motif. Immediately after the above scene, we cut to Beth and David in their cottage. David is writing, and Beth is busying herself with tea in the background. They discuss Julia's departure, and Beth asks, 'Did you like her? You never really told me how it went when you went for that terrible, serious chat of yours [about Blades].' David, with his back to Beth and facing the camera, does not answer immediately but compresses his lips, as if he wants to hold something back, and not speak (figure 9). Finally he answers vaguely, 'Oh, it went all right, really.' He breathes out heavily, as if somewhat exasperated or dissatisfied, and, in an unusual action for his character, impetuously rises from his chair,

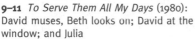

9–11 *To Serve Them All My Days* (1980): David muses, Beth looks on; David at the window; and Julia

moves to the window and opens it. We hear a gentle breeze, making us aware of restless movement in the world outside. David comments, 'She was a strange woman.' Beth asks, 'I wonder if we'll ever see her again, Davy. Do you think we will?' There is a cut to David, who is distracted, deep in thought, and pays little attention to Beth's question. He is softly lit by light coming in through the window, which warms the white shirt he wears (figure 10). Significantly, a sustained high note on the violin introduces the rare musical theme, which indicates emotional signi-ficance. Beth repeats, 'Davy?' David's response, 'Hmmm … What? Oh, er, no, I shouldn't think so', sounds unconvincing and unconvinced, given the connection forged between himself and the absent Julia, through the open window motif and the musical theme. The connection is reinforced with the next and final shot, of Julia on the train. She removes her hat, smiles as if she knows the truth of the situation, and settles in for her journey (figure 11). The presence of a cream window frame and seat cover echoes the soft white of David's shirt in the pre-vious scene and hints at a future romantic connection between the two, which is further confirmed by the use of a mix rather than a cut, so that their images are momentarily superimposed. Most importantly, the suggestion of Julia's future significance keeps alive the enticing possibility of the kind of sexual passion that Howarth wished to exclude from the world of Bamfylde, and that David denies appeals to him.

The window motif is interesting because it implies that Davies, supported by director Ronald Wilson, does not want Julia to lose as Delderfield forces her to. Delderfield's novel arguably depicts Beth as the most favoured female character. She is bubbly and intelligent, but also quick to abandon her independence and career in order to settle down with David at the school, have children, and be a housewife. Though she does participate in school life, this is primarily in domesticated ways – holding tea parties for the young boys, for example (this contrasts with Chris Forster's more ambitious and energetic engagement with the educational activities of the school). A modern reader/viewer might find the valorisation of Beth rather difficult to swallow, and she certainly does not seem to exhibit the features of a classic Davies heroine such as those seen in his later classic-novel adaptations, lacking the sparkiness, cunning, wit and seductiveness of his more renowned female protagonists. We have already seen that Julia is given a greater voice in the adaptation, implying that she stands for important qualities which might be lacking at the school, and even in David and his peers. In an added scene in part 4 in which Julia visits Beth for tea, a comparison between the two is made clear, and is recast as a tentative critique of Beth's pre-feminist attitudes and behaviour.

The tea takes place after a dramatic incident in which a section of the school catches fire. Beth concludes that 'It's all over now', and Julia remarks, 'And Bamfylde returns to its usual tedium.' Beth ignores the comment, but Julia refuses to let the idea rest. Moving to the window, Julia finds that she cannot gaze out of it, for it is covered in nets, and *sotto voce* she asks, 'How do you live here?', the intonation implying a statement of disbelief rather than a genuine enquiry. When asked to repeat the question, she amends it to something less overwhelming:

> Julia: What do you do with your time?
> Beth: Well, the twins take up most of it now.
> Julia: Oh yes, there is *that* about them ... And that's plenty for you, is it, Beth?
> [Beth avoids a direct answer to the question, instead describing the activities that keep her amused during the day.]
> Julia (somewhat impatiently): Yes, of course, but I mean, *before* this you ... you did have a job before you were married?
> [Beth replies that she was a nurse. Julia expresses her frustration with Bamfylde and her desire to do more, and see more of life. Finally Beth responds.]
> Beth: You make me feel so dull.

Julia's questioning of Beth's choices, set alongside Julia's personification of appealing vitality and passion, constitutes an implicit critique
of Beth, who represents the perfect model of domesticated, maternal
femininity, and whom David seems to idolise[19] (though his performance in this episode, as we have seen, implies the presence of repressed
feelings and desires). Thus Davies reshapes Julia's character to allow
space for an alternative voice, and an alternative woman. This affects
not just the characters' relationships but the depiction of Bamfylde itself
and its values. Julia cannot settle in Bamfylde, and describes it to David
as 'a bloody awful, stifling place'. Even the way in which she personal-
ises her rooms – her space in the school – indicates her differences
from the men and from Beth. Later in this episode, a cut from Beth in
her apron, hair tied up, undertaking domestic tasks, takes us to a contrasting shot of Julia, with her wavy long hair loose, relaxing in her
room, which is furnished in vibrant colours (pink carpet, red chair), and
decorated with freshly cut flowers – both an indicator of a romantic
femininity and an attempt to bring something of the outside world into
her space. Thus Julia offers an implicit critique not just of Beth's version
of femaleness but also of Bamfylde's values. She is a dangerous force
within the school, one who questions and challenges its safe, tame security.

Davies's female protagonists are justly renowned, and appeal to male
and female viewers alike, combining ambition, cleverness, determination
and wit with good looks and seductiveness. Importantly, these women
are ordinarily not free (of social restrictions, of material constraints, of
repressive relationships) but they struggle to be so.[20] It is in Julia, and to
some degree in Chris Forster, that we see these qualities most strongly
here – not in Beth. It is important that both Chris and Julia challenge
the values of Bamfylde, not because the adaptation wishes critically to
undermine those values, but because the act of critique and challenge is
in itself vitally important, for it opens up a dialogue within the
programme between different ideologies and world views. In a sense,
Davies converses with Delderfield through his reinterpretation of his
work (aided by a sympathetic director). This dialogue, this arena for
gentle debate, concords with both Davies's and Delderfield's attachment to broad-minded, wide-ranging liberal values.

Two single plays followed *To Serve*, both of which continued Davies's
focus upon characters seeking resolution and maturity as did David
Powlett-Jones. In 1985, Davies adapted Molly Keane's book *Time after
Time*: four elderly siblings and their vast collection of pets live together
in their family home, until their peaceful if eccentric existence is upset
by the arrival of a childhood friend. The programme explores the
persistence of the past (through mementoes, places and memories) and

its enduring influence in the present, alongside the power of childhood relationships in shaping adult personality and behaviour. *Lucky Sunil*, produced in 1988, is a comic tale based on a story by Tariq Yumus, which traces the adventures of Sunil (Kulvinder Ghiv) as he moves to England and adapts to its strange culture.

A greater means of expression: stylistic developments in Davies's 1990s adaptations

In the 1990s, Davies explored new avenues in terms of characterisation, developing more ambivalent characters like Julia in *To Serve*. After the broadly affirmative world view offered in the Delderfield adaptations, he turned to something entirely different in his three adaptations of Michael Dobb's novels: *House of Cards* (1990), *To Play the King* (1993) and *The Final Cut* (1995). Here the protagonist was not a good guy like David Powlett-Jones or Stephen Daker; it was the clever and ambitious, but predatory and self-interested, Francis Urquhart (played by Ian Richardson).

Davies has said that 'there are some characters I particularly enjoy inhabiting – often brutally articulate, right-wing characters like Bob Buzzard in *Peculiar Practice* or Francis Urquhart',[21] and indeed the latter seems to be written with a certain relish. Davies chose to turn Urquhart 'into a full-scale Richard III-type villain, with asides to camera' (Davies, 1994). Thus the character speaks directly to the viewer, through direct address. As John Ellis (1982) notes, direct address is a much used, defining feature of television, distinguishing it from film. However, it is not customarily used in dramatic and fictional programmes, so Davies's employment of the device here was a striking stylistic anomaly which defied contemporary television conventions.[22] Davies reused this technique, developing it further, in his later adaptations of *Moll Flanders* and *Othello*.

As a mode of address, direct speech to the camera is a powerful communication with the viewer, and is usually used to provide inform-ation or guidance. Its register is adaptable to drama, for it is an intimate form of address 'whereby viewers are spoken to in a register deriving more from interpersonal than from mass-public communication' (Corner, 1999: 40). In the Dobbs adaptations, Davies presents to us the thoughts and feelings of an unsympathetic character, compelling us to engage with him. The programme grants us access to Urquhart's sub-jectivity and voice, simultaneously sustaining a critique of the character by allowing us to see the broader picture and judge the truthfulness, validity and value of his words. Perhaps most interestingly, the use of direct address alters slightly across the three series, playing upon the theatricality of the device. By the last series, *The Final Cut*, Urquhart speaks to the camera more frequently when other characters are present, defying television's dominant mode of naturalism; his mono- logues constitute theatrical asides which demand that other characters act as though they were oblivious to them. This reflects Urquhart's more overt ambition and unconcealed recklessness; he takes bigger risks, arrogantly assuming that he will not be found out (or overheard).[23]

The 1990s saw considerable aesthetic achievement on television, with many practitioners striving to impress the audience with the filmic qualities of their work. 'Quality' drama programmes exhibited more varied and fluid camerawork, more subtle and precise gradations of colour, and greater integration of sound and image. Davies, and directors of his work, strove similarly to achieve greater complexity and express- iveness (as well as humour and irony); these are later honed in the classic- novel adaptations discussed in the next chapter. Greater financial and artistic investment in television was also apparent in this period, and Davies was aided in his artistic development by bigger budgets and by sympathetic, responsive and inventive directors. This can be seen *Anglo Saxon Attitudes* (1992), a fine adaptation of Angus Wilson's novel, directed by Diarmuid Lawrence. New levels of stylistic expressiveness are especially visible in Davies's 1992 adaptation of Kingsley Amis's novel *The Old Devils*. The serial also displays some interesting traces of Davies's authorship, in that it seems to reflect upon the process of writing, expression and adaptation.

The Old Devils (1992)

In Amis's *The Old Devils*, Alun Weaver (John Stride) returns with his wife Rhiannon (Sheila Allen) to his homeland, Wales, to revisit the places and people of his youth. His arrival stimulates poignant memories in his childhood companions, and they struggle to deal with the repercussions of the past that his presence recalls, and to address the problems that exist within their current relationships. The novel is 'one of Amis's most dense novels, its many different characters and their stories diverging, interweaving, and dovetailing with a striking precision that requires the utmost concentration of the reader' (Salwak, 1992: 243); its thematic concerns chime with Davies's preferred focus on individual relationships and his interest in 'the past and its impingements upon us all' (Salwak, 1992: 245).

First impressions: a sense of style

The opening shots of this programme layer images and sounds to create an engaging pastiche that echoes the complex structure of its source. The episode title, created for the adaptation, echoes the programme's literary roots, exploiting the expressive potential of words: 'Love, lust and litre bottles'. The use of alliteration denotes a literary register that is even more pronounced than that found in the chapter headings of the source text (where character names are used as titles). The music is a striking jazz piece, with a driving drum beat and brushed cymbals conveying a sense of period (the 1950s, during which the central characters first met) and also an air of excitement and anticipation.

Further, the structuring of the sequence is fragmented, opening up various narrative possibilities, and requiring concentration from the viewer. The camera cuts not just between the central characters (Malcolm and Gwen, Charlie and Sophie, Peter and Muriel – and Alun Weaver is referred to by the others), but also between past and present, including Malcolm's sepia-tinted (rose-tinted) memories of a golden beach and a golden girl (Rhiannon).

Framing and constraining – theme through style

The camera movements in *The Old Devils* are more stylised and conspicuous than in previous adaptations, and they frame and link objects meaningfully. Near the beginning of the programme, Alun holds forth to a reporter about his love of Wales, his 'home', in an overblown and over-enthusiastic manner. The camera initially frames Alun and the reporter, viewing them from outside the railway station shelter in which they sit, but subsequently, as if bored by Alun's oration, it begins to track and pan to the left, Alun disappearing out of shot first, and then the reporter (who is distractedly blowing his nose). It continues to move across the wall of the platform, on which two near-identical posters – one in Welsh, the other in English – advertise a local craft showcase, and finally comes to rest upon the window of the station waiting room, where Rhiannon waits patiently for her husband.

The framing of a scene within a window frame – and our corresponding point of view on the contents – is a visual motif repeated throughout the serial.[24] In this instance, the effect is to separate us somewhat from the interior depicted, as we view it from outside, through glass, which gives rise to a sense of detachment in the viewer. However, the sounds of a fruit machine, on which a youth is playing, permeate unnaturally through the window, so that it seems as though we have privileged access – if only aural – to the world behind the glass. Further, the sense that this image has been picked out and framed for our attention endows it with a special status, encouraging in the viewer greater exploration and engagement with details of the picture. Here, we notice the placing of the characters within the frame, and the objects around them. In particular, Rhiannon sits low in the left of the image, as if she is only of marginal interest – which, in terms of her husband's greater status (the reason she has been abandoned to the waiting room), she is. Yet her feminine attractiveness and vitality are echoed in the vase of fresh flowers that shares the bottom left corner of the window. Dominating the image are two large fruit machines, between which a bored youth wanders, and an open door behind Rhiannon, with a large EXIT sign visible above it. A temporary alignment of Rhiannon and the open door, and the additional liveliness of the flowers, convey potential freedom or escape for her; the possibility is implied that although she is currently marginalised, seemingly rather insignificant, she is potentially a source of vitality and has the potential to escape her supporting role.[25] However, as the camera continues to move, the doorway is lost from the frame and Rhiannon is caught again with only the fruit machines and the youth for company.

Rhiannon is perhaps the most obvious candidate in *The Old Devils* for the role of the ideal Davies protagonist. Beautiful, composed and confident, she is to some degree trapped in her marriage to Alun. Although they enjoy each other's company, have a good sex life, and she respects, even admires, Alun's ambition and success, her unhappiness in the marriage, which is faithless on his side, becomes clear when she meets Peter Thomas (James Grant) again, and rediscovers a long-held affection for him. The feelings between them quickly develop, until it seems that they reach a dead end: Rhiannon cannot (or will not) leave Alun, and Peter cannot (or will not) leave his wife Muriel (Anne Stallybrass), and Rhiannon declares the unconsummated love affair 'hopeless'. Yet again, as with Davies's other female protagonists, it is Rhiannon's liveliness and enthusiasm for life and love, reined in by her superficial composure and her constraining circumstances, that draw us to engage with her rather than the other female characters.

The sense of limited and conforming lives is pervasive throughout the serial, constituting one of its clearest themes. In one scene, Malcolm (Bernard Hepton) speaks tenderly of the young Rhiannon, and a saxophone plays low in the background, bringing romantic associations to the moment, and yet he and his group of friends are trapped within the frame, just as Rhiannon was trapped earlier. This time the frame is created not by the edges of a window but by the bar in their local pub. The shot is taken from behind the bar, so that the camera is positioned on the barman's side, and the group is pictured within a 'window' created by the sides and top of the bar and the barman himself. Their reminiscences of youthful freedom and abandon contrast with this severely contained framing, again implying that with age come restrictions – restrictions that we ourselves choose to conform to. The fact that the conversation focuses on Rhiannon reiterates her importance to the group as an emblem of their youth and enduring zest for life. Similarly, despite their awareness of his flaws, the group expresses grudging admiration for Alun simply because of his enthusiasm, his desire to move forward, press on, and grab every opportunity. Alun and Rhiannon are the dynamic couple at the centre of this rather staid group. We see them dining together, captured behind French windows, the bright yellow glow of their space marking out a refuge amidst the inky blue of the night outside; although they are trapped, they are together. A subsequent montage of the other characters reveals them to be isolated individuals, as they lie awake and alone, in separate rooms from their spouses, or in bed with their partners who sleep, oblivious, next to them. Muriel sums up the stagnation of their lives in comparison with the 'golden couple', accusing Peter of emanating 'hopelessness and resentment and boredom and death'.

Places, spaces and fragments

As we have seen, the placement of characters within a frame, and the use of vertical and horizontal lines to divide the screen and create frames within frames, can be regarded as expressing containment and restriction (and occasionally a sense of isolated security). But *The Old Devils* utilises framing in more ambivalent ways. It exploits the visual features of television such as its two-dimensional surface and its depth of field to demonstrate an enhanced sense of fragments of space and

12 *The Old Devils* (1991): Charlie dances; and Peter and Rhiannon express their affections

time, revealing the two to be interlinked, and thus creating the impression of salient moments, captured by chance. It also employs spatial elements thematically, conveying the importance of space(s) to collective and individual identity. Doorways and room divisions divide characters into separate groups, creating a sense of compartmentalisation and potential conflict. Temporal and spatial aspects are then combined so that particular moments in different spaces are played out alongside one another, one overlapping the next, encouraging the spectator to draw out connections, contrasts and conclusions.

A shot of Charlie (Ray Smith) shows him dancing to jazz, alone in his house, across the frame of a doorway (figure 12). In breaking that frame, his performance expresses joyous freedom, and a pleasure in the music and his movement. It is a positive image of solitude and contentment, as Charlie revels in his own space and his own time, creating a space and a moment for himself.[26] Charlie's recurring nightmare is of rough seas – the open expanse of water being threatening compared with the comforting reassurance of a homely space, with its boundaries and frames.[27] Here, then, unlike in other moments, restricted space is presented not as negatively constraining but as reassuringly supportive.

Another scene similarly employs divisions of on-screen space to create an impression of significant moments in time. The central characters all attend a house party, but the group is quickly divided by placing them in separate, compartmentalised spaces within the house. These are marked out not just by vertical and horizontal lines (e.g. door frames) but also by bold blocks of colour: settings and lighting are manipulated to create red, yellow and blue sections, giving a sense of fractured space, and implying broken connections between the characters. This scene ends with a sequence that uses these fractured spaces to echo interruptions in a conversation between Peter and Rhiannon, and to reiterate the divisions and divided loyalties that keep them apart.

Outside the house, the camera pans and tracks to the left along the house's walls, in a movement reminiscent of the shot of Rhiannon in the train waiting room; this time, however, it finds its protagonists outside the building. A striking use of colour is again apparent: the night sky is a bright, deep blue,[28] reflected on the walls of the house, but the scene inside the house, in the window frame, is dominated by warm, vibrant reds and yellows. This clearly demarcates the two spaces (outside/inside). The camera moves from the wall of the house, across the window, and to the porch. It is raining. Peter and Rhiannon sit alone there (figure 13). Alternate close-ups of the two accompany their conversation:

Rhiannon: Look, I know I'm rushing things a bit, but er, it could be ages
before we're on our own again and these days, you never know how
long you've got. I ... just wanted to tell you, you know, before ... anyone starts dying ... that it was *lovely* [referring to her past relationship
with Peter].

Peter: Yes, it was. (He looks down, then looks up at her) *Is.*

[We cut to a scene inside the house, in which Muriel, Peter's wife,
accuses Alun of being a fraud, claiming that his writing is only a pale
imitation of that of the late Brydan Hughes, an esteemed local writer
whom they all admire. Cut back to exterior scene. Rhiannon declares
that the situation is hopeless, and leaves Peter, his hand outstretched
after her in a lame attempt to hold on to her. A record is played in the
house; we hear its opening words, 'What good am I without you?' The
camera tracks back as Peter rises from his seat.]

The scene captures the misfortune of mistimed moments and the
poignancy of missed opportunities. The use of space, colour and sound
echo the notes sounded in Davies's dialogue, reflecting the situation
between Peter and Rhiannon; in particular, the themes expressed in the
dialogue are inflected by the cross-cutting between demarcated spaces.
That is, the presentation of spaces communicates underlying tensions
that are present between the couple.

The tracking camera echoes and calls to mind the earlier scene
which found Rhiannon alone in the train station waiting room, thus
highlighting the fact that with Peter, she is no longer abandoned.
Placing Rhiannon and Peter within their own space, separated by
internal frames and stark colour blocks, the scene implies the potential
for them to break away and create their own space together; it highlights
their isolation from the other partygoers, and the fact that they are
outside, no longer trapped. However, by placing them in a dark blue,
rainy location, and imbuing the internal scenes, as seen through the
window, with warmth and vitality, it is also implied that their future is
not rosy, and that an elopement would bring only more isolation for the
couple. Yet the interruption of their conversation by the scene inside the
house, when Muriel attacks Alun, creates a further fluctuation, emphasising that the view of the group we saw from outside, through the
window, is not realistic. The party is not the communal expression of
warm-hearted cheer amongst close friends that we might have mistaken
it for, but the gathering of a group within which reside deep divisions,
grudges, and antagonisms. We realise then that Rhiannon and Peter
have little to lose (Alun and Muriel, respectively) and much to gain,
which makes Rhiannon's decision to leave – and Peter's decision not to
call her back – all the more regretful.

The presence of Davies? Writing, adaptation and self-expression
In *The Old Devils*, the inventiveness of the director, Tristram Powell, and other crew members, underlines and enhances fluctuations in tone within Davies's writing, and creates meaning beyond that which is overtly present in the dialogue. Through the manipulation of space, sound and colour, through careful framing and editing, the work of the crew complements and supplements Davies's writing. It cannot be claimed that Davies is the sole author of the programme.

However, the dialogue in the programme is more pointedly authored by Davies, offering as it does an intriguing reflection upon his own relationship with writing, self-expression and how these things relate to adaptation. Within the characters' words, it is possible to discern traces of Davies's authorship, and to relate these to his own authorial role. Davies appropriates Amis's words and makes them his own, rein-flecting them within the adaptation to convey both literal meanings and his own metaphorical ones. Specifically, the characters' attempts at writing and 'translation' appear to offer a commentary upon the very process of adaptation that Davies so frequently undertakes.

Alun is a writer who finds his identity constantly under threat. He is, on a visit to the local pub, confused with a regional sports commentator, and accused of not being Welsh. Most importantly, he cannot break away from Brydan Hughes, a respected author who was initially his role model. He finds that in constantly returning to his mentor for inspiration, and drawing upon his work, he is unable to create original writing of his own. He asks Charlie for his frank and honest opinion of his latest draft:

> Charlie: Pure bullshit. 100 octane bullshit. It's not just that it's like Brydan. It's like a whole way of writing that it's impossible to tell the truth in.
> Alun: So there's nothing there at all? Nothing to be ... salvaged?
> Charlie: Nothing that I could see. Sorry.

Later, Charlie advises Alun, as they linger in the graveyard in which Brydan is buried, 'If you want that novel to be any good at all, you have to scour Brydan right out of it, so that not a single word reminds me of him, even vaguely.'

Alun realises that while he can retain his esteem and love for Brydan's work, he must break away from him artistically, 'scour [him] right out of it', if he wishes to find his own voice. The extent of Alun's psychological entanglement with the deceased author, and its effect upon his sense of identity, becomes clear when he reads some poetry to Rhiannon, who asks, impressed 'Gosh, is that you?'; Alun replies, deflated, 'No, it was him.' Rhiannon thus conflates Alun with his work ('is that you', not 'is that yours') and simultaneously mistakes Alun for Brydan. Alun refers to Brydan simply as 'him' – an ever present other, as if he is haunted by the man.

The programme ends with Alun's funeral, at which, despite the deceased man's stated wishes, an audio tape is played of Alun reading out his own work, not Brydan's. The work is a poem about the last pit death, and borders upon the pretentious and mawkish. The words are Alun's own, but in trying to ape Brydan, Alun ultimately succeeds only in sounding second-rate and insincere. One can see how mediocrity and insincerity are inevitable risks when building upon another's work; in adaptation, they are the result of attempting to quash one's own concerns and way of speaking, and trying to take up the voice and identity of another. In this way, Alun's failure offers a sceptical but realistic commentary upon the pitfalls of adaptation.

If aping another's voice is a project doomed to failure, the final conversation of the programme proffers an alternative mode of adaptation, presented by Malcolm. He has been busying himself with a piece of writing throughout the serial. Finally, his wife Gwen asks, 'What is that you keep fiddling with?' Malcolm replies, 'Oh it's just a translation. Well, it's a free adaptation, really. [He reads the sentences in Welsh first, then translates into English:] Brighter than the fringe of foam on the murmurous waves she was [he imagines, and we see, young Rhiannon], And dearest to him because ... she was the only woman who had ever cried for him.' Malcolm rejects 'translation' – the faithful (potentially slavish) reproduction of one person's work by another – for 'free adaptation', which involves reiterating the spirit of the source in another language, bringing to the process his own memories (of Rhiannon) and motives. Significantly, he also brings to his 'free adaptation' fresh *images* that were not available to the writer working in a literary medium. In this he expresses something of Davies's successful approach to adaptation.

Davies returned to Amis in 2000, when he adapted *Take a Girl Like You*, which is set in the late 1950s and follows the antics of debonair, dissembling charmer Patrick Standish (Rupert Graves) in his pursuit of the naïve, sincere Jenny Bunn (Sienna Guillory). Period is successfully evoked through the use of similar motifs as those employed in *The Old Devils*: period details of settings, costumes and props are combined with an evocative musical soundtrack, allowing Patrick's urbane modern jazz to dominate over Jenny's preferred choice of old-time songs, and implicitly reinforcing the challenge she faces in adapting to this new world. The clash of musical tastes is echoed in the presentation of

Patrick's and Jenny's contrasting views upon the action, which are conveyed through both point of view shots and voice-overs. The inclusion of two characters' explicit, powerful voices within the text, and the resulting dissonance between them, creates an engaging frisson that encourages the viewer to evaluate alternative views (this is an attribute that is prevalent Davies's classic-novel adaptations, explored in Chapter 5).

Davies's version of Angela Lambert's *A Rather English Marriage* (1998) revisits similar themes to those in *Pythons on the Mountain*, *Time after Time* and *The Old Devils*. It explores the developing relationship between two very different widowers, ex-squadron leader Reggie Conyngham Jervis (Albert Finney) and retired milkman Roy Southgate (Tom Courtenay). The pair are thrown together after their wives' deaths, and forced to reflect upon their past lives, present predicaments and uncertain futures. As in the previous texts mentioned above, *English Marriage* achieves a subtle and moving exploration of the men's tentative steps towards a mutually rewarding friendship, and reveals how, as they negotiate their differences, each man alters in response to the other. Again, the programme bestows sentimental value upon the details of everyday life, as they enrich the men's experiences with mementoes of the past (the photographs and music that remind the men of their deceased wives), and with enduring, familiar, daily pleasures (such as Reggie's favourite cigarettes, smuggled illicitly into his hospital ward by Roy). The potential for companionship and consolation that may be found within the men's newly established relationship with each other is underscored at the end of the programme, as they dance together, listening to their favourite old tunes and enjoying both their recollections of past youthful dances and the warmth that the present moment provides in its own right. Thus while the past is valued, the present is celebrated (echoing the tone of Davies's *To Serve*).

The influence of generic and cultural expectations

The programmes explored above exhibit varied merits that I have attempted to elucidate. However, within such a large body of work as Davies has produced, it is inevitable that some of his programmes are less complex, subtle, powerful or enduring. The reasons for this are many, and one may wish to refer to authorial mistakes – failures on Davies's part – to explain these less successful texts. However, that is to underestimate the influence of the various contexts within which Davies must work. As I mentioned at the beginning of this chapter, Davies has often been constrained by aspects of context less tangible than financial, technological or institutional ones. He has had to work within particular generic boundaries, which determine to some extent directors' and audiences' expectations of texts. Working within popular formats or genres necessarily places upon a screenwriter particular limitations.

Generic frameworks do not necessarily impact negatively upon the final texts. In collaboration with director Ben Bolt, Davies produced two effective 'genre pieces'. With *Wilderness* (1996), a three-part adaptation of Dennis Danvers's lycanthropic tale, Davies ventured into a supernatural genre with some success, and although it lacked the finesse of some of Davies's other work, Bolt, who had directed science fiction and supernatural drama previously, created a successful genre piece. Even more notably, an adaptation of Davies's own novel, *Getting Hurt*, for a series of television plays grouped under the title 'Obsessions', was enhanced by the imposition of an appropriate generic framework that drew upon recognisable filmic codes.[29] Davies wrote the screenplay for the adaptation himself, but credit for the transformation of a reasonably good popular novel into an utterly filmic, stylish, witty thriller is also due to the creative boldness of Bolt.

The opening of *Getting Hurt* immediately establishes its generic reference points, alluding as it does to film noir, and echoing more recent televisual rewritings of noirish traits, such as those seen in Dennis Potter's *The Singing Detective* (1986). A male voice-over introduces himself as the protagonist, solicitor Charlie Cross (Ciaran Hinds), establishing the kind of bitter, retrospective reflection seen in old detective movies: 'I was a very respectable man ...' The music is noirish. We observe Charlie framed within the window of his flat, sitting at a table in a sparse room; while the window motif is borrowed from other Davies programmes, the particular use of lighting and colour brings new connotations to the shot. Darkness surrounds the window, and the scene inside is dominated by bold green and yellow tones. This is an unapologetically bold generic image; it is also visually striking, with its clear echoes of Edward Hopper's paintings. The use of saturated primary and neon colours is sustained throughout and creates a sinister but appealing (under)world into which Charlie is seduced by the femme fatale, Viola (Amanda Ooms).

The adaptation of *Getting Hurt* is more successful than the source book, for it feels more fully realised, primarily because of the powerful and engaging stylistic and thematic elements that arise from its generic framework. It is also striking that the programme employs clichés of the thriller/noir genres in a knowing fashion, bringing it closer to Potter's work than to naïve or conventional examples of these genres. However, such generic reflexiveness is unfortunately lacking in other examples of Davies's work. This chapter concludes by considering how generic and cultural expectations adversely affected other Davies adaptations from the 1990s.

In 1993, Davies wrote the pilot episode 'Headcase', for an LWT serial entitled *Anna Lee*, which was based one of the books by Liza Cody that traced the antics of the eponymous heroine.[30] Imogen Stubbs starred as Anna Lee, a kooky young woman who had left the Metropolitan Police to pursue a career as a private investigator. The programme was light-hearted in tone, despite some dark plot twists, but it was ultimately shallow in its characterisation, with Anna's wackiness emphasised through 'conventionally unconventional' behaviour (for example, her early morning routine of a cigarette, followed by a jog in the park). Other characters, like the cerebral, unemotional academic who claimed 'I'm not really interested in people', were equally one-dimensional. In competition with other contemporary 'female cop' shows such as the innovative *Prime Suspect 3* (1993), which Davies himself greatly admired,[31] the programme failed to break free of conventions and engage the audience.

Harnessing Peacocks (1993) was even more overtly stifled by generic constraints; specifically, directorial decisions based upon a perception of the source material's genre undermined any attempt at subtlety or profundity. The source text by Mary Wesley can be classified loosely as a romance, and was clearly marketed to female readers who enjoyed popular romantic fiction. The director, James Cellan Jones, evidently wished to sustain the generic elements of romance and pulp fiction in the adaptation; unfortunately the effect is that the programme is trite and clichéd, lacking subtlety and style. In attempting to establish bold dichotomies within the text, the director cudgels the viewer with blatant, overstated imagery and symbolism.[32] The protagonist Hebe (Serena Scott Thomas), whose name in itself, taken from the source book, is over-weighted with symbolic connotations,[33] dressed in a white shirt and purple patterned skirt, and with her long blonde hair tumbling loosely over her shoulders, gambols in bare feet, in a meadow, alongside white peacocks and her white horse. The scene recalls a long-running and much parodied advertisement for Timotei shampoo. The conno-tations of youthfulness, purity and nature already implied in her name are piled up in the accretion of conventional symbols, as if there are fears that the viewer might not understand the references. Though Hebe's association with the purity of nature is later sullied, as we learn of her prostitution, the serial (following the source novel) insists upon her fundamental goodness, and so this opening sequence is not deliberately ironic, but an attempt to express a truth about the character. Like Anna Lee, Hebe is conventionally unconventional, and the programme fails to offer any serious exploration of her situation or character.

Mother Love (1989), a four-part serial based on Domini Taylor's book, does not lack redeeming qualities. Diana Rigg's performance in the central role of Helena Vesey, a possessive, unstable, and embittered mother who lives her life vicariously through her adult son Kit (James Wilby), won her a British Academy Award for best actress. Indeed, one of the most successful aspects of the programme is the way in which her character is presented: the text gives space and power to this protagonist's subjectivity, through voice-over and, in particular, the gradual uncovering of her childhood memories, resulting in the revelation of a disturbed, dangerous and initially intriguing character. In this, *Mother Love* echoes Davies's more adventurous work, which focuses upon amoral and immoral protagonists and utilises voice in powerful ways. There are some interesting stylistic motifs, with memories, fantasies and dream sequences conveying a keen sense of unreality through the use of striking colours and distorted sound.

However, as in *Harnessing Peacocks*, there is a lack of subtlety in both performance and direction. Diana Rigg's mode of performance is attuned to the melodramatic genre of the programme, and as such is somewhat exaggerated and unrealistic.[34] While the presentation of her subjectivity through the other techniques mentioned above compensates for this and rescues her character from stereotype, other elements of the text are similarly overstated. Too often, Helena expresses her anger, resentment and malevolent intentions in dialogue when these motivations are already conveyed or implied through her actions; the dialogue and images thus assert (or make) the same point, which again implies little faith in the audience's intelligence and interpretative skills (or perhaps suggests that the director lacked confidence in the ability of Davies's script to communicate the themes effectively). Much more recently, *Tipping the Velvet* (2002), from Sarah Waters's historical romance, makes similar mistakes, being rather clumsily executed, relying upon excessive stylisation and overstatement.

The tentative claim could be made, looking at these last four examples, that there appears to be a set of assumptions regarding how 'women's novels' (novels dealing primarily with interpersonal relationships, written by women for a female readership – this would include romances and 'chick-lit') ought to be adapted. Despite considerable differences in quality and style of the source novels, the adaptations discussed above have tended to pick up on the melodramatic and intimate focus of their sources to create rather over-indulgent and clichéd programmes. The audience for the adaptations is expected to favour romance, melodrama and spectacle, and subtlety and depth are forgone in favour of unambiguous simplicity, so that no meaning can be missed. In a sense there is an excessive presence of 'intentionality' within the adaptations, so that the burden for forging connections and creating symbolic readings has been taken entirely upon their makers' shoulders, leaving the audience with little scope for intellectual and interpretative activity.

The source texts themselves exhibit particular and varying concerns, themes and stylistic features, and lend themselves to different levels of analysis and evaluation – some of them may not permit transformation into challenging, thought-provoking, moving adaptations. However, it must be recognised that the generic preconceptions that television makers and viewers bring to 'feminine', primarily romantic novels give rise to different conventions in their adaptation to the screen – this includes differences in acting styles, the use of motifs and symbolism, the structuring and management of emotional climaxes, and so on. I would contend that such preconceptions work to the disadvantage of adaptations of the kind of 'feminine' novels described above, for they do not improve upon the source texts but limit their possibilities for subtlety, profundity and stylistic achievement.

In contrast, the next chapter considers Davies's highly successful adaptations of 'universal', great literature – eighteenth- and nineteenth-century classic novels, allegories, and satires concerned with larger social, political or moral questions. We have seen in this chapter benevolent and malign influences of genre. In Chapter 5, we will see its potentially animating power, as we explore how one particular genre has inspired Davies to create intelligent, bold, innovative and complex television.

Notes

1 This chapter does refer to Davies's recent non-classic adaptations, of which there have been a few, but most of the programmes dealt with in this chapter were produced earlier in his career than the classic-novel adaptations covered in Chapter 5.

2 There are some continuities in focus across Chapters 4 and 5, though: both consider, to different degrees and in varying ways, questions of authorship, genre and voice.

3 Readers who are interested in the general subject of adaptation may find the overview of the field and the bibliography in *Adaptation Revisited* (Cardwell, 2002) useful as a guide to further study.

4 Quote from my interview with Davies, 21 February 2003.

5 Dickens's original story is included at the end of this book (Appendix 1), and the programme is readily available on videotape and DVD; interested readers who are not familiar with these sources may like to (re)acquaint themselves with them before reading the following analysis.

6 When *The Signalman* was first shown, it was described as a 'classic ghost story for Xmas'; when it was broadcast again in 1991, it was as part of a 'Classic TV Christmas' season. This classification draws upon the abiding popular connection made between Dickens and Christmas.

7 Other examples include metaphor and simile. The untranslatable nature of these literary devices in relation to film and television arise from the precise and symbolic nature of language as outlined in this section.

8 This effective repetition is also dependent upon the flexibility of language referred to above: the word 'figure' is a general noun that can be applied to any number of individuals, thus allowing ambiguity with regards to its referent, and implying a connection between the narrator and the 'ghost'.

9 This preoccupation with words and language, and the limits of their meaningful and communicative power, can also be seen in other Davies texts, such as *Peculiar Practice*.

10 Because this sequence follows a dream sequence, its status as objective reality is under question to some extent. The level of subjectivity of the image is thus unclear, which contributes to the broader ambiguity of the programme. That is, we cannot be certain whether the bell really hums, or whether this is subjectively perceived sound – a figment of the characters' imaginations being presented to us.

11 Edvard Munch, *The Scream*, 1893.

12 The source for the adaptation was actually Delderfield's *The Green Gauntlett* (1968), the third book in a saga of three novels entitled *A Horseman Riding By*.

13 Having said this, one advantage of the term 'dramatisation' is that it draws attention to the importance of performance and crew in shaping the final television text (that is, it draws attention to the human agency that must interpret the novel/script for the new, dramatic medium).

14 There is a difference here between source text and adaptation. In the programme David's wife, Beth, and their twins are killed; in the novel one twin, Grace, survives and grows up at Bamfylde with her father.

15 *To Serve* and *Peculiar Practice* differ, then, from *Bavarian Night*, *Marmalade* and *Boot Street* not just in their genre but also because they express a healthy respect for the values of traditional liberal education. They do not value anarchy, rebellion and unthinking pluralism. Although *To Serve* is set in the past, it shares with *Peculiar Practice* the potential to speak to contemporary viewers concerned about a detrimental drift in education – and indeed the serial's exploration of the values of education and community is still pertinent today.

16 Other threats are also explored in *To Serve*: parts 7, 8 and 9, for example, address a conflict between the drive for greater profits, a new emphasis on economy and sanitation, and an emphasis on teaching.

17 The programme couches its political concerns primarily in terms of a potential conflict between the individual and the institution, in an interrogation of the notion that 'the personal is political'. Part 6 explores the question of 'belonging', depicting David as torn between loyalty to his home (which is explicitly related to his class roots and socialist affiliations) and his alliance with the traditional, conservative milieu of Bamfylde. This is developed in part 9, when Chris claims that Bamfylde 'institutionalises rebellion', and when her explicit engagement in real politics is contrasted with David's relative apathy in the matter of party politics. David is questioned throughout by Chris, by his relatives, especially his brother, and by others who are outside Bamfylde, forcing him to reflect upon

himself and his actions in political terms.

18 This concern with the roles that people, especially women, are compelled to play, resurfaces in Davies's classic-novel adaptations (such as *Moll Flanders* and *Vanity Fair*).

19 Beth persists as a powerful presence within David's life; we still see her photograph placed centrally on his desk in part 11 of the serial, long after her death and his subsequent relationships with Julia and Chris.

20 This is perhaps why the female protagonists in Davies's later classic-novel adaptations, bound by eighteenth- or nineteenth-century social conventions, are so striking and memorable. It also possibly explains the relative failure of *Harnessing Peacocks*, discussed later in this chapter, in which Hebe seems to have absolute freedom to behave as she chooses; once she reaches adulthood, the greatest risk she runs appears to be that of mild disapproval from those around her. While the programme wishes to depict her as a rebellious free spirit, one is tempted to ask what she is rebelling against, and what further freedoms she might require.

21 Quoted from Davies's e-mail communication to me, sent in February 2004.

22 Direct address is more often used in certain areas of 'quality' television drama, such as Shakespeare adaptations. However, it is still rare in most popular drama programming, and most adaptations, especially those based on classic novels, eschew the technique.

23 It should be noted that this device draws attention to the actor's performance, alienating us slightly from the diegetic world. This is a technique reused in Davies's later *Moll Flanders* and *Othello*.

24 This motif is carried over from Davies's earlier work, and its deployment is discussed in Chapter 3.

25 In this, Rhiannon clearly echoes the depiction of Julia (e.g. in her room at Bamfylde) in *To Serve*.

26 Charlie is a vitally important central character. He is valued for his honesty and peace with himself, his lack of concern about his public appearance, and his ability to find satisfaction in music and thought. His character is crucial in establishing, as in this scene, the importance of feeling a genuine attachment to a place, and of finding a space in which to be truly at home. This is contrasted with Alun, who is unable to form meaningful connections with places. His crass voice-over to his new television series, *In Search of Wales: A Television Essay in Six Parts*, describes it in typically overblown fashion, as a 'private journey seeking the real Wales, the essential Wales, the Wales we all carry around inside us'. Alun's inability to distinguish between a 'private journey' and a public lecture is typical of his failure to demarcate public from private space. He also fails to recognise the true nature of the real people and real places around him. His panegyric, accompanied by soothing, humming music, waxes lyrical about Wales and its people, 'their passion, their poetry'; accompanying this, we see decidedly unromantic, quotidian, 'real' images of the other characters going about their everyday business.

27 Charlie's fear of the open water may also be linked to his memories of Rhiannon on the beach, in his youth, and the unresolved feelings about her that still trouble him. The nightmares do not reflect any actual adverse experiences with water; instead, the scene must be read metaphorically.

28 The blueness of the sky here is unrealistic in its intensity and brightness of colour; it appears artificial. The effect of this is to highlight the blocks of bold primary colours that demarcate the scene, emphasising the sense of separated but interrelated intimate moments.

29 Another of Davies's books, *B. Monkey*, was also adapted for the screen. However, after many disagreements during the production process, Davies withdrew from the project, and the script was written by Chloe King, Michael Radford (the

director) and Michael Thomas. Davies disliked the final film, and dissociates himself from it, as he stated in an e-mail correspondence with me in February 2004.

30 The pilot was based on *Head Case (An Anna Lee investigation)* (1985) by Liza Cody. The book *Head Case* was the third in the Anna Lee series, following *Dupe* and *Bad Company*. The programme did get commissioned, and several episodes were produced, but Andrew Davies did not script these.

31 Davies stated his esteem for *Prime Suspect* in his Huw Wheldon Memorial Lecture, 1994.

32 The use of symbolic dichotomy is not a flaw in itself, of course, as is demonstrated in Davies's successful adaptation of *The Signalman*. Here, however, the execution is clumsy, and seems to expect little of the audience.

33 In Greek mythology, Hebe was the daughter of Zeus and Hera, and was a personification of youth.

34 It could be argued that the performance appears overplayed only to a twenty-first-century viewer, and that it can be more positively received if one considers it in the context of television melodramatic conventions of the 1980s. However, this does not alter the fact that other, much earlier (melo)dramas discussed in this book have endured much more successfully than those covered in this section. This implies that the problem lies in the narrow and unthinking deployment of generic conventions in these programmes, their mode of address and, relatedly, the actors' performance style.

The classic-novel adaptations: voice(s) and genre

5

Davies's best-known adaptations are taken from major, canonical eighteenth- and (especially) nineteenth-century novels. These classic-novel adaptations, most of which were produced between 1994 and 2002, are the focus of this chapter. As I mentioned earlier, Davies adapts with a flair and creativity that is occasionally lacking in his original screenplays, and interestingly, it seems that the more intimidating the source novel (the more respected, even revered, it is), the more success-fully Davies is able to create engaging and complex television. Thus his adaptations of Austen, Eliot, Defoe and Thackeray outshine his previous adaptations of potboiler/genre writers like Mary Wesley, Liza Cody and Domini Taylor. Without doubt, the trends detected in Chapter 4 persist in Davies's more recent adaptations: they have benefited from technological advances in television production, and the consequent stylistic and artistic development that can be seen within the medium; similarly, the directors and producers assigned to Davies's projects have been increasingly willing to experiment and utilise their creative free-dom compared to some of his more prosaic colleagues from previous years. One of the aims of this chapter is to expose the general movement within Davies's classic-novel adaptations towards greater subtlety and complexity, and the maintenance of a distinctive authorial voice.

Voice

For the moment, it is simplest to understand 'voice' as comparable with 'discourse': the way in which a story is told, and the point of view that appears to be offered on the story. Davies has said, 'I would have thought that the notion of an authorial voice in any work of drama is a tricky thing to handle. And especially so when the drama is an adapta-tion of someone else's work'.[1] One of the aims of this chapter is to consider this thorny subject, and to discuss the various voices that may be present in a television programme (authorial, narratorial, and those of the characters).

Adapting voice: from literature to film/television

Brian McFarlane characterises one of the most important distinctions between literature and audio-visual media such as film and television as being, respectively, the difference between 'telling' and 'presenting' (or 'showing') a story, and pinpoints what he calls the narratorial voice (the voice through which the story is told) as one of the salient features that distinguishes novels from their screen adaptations:

> [One] aspect of the distinction between telling and presenting is located in the way in which the novel's metalanguage (the vehicle of its telling) is replaced, at least in part, by the film's mise-en-scène. In a sense, the film's story does not have to be told because it is presented. Against the gains in immediacy, the loss of the narratorial voice may, however, be felt as the chief casualty of the novel's enunciation. (McFarlane, 1996: 29)

The sense of loss felt by critics and viewers on watching an adaptation of a favourite, esteemed novel does indeed seem to arise from changes relating to voice, as the observations made about Davies's adaptation of *Middlemarch*, cited below, bear out.

Importantly for our purposes here, McFarlane does not suggest that the loss of the original novel's narratorial voice necessarily leads to an anonymous adaptation, though. He notes the challenges inherent in adapting the voice that defines a novel, and that contributes so much to its elusive 'spirit', recognising that this process is neither effortless nor straightforward; however, he also asserts that aspects of this voice, such as tone and attitude, can be reproduced on the screen – if the adapter so chooses.

> The camera ... becomes the narrator by, for instance, focusing on such aspects of mise-en-scène as the way actors look, move, gesture, or are costumed, or on the ways in which they are positioned in a scene or on how they are photographed: in these ways the camera may catch a 'truth' which comments on and qualifies what the characters actually say. (McFarlane, 1996: 17)[2]

We shall see in this chapter how such techniques are deployed within Davies's work to create a sense of a narratorial voice within the adaptations – a voice that presents the story to us, simultaneously offering its own point of view upon the action.

The distinction between author and narrator

An important distinction to grasp before approaching Davies's later adaptations (such as *Emma* and *Vanity Fair*, the latter of which I shall consider in some detail in this chapter) is that between author and narrator. Above, McFarlane discusses the 'narratorial voice' present in a novel. This voice is the one that 'speaks' the words we read. In some cases, this may appear to be indistinguishable from the authorial voice, for the author of a novel is, of course, the actual person who writes the words we read. However, in other instances, a novel might be written from the point of view of a fictional narrator – a character invented by the real author (this occurs particularly whenever there is an unreliable narrator present). In these cases, there is a clear distinction to be made between the *author* and the *narrator*, and then the *authorial voice* can be distinguished from the *narratorial voice*.[3]

McFarlane makes the mistake of conflating the author with the narrator. This leads him to assert that novels and films/television programmes have different kinds of narrator. He states that the narrator of a novel exists entirely *within* the novel (for the narrator's words constitute the novel itself), but that the narrator of a film/television programme, understood to be the camera that presents the story to us (as the words of the novel do) is *outside* the story being presented: 'the camera – here used metonymically to denote its operator and whoever is telling him what to aim it at, and how – is outside the total discourse of the film, whereas the omniscient narrator is inextricably a part of the novel's' (McFarlane, 1996: 18).

However, McFarlane leaps too quickly to assert a fundamental difference between novel and audio-visual text. It makes sense to equate the television camera (and its director/operator) not with the words of the novel (the text), but instead with the writer and his pen, for in both cases they are the persons and tools that capture a story – they are the 'authors', loosely speaking. In neither case, therefore, is the author present within the final story itself. The author of the novel remains in the real (actual) world, outside the novel; the screenwriter and the director/camera similarly remain outside the film/programme. What may be present within a novel is a narrator – a character who is separate from his creator/author. Similarly, one can find a narrator in some television programmes and films. The distinction between 'external' author and 'internal' narrator is an important one to bear in mind. While authors are necessarily omniscient and omnipotent, and where the notion of 'truthfulness' is irrelevant to the author of a fiction, not all narrators are omniscient and truthful. Indeed, a narrator may be blinkered and unreliable, and not at all disinterested and objective. Some novels, such as *Vanity Fair*, exploit this distinction to great effect.

Whose voice? Characters, authors and narrators in Davies's work

Davies's television work is rich in voices, which sometimes speak in unison, sometimes differ from, and sometimes contradict one another. The resulting tensions between numerous disparate voices make Davies's recent adaptations more complex, ambiguous and intriguing. They compel the audience to weigh up the material being presented, to assess different points of view upon the action, and to postulate alternative interpretations. It is this increased potential for viewers' involvement that makes these programmes so engaging, and it is for this reason that voice is one of our foci here. As I argued in Chapter 4, adaptation compels Davies to step outside his own world view and speak with the voice(s) of another.

The characters

The voices that can be most easily pinpointed within the programmes are those of the characters. 'Voice' here includes what the characters say and how they say it, as well as the point of view that they thus offer upon other characters and events. With his long-established concern for his characters, it is unsurprising to find Davies asserting that 'I find that most of my efforts are concentrated on making sure each of the characters has his or her individual voice'.[4] In recent work, both original and adapted, Davies has moved away from allowing singular protagonists the last word, and has more confidently permitted a range of voices to present differing views. The resulting conversation and conflict between characters is more finely balanced than in his earlier work, with less emphasis on establishing one particular character as the voice of reason. In *Moll Flanders* and *Vanity Fair*, for example, although Moll and Becky Sharp are the respective protagonists, and are presented sympathetically, their voices do not dominate and subordinate those around them, and other characters comment upon the two protagonists, compelling us to evaluate them in a sympathetic but critical manner. At this level the adaptations are already clearly more multivocal in comparison with earlier work.

The author(s)

Davies's authorial voice is strongly yet subtly asserted in the adaptations. There are two ways in which knowledgeable viewers are alerted to the fact of his authorship (shared with others) of the programme. The first is that Davies selects source novels that, although varied, contain specific common elements that he subsequently highlights. Although the popular press (encouraged by Davies) regards as a key feature of his work an increased emphasis on sexual content, close attention to his adaptations reveals that this is not really an accurate depiction of his work. In fact, more striking is Davies's preoccupation with strong female protagonists. In recent work, as I have noted above, there is also a discernible tendency towards ensemble dramas which present a range of characters, rather than single protagonists supported by a backing group of minor and incidental characters. Hardest to define, yet clearest to the regular viewer of Davies's adaptations, is the presence of a tone or attitude towards the story being presented: it is a tone which arises from his liberal, concerned appreciation of others' situations (such as was seen in his earlier work), his astute observations of characters and their situations, and his love of wit and satire. Socially aware and humorous, his work might be described as displaying *sympathetic irony*: Davies tends to foreground ambivalent or morally dubious characters, presenting them sympathetically but also creating a sense of critical distance from them, allowing us to watch them ironically. He embarks upon the process of adapting a 'great' novel sincerely, thoughtfully and affectionately, but ready to place his tongue in his cheek.

Second, Davies has been aided in the development of an authorial voice or signature by a positive feedback loop, in which the more famous Davies becomes, the more choice he has about which projects to do and the more say in how they are executed. Thus Davies is chosen as the adapter for a project because a producer seeks the very elements that define his style – producers want a 'Davies adaptation' of Austen, Dickens, Eliot, containing his trademark traits of content, style and tone. Davies has thus acquired the freedom to consolidate and confirm his particular approach to adaptation and his resulting authorial voice.

In the case of adaptation, the author of the source text is always somehow present, lingering in its history. Davies engages in what one might regard as a conversation with the authors of his source texts, not just selecting elements of content that suit his agenda, but also adapting his own preferences of style and tone to echo aspects of the author's particular voice. He has even said that 'sometimes I'll want to have a little quarrel with the author',[5] which implies a tussle for authorship behind, and within, the texts. This further enhances Davies's ability to present multifaceted points of view – a range of voices – in one adaptation. As we shall see, for example, he claims to find Jane Austen 'easy to adapt', and feels in sympathy with her agenda and her voice; the result is that his Austen adaptations have considerable positive qualities, but are somewhat univocal and constricted in viewpoint. When Davies tackles Eliot, Defoe and Thackeray – novelists whose work can be in part defined by their unusual and striking use of voice, and who thus pose potentially greater challenges for an adapter, he appears inspired by their innovations and their difficulties, and his management of a plethora of voices within the programmes is more skilful and impressive.

The narrator(s)

In literature, both authorial and narratorial voices result from the stylistic, structural and generic choices made by the author. Each of those voices has a discernible character, and each expresses an attitude towards the events and characters depicted. Each contributes significantly to the mood or tone of the work. When we read literature, it is important that we perceive, understand and distinguish these voices, because they guide us in evaluating characters and events.

In the case of television, unravelling authorial and narratorial functions and voices is rather trickier. An actual person (or a number of people, such as Davies, the director and the editor) composes the material, records it, and constructs it through editing. These are authorial tasks, performed outside the programme before its completion and reception. When the viewer perceives a strong sense of premeditation or intention within the programme, it directs his/her attention outside the text, and they detect an authorial influence or voice. However, once the authorial role has been undertaken and completed, commentary can be created that exists only within the text (and may not even be intended by the 'authors'). An example would be when two shots are juxtaposed so that a meaning (intended or unintended) is created by their combination; in this case, it is not the author or the camera that is saying something about the characters and the scenes, it is the juxtaposition, which is a result of the camera's/author's actions, just as the narrator is the result of the author's actions. The comment made by this juxtaposition may be regarded as a narratorial one, as it is constructed entirely within the programme: although the sequence is created by a real person (an author), the meaning seems to be narrated by the juxtaposition/shots themselves; it arises from within. We can infer an authorial voice here, of course, but we need not. The sensation for the viewer is that the sequence is not *illustrating* a point of view (the author's) but *creating* a point of view (the narrator's).

So voice incorporates the literal voices/points of view present within the work through the characters, and more obscure voices including the narrator and Davies's own authorial voice. As these aspects are created by the interweaving of elements of sound and image, the exploration of voice thus involves attention to elements of content (e.g. characters' dialogue), elements of style (e.g. the choice of camera angle, offering the point of view of an implied narrator), and elements of tone (the interrelation of sound and image revealing a narratorial attitude towards or authorial commentary upon the events and characters depicted). These will therefore form the focus of the analyses in this chapter.

Genre

A word about genre is necessary at this point. When viewing the adaptations discussed in this chapter and the last, the most notable difference is that the adaptations in this chapter are not just classified within the group 'adaptations', but are also recognisable members of the genre 'classic-novel adaptations'.[6] In a sense, this has become Davies's trademark genre.

It is important to recognise that in building his own oeuvre and strengthening his authorial voice through these programmes, Davies has also made a significant contribution towards the genre itself, and has played a vital role in its development. Indeed, one could go so far as to say that he has shaped the genre on British television, as this chapter will reveal. With two of his most famous adaptations, *Middlemarch* (1994) and *Pride and Prejudice* (1995), he consolidated the generic norms of classic-novel adaptations. In adapting *Emma* (1996), Davies seemed briefly constrained by these norms, and by the dominant voice of Austen (and the conventions of adapting her), and his movement away from Austen after *Emma* marked a fresh period of experimentation in his work. Further, the heroine of *Emma* precipitated two of the most memorable of Davies's female protagonists: Moll Flanders, in *The Fortunes and Misfortunes of Moll Flanders* (1996) and Becky Sharp, in *Vanity Fair* (1998). *Daniel Deronda* (2002) continued Davies's successful run of innovative, engaging adaptations. These latest works have successfully propelled the genre into the twenty-first century and sustained its freshness and vitality.

The programmes' generic context is therefore important when interpreting and evaluating them. Davies's sustained work within the same genre has allowed him to develop a keen awareness of its conventions, to the extent that he has become a major author of it. Indeed, this genre has proved to be one of Davies's most productive working relationships. Perhaps the key to the successful match is that the genre of classic-novel adaptations (unlike others in which he has worked) uses restriction and restraint in positive ways: emotions are both central and yet presented as necessarily repressed; Davies's powerful female prota-gonists are both expressive yet simultaneously constrained by societal mores and the generic conventions determining the depiction of women. Davies must work within a framework composed of generic conventions, the public's expectations of the genre and the source novel. These restrictions give Davies something consistent to work within, and indeed to work against, compelling him to express himself more innovatively and in more diffuse ways.

Below, then, I chart Davies's work in the genre throughout the 1990s. An extended exploration of *Vanity Fair* (1998) is included as a case study, and this programme is located within its generic context and within Davies's oeuvre. Through a consideration of details of content, style and tone, I highlight issues of voice and genre as they relate to Davies's authorial development.

Middlemarch (1994), *Pride and Prejudice* (1995) and *Emma* (1996)

Middlemarch

Davies's *Middlemarch* was a careful, responsive adaptation that was critically well-received. Unlike the subsequent *Pride and Prejudice*, it was aesthetically (and generically) understated: in the actors' performances, in the camerawork and editing, and in the settings and costumes. This uncomplicated approach to the adaptation emphasised its novelistic roots, guiding our attention to the dialogue, to the rhythms and tensions it creates. The slow pace of the serial, created by long scenes, long takes and limited cutting, was also noted; Robin Nelson praised this pace because it encourages a similar response and engagement from viewers to that elicited from readers of the novel: 'it is this aspect of the series which, with some success, attempts to retain the textures and moral seriousness of the novel' (1997: 147). (Interestingly, the adaptation's exhibition of such features was primarily due to the persistence of the director, Anthony Page, who battled with Davies over details of the programme. Davies wanted to make the programme more 'visually exciting', arguing that 'this is supposed to be a visual medium', but Page asserted his authority over the final text, which ultimately reflected his desire that Davies's scripted dialogue carry the greater weight and be prioritised over the images).[7]

Of course, there were some negative responses to the adaptation, particularly from writers whose affiliations lay firmly with the novel. Amid the usual concerns regarding fidelity, the tricky issues of authorship and, particularly, voice were critical in shaping these critics' responses. Several writers bemoaned the loss of the novel's authorial and/or narratorial voice from the serial, as Margaret Harris notes: 'the commonest criticism I have encountered of the TV *Middlemarch* concerns the absence of a narrating voice, or of George Eliot' (1995: 98). Such comments echo McFarlane's observation that voice is central to readers' perceptions of a source novel, and that it frequently arises as a problem in screen adaptations from literature.

Pride and Prejudice

Following *Middlemarch*, Davies embarked on adaptations of two of Austen's most famous novels: *Pride and Prejudice* and *Emma*. As I mentioned above, Davies has asserted that he likes adapting Austen, saying there is very little he has to do to her work, as 'she has perfect structure and very good dialogue that just needs trimming. So you don't have to solve or disguise problems in the story structure. You don't have to reinvent the characters because they're all just as they should be. You don't have to make up the way they talk because it's all there, so that's fine' (Davies, quoted in Ransome, 2001: 39).

Indeed, Austen's and Davies's work appear to exhibit some common features. Each of them chooses to emphasise interpersonal relationships against a social background, rather than focusing on social structures and problems. Each of them develops a point of view that is observational, witty and ironic. Yet despite Davies's protests that Austen's novels are 'perfect', it is clear that he feels the need to spice up her work. In these moments there is a productive tension between what viewers feel is 'authentically' Austen and what they feel is 'Davies' (e.g. when he emphasises the sexual tension between Elizabeth and Darcy), which causes us to reflect upon what Davies's own concerns and draws our attention to his authorship.

Thus it is vital to recognise the nature of the synergy between Austen and Davies – his empathy with her preoccupations and voice, but also his desire to assert his own voice and concerns. Interestingly, he refers to this latter desire as if it were a critical reading of Austen, not a colonisation of her work or an overriding of her ideas. He writes,

> It's like Leavis's classic thing, the conversation – 'it's like this, isn't it?' And then someone says 'yes, but'. But it is like giving a reading, literally, using my voice to show the emphasis Jane Austen intended (in my view). When I taught Jane Austen to North London sixth formers, I used to read her aloud to them – only then did they seem to get the jokes. Once they'd got the tone, they could carry on by themselves. So it's a bit like that.[8]

It is interesting to note that Davies refers to Austen's intended emphases and tone, rather than to plot, character and theme. This explains why he chooses to amend details of the latter elements, in his desire to capture the former ones. He characterises his amendments and additions as alterations made in the spirit of suggestions, not improvements or criticisms; of the famous moment when Darcy dives into the lake to cool down after an energetic horse ride, and to quench his desire for Elizabeth, for example, he claims that 'I just saw that scene as a scene Jane Austen chose not to write, because of the rules she made up for herself about men on their own'.[9] In moments like this, when the question of authorship is muddied by the detectable presence of Davies's authorship, we become aware of the existence of two voices in conversation (and potentially in disagreement): Austen's (or more precisely, Davies speaking for Austen) and Davies's.[10]

One further aspect of Davies's *Pride and Prejudice* implicitly asserts his authorship over the material, and places it firmly within a televisual rather than literary context: the programme marked a peak in the genre of classic-novel adaptations, utilising all its most recognisable features to the fullest degree. It provided stunning long-take long shots of stately homes and rural landscapes; beautifully designed, colourful costumes (and most impressive cleavage sported by the female characters); fine interior 'heritage' settings; and a mode of performance in which the protagonists appear realistic but the more minor characters are exaggerated and embellished to work as entertaining, comic caricatures (Elizabeth's silly, fussing mother, played wonderfully by Alison Steadman, for example). It was a work that could not have been repeated without seeming tired, and could not have been further embellished without descending into parody and cliché. *Pride and Prejudice* consolidated the genre of classic-novel adaptations as it existed in the 1990s.[11] It also marked a pivotal moment in Davies's oeuvre, with his subsequent writing working with an awareness of *Pride and Prejudice*, and to some degree in response to (and against) it.

Emma

Partly because of Davies's own work, by the 1990s, 'the choice of a book by Austen as the source text for a screen adaptation implied a conscious decision to work within the bounds of the classic-novel adaptation genre, which had itself been consolidated by previous (Austen) adaptations' (Cardwell, 2002: 134). Davies's adaptation of Austen's *Emma* betrayed intriguing signs of strain as Davies attempted to work again within the restrictive framework of the genre and the expectations that accompanied an 'Austen adaptation'. The willingness of Davies to subjugate his own voice to Austen's was tempered by his increasing boldness in projecting aspects of his own voice into his work and in experimenting with the generic conventions established in earlier adaptations.

The opening of the programme reveals a conscious departure from the source novel. While the novel opens with a lengthy introduction to the protagonist, Emma Woodhouse, the adaptation makes use of a fast-paced editing rhythm, with quick and disparate scenes placed side by side. The first scene, set at night, shows chicken thieves, lit by moonlight, stealing fowl from Mr Woodhouse's property; Emma (Kate Beckinsale) watches, bemused, from one of the upstairs windows. This is followed by a more conventional scene of a carriage departing from the house, conveying Emma, her soon-to-be-married governess Miss Taylor (Samantha Bond), and her father Mr Woodhouse (Bernard Hepton), who exclaims dejectedly that it is all 'too much': 'Six good hens and now Miss Taylor. It's a sad business.' Unlike *Middlemarch*, the programme uses familiar televisual techniques, rather than attempting to find correspondences with its literary source, and it goes beyond the generic fidelity of *Pride and Prejudice*, offering a more fragmented structure, upping the tempo, and placing a heavier emphasis upon comic juxtaposition.

The novel contains a clear narrator's voice, which one instinctively associates with the authorial voice of Austen. The opening lines are characteristic in their tone: 'Emma Woodhouse, handsome, clever, and rich, with a comfortable home and happy disposition, seemed to unite some of the best blessings of existence; and had lived nearly twenty-one years in the world with very little to distress or vex her' (Austen, 1816: 37). While on the surface this is a straightforwardly descriptive account, it also offers an implicit commentary upon Emma, and conveys a sense not just of narratorial observation but also of authorial prescience. Emma is presented as fortunate, and also as cosseted, implying a rather unworldly soul who is likely to be possessed of a high level of self-confidence. As we enter the story at a relatively precise moment in Emma's life (she is almost twenty-one), it is suggested that the story begins at the moment when this state of equilibrium is to be disrupted, and that Emma's carefree existence will be complicated by events coming later in the novel. This implies an awareness of what is to come, which discloses an *authorial* voice, for only the author knows what is to come (the narrative is presented in the present, so the narrator would not have the advantage of retrospective knowledge). The narratorial and authorial voices are merged so that they appear to be one and the same.

In the adaptation, there is a discernible distinction between author and narrator. At times, a witty, implicitly commentating narratorial voice is present, such as when Frank Churchill (Raymond Coulthard) announces his plans for an outing to his father (James Hazeldene):

> Frank: Father, I believe I must go to London tomorrow.
> Father: To London? Whatever for?
> [Cut to Mr Knightley (Mark Strong), in a new scene, who expostulates, disbelieving and outraged: 'To get his *hair* cut?']

Here, a wry reflection is created through the editing and juxtaposition of scenes, which expose Frank's vanity, extravagance and duplicity. As the reflection is created entirely within the text, through the synergy of two shots, and through Knightley's words, it is most reasonably regarded as expressing a narratorial voice, with the narratorial role being temporarily assumed both by Knightley and the camera/editing.

Davies's authorial voice – his sympathetic irony – is also detectable in *Emma*. The programme depicts rural life in rosy terms, with idyllic scenes of harvesting that appear to be taking place in golden Mediterranean sunshine. There is little evidence of revisionism and social critique. However, there is a light jibing, mocking tone discernible, which inflects the presentation of some scenes, and indicates Davies's retrospective view on Austen's text. When the protagonists set off for their countryside picnic, for example, a long shot lingers upon the stream of servants carrying food, hampers and furniture up a hill, so that the protagonists may dine at its summit. This shot, which defies generic expectations, appears strongly intended – and thus strongly authored; we perceive Davies's direct influence upon the text.

Finally, there are the characters' voices. The presentation of characters' points of view in *Emma* is intriguing. Davies incorporates and extends Emma's sensibility in a way that is developed in his next two adaptations (*Moll Flanders* and *Vanity Fair*). We have seen how the camera can be used to present the story, and to 'speak' with a narratorial or authorial voice. Here, it is also used to convey Emma's thoughts and emotions, speaking with another, subjective voice, within the context of a more sustained outside view. A critique is made of Emma through the presentation of her fantasies, for instance; they are depicted visually (such as when she imagines the wedding between Harriet Smith (Samantha Morton) and Mr Elton (Dominic Rowan)), but it is made clear that Emma is deluded in her imaginings. Thus her point of view is prioritised and she is sympathetically given a voice, but what she 'says' is simultaneously shown to be flawed.[12]

The consequence of this use of the camera to present a range of voices is that occasionally the authorship and subjectivity of scenes are troubled, and it is unclear whose subjectivity is being presented. As Emma gazes upon the portrait of Frank Churchill, he is vivified, and reaches out to her, saying, 'We meet at last.' Interestingly, this moment is replayed further on in the story when Emma meets the real Frank, suggesting her as yet another potential 'author' of events. Later, Knightley imagines himself marrying Jane Fairfax, but at the end of his daydream Emma appears to interrupt the happy event, and we cut to Emma waking up in bed with a jolt. Knightley's daydream becomes Emma's nightmare, and doubt is thus cast upon the 'ownership' of the scene: who is speaking here? Does the speaker have authorial control? In this way, such moments offer pause for thought concerning questions of voice, control and authorship.

Similarly, the end of the serial appears to offer an implicit reflection on the part of Davies regarding the current and future state of the genre in Davies's hands. Knightley speaks to the villagers, reassuring them that despite his moving away from his estate, he will still retain ownership, and that 'There will be stability. There will be continuity'. This continuity implies the continued acceptance by everyone of existing iniquitous social hierarchies and customs; it also includes the chicken thieves, who return in the final shot of the serial, and who thus have the last word. Their presence implies the ongoing existence of tensions and inequalities within that stable world, and presages Davies's subsequent work within the genre, which is decidedly more experimental and edgy, challenging old structures and hierarchies, and combining generic traditions and conventions with stylistic innovations and new voices.

The Fortunes and Misfortunes of Moll Flanders (1996) and Vanity Fair (1998)

There are several notable continuities between these two serials. Both have central, powerful women protagonists who differ from the conventional 'good' women found in many classic-novel adaptations. The programmes are marked by Davies's sympathetic irony, encouraging the audience to engage in a more active and thoughtful manner. Davies's humour and enjoyment of the burlesque is allowed a freer reign in adaptations of Defoe and Thackeray, and these two programmes exhibit bawdy, satirical qualities that mark a departure from the traditional world of the classic-novel adaptation.

The condition of 'classic' status is still applicable in the cases of these two source books, as is the productive constraint of working with someone else's characters and stories. However, the source novels are less widely read than *Middlemarch*, *Pride and Prejudice* and *Emma*, so Davies was able to take more liberties with the texts. As television reviewer Kathryn Hughes puts it, with reference to two of Davies's most recent adaptations, 'Change a single word of *Middlemarch* or *Pride and Prejudice* ... and you will find yourself up against a small army of outraged fans, devoted to maintaining the purity of their favourite text. Swap bits of *Daniel Deronda* or *The Way We Live Now* around and not only are people less likely to notice, they probably won't care' (Hughes, 2002: 64).

It is perhaps the central characters (Moll and Becky) that constitute the most famous elements of their respective novels, and Davies's adaptations respect the cultural importance and endurance of these two characters. Perceptions of Defoe and Thackeray as being different from commonly adapted authors such as Austen, Dickens, Eliot and Hardy extend beyond the audience's awareness of differences in period, subject matter and writing style. Both authors have colourful life stories that bring additional frisson to their work.[13] Davies was able to use these distinguishing factors to create two innovative, alternative classic-novel adaptations.

The issues of genre and voice are even more interesting in these two cases. First, each book focuses not on the tidy social (if messy emotional) lives of middle-to-upper-class families, but on those struggling to survive: the working classes, the criminal classes, those women forced to work or marry to survive, and so on. This means that Davies is required to adapt the genre beyond his mild tampering with it in *Emma*. Familiar tropes of content and style (such as long-take long shots of manor houses) and of mood or tone (nostalgia) may consequently need to be abandoned. Second, each book has an authorial voice that is in some sense unreliable; that is, we cannot entirely trust the narrator, and there is a clear distinction between narrator and author – and Davies took on the challenge of recreating this in his adaptations.

In terms of our interests here, the programmes share three notable aspects: the depiction of a cunning, duplicitous and morally ambivalent female protagonist; the manipulation of generic conventions so that they offer a critique of the most formulaic and reactionary aspects of the genre, and a simultaneous social critique; and the discernible presence of Davies's voice, creating an attitude of sympathetic irony towards the protagonist and her situation. Having dealt with *Moll Flanders* in a previous work,[14] I shall focus here on *Vanity Fair*.

Vanity Fair: the novel

Thackeray's novel *Vanity Fair* was published in serialised form from January 1847 to July 1848, and first published as a novel in 1848. Thackeray made some amendments to the text when it was republished in 1853, and the second version is generally accepted as the definitive text.[15]

The title of the novel refers to the fictional Vanity Fair, from John Bunyan's *Pilgrim's Progress*. In this moral allegory, a fair is established by Beelzebub and his accomplices in the town of Vanity, in an attempt to seduce the earnest pilgrims on their journey:

> a Fair wherein should be sold of *all sorts of Vanity*, and that ... should last all the year long. Therefore at *this Fair* are all such Merchandize sold, as Houses, Lands, Trades, Places, Honors, Preferments, Titles, Countries, Kingdoms, Lusts, Pleasures and Delights of all sort, as Whores, Bawds, Wives, Husbands, Children, Masters, Servants, Lives, Blood, Bodies, Souls, Silver, Gold, Pearls, Precious Stones, and what not.
>
> And moreover, at this Fair there is at all times to be seen Jugglings, Cheats, Games, Plays, Fools, Apes, Knaves, and Rogues, and that of every kind. Here are to be seen too, and that for nothing, Thefts, Murders, Adulteries, False-swearers, and that of a blood-red colour. (Bunyan, 1678: 107–8)

Thackeray draws upon Bunyan's moralising view of the sinfulness of Vanity Fair, but presents its temptations as understandable.[16] He critiques a world in which possessions and commerce are equal in value to (or greater than) virtue, compassion and moral strength, and, like Bunyan, he bemoans commodification and the notion that anything may be bought or sold (from houses, through kingdoms, through people, to 'blood, bodies and souls'). However, Thackeray does not utterly condemn the temptations of the world but recognises their power to amuse, entertain and indeed move us.[17] The novel is satirical, but is not a moral allegory or social critique.

Voice

> One could say that of all the characters in *Vanity Fair* the narrator is (or perhaps narrators are) the most interesting in the book. This is a proposition totally lost on the makers of movie versions of the novel whose only technique with which to introduce the narrator is clumsy voice-overs. But the voices of the speaking narrators and the (silent) voice of the author that stands behind them make all the difference in a reader's perception of the story and the characters. (Shillingsburg, 2001: 1)[18]

Peter Shillingsburg accurately pinpoints one of the most important features of Thackeray's novel: its use of voice(s). While he uses this observation to justify a biographical approach to Thackeray's work, I am interested in how this feature may be related to Davies's adaptation of the novel.[19] As Shillingsburg asserts, the novel contains both narratorial and authorial voices, which comment upon the characters and situations. These voices initially appear judgemental, but are actually frequently ironic, and should thus not be taken at face value, as we shall see.

The characters and the narrator/author

First, let us make a distinction, as far as is possible, between Thackeray's authorial voice and other narratorial voices within the novel. These voices reflect each other and are closely related, but they are not identical, and they bear different relationships to the characters; indeed, they appear to disagree in their judgements of those characters. Through Thackeray's authorial voice, we can perhaps observe his changing feelings towards different characters during the writing and serialisation process.

Thackeray felt a strong connection to the characters he had created, so that they seemed to take on a life of their own: ' "How curious it is! I believe perfectly in all those people, and feel quite an interest in the Inn in which they lived", he wrote in a letter of 1848, announcing that he was off to see the Hotel de la Terrasse in Brussels, where Becky had stayed' (Carey, 1977: 177). For a moment, it is almost as if Thackeray's relationship with the characters is transformed from that of creator to that of observer, as he feels that the constitutions of the characters themselves begin to determine their actions, rather than he as omnipotent author. This places him almost in the position of a narrator, rather than an author, and indeed there is some blurring of this distinction. Thackeray frequently includes the reader within a 'we' that observes and judges the actions of his characters, giving a conspiratorial air to the writing, rather than establishing a relationship between ignorant reader and omniscient, omnipotent author. At one point he writes, 'a few pages back, the present writer claimed the privilege of peeping into Miss Amelia Sedley's bedroom, and understanding with the omniscience of the novelist all the gentle pains and passions which were tossing upon that innocent pillow' (Thackeray, 1853: 192). It is interesting that Thackeray, whilst claiming an authorial voice and perspective here, claims for himself only omniscience, not omnipotence, implying the continuing existence of the characters outside his construction of them (he peeps into Amelia's bedroom to find her pining, rather than conjuring her up, and making her pine).

Thackeray's authorial voice tends to take a particular attitude to the characters, and it is one that is interestingly similar to Davies's:

[Many readers see in Thackeray] a writer whose voice is sometimes detached and ironic and other times marked by humility and compassion. And they find in these contraries and contradictions an attractive complexity ... He neither idolized heroes nor dismissed villains; for they are, like ourselves, a mixed lot. (Shillingsburg, 2001: 5)[20]

This authorial voice is created, intriguingly, by the presence of unreliable and biased narratorial voices that we are asked to judge, so that an authorial voice is implied by the mixture of narratorial voices (with an intriguing reversal, by which the authorial voice is created by narratorial ones, while the author creates the narrators). Let us consider the question of authorial and narratorial voices in relation to the presentation of and attitude to characters.

The character of Becky Sharp, the protagonist, is constructed partly in opposition to the character of Amelia Sedley, against whom she is contrasted. At first, it seems that the narrator (and Thackeray as author) favours the virtuous Amelia:

as we are to see a great deal of Amelia, there is no harm in saying, at the outset of our acquaintance, that she was a dear little creature; and a great mercy it is, both in life and in novels, which (and the latter especially) abound in villains of the most sombre sort, that we are to have for a constant companion so guileless and good-natured a person. As she is not a heroine, there is no need to describe her person; indeed I am afraid that her nose was rather short than otherwise, and her cheeks a great deal too round and red for a heroine; but her face blushed with rosy health, and her lips with the freshest of smiles, and she had a pair of eyes which sparkled with the brightest and honestest good-humour, except indeed when they filled with tears, and that was a great deal too often; for the silly thing would cry over a dead canary-bird; or over a mouse, that the cat had haply seized upon; or over the end of a novel, were it ever so stupid. (Thackeray, 1853: 43)

This creates a vivid image of Amelia, and communicates both narratorial and subsequently authorial attitudes towards her. Initially, the narrator appears sympathetic to Amelia, praising her virtues, but other features undermine this positive view. First, the tone alters towards the end of the section, as Amelia is implied to be rather over-sensitive, silly and soft-hearted (this contrasts with Becky, who is calculating, cunning and practical). Second, Amelia does not become our 'constant companion', as the narrator promises here – Becky does, and Amelia is absent for long periods in the novel. There is a marked fluctuation in attitude to Amelia in the novel, which implies that the intentions declared by the narrator (for Amelia to be a protagonist) are undermined by authorial whims (as Thackeray changes his attitude towards her, as he writes the serialised parts). Indeed, the authorial voice, when present, is inconsistent in its attitude towards Amelia. Having emphasised that she is no heroine, he later names her as the heroine of the novel;[21] his commentary upon her actions is often ambivalent – he offers genuine praise for some of her virtues (her sincerity, for example), alongside cutting criticism of her naivety, selfishness and dullness.[22]

The claim that Amelia is not a heroine reinforces a distinction between authorial and narratorial voices. She is not a heroine because she does not 'look the part'.[23] Thackeray, as author, could of course have designed her to fulfil the requirements of a beautiful heroine. This implies firstly that he does not wish to do so, implying his ambivalent attitude towards Amelia, and secondly that the person speaking here is not an omnipotent author, who can design, but a narrator, who may only describe and comment upon what is already created.[24] There is a sense of something/someone else controlling and designing the world that the voice comments upon. This makes it clear that the voice we hear is that of a narrator, which encourages us to reflect upon its veracity and trustworthiness in a way that we might not have done with an omniscient, omnipotent authorial voice. (One could say that while Thackeray is clearly the author, the unreliable narrator is the part he plays within the novel.)

Defying conventions
Becky is contrasted with Amelia:

> Becky Sharp is, possibly, the most famous female character from Victorian fiction ... Becky is one kind of Thackerayan woman ... intelligent, headstrong and wily. These beautiful, accomplished, manipulative, calculating women stand out primarily because they run counter to the more commonly admired women of Victorian fiction of whom Amelia Smedley has been called the epitome: the reticent, retiring, subservient, helpless Victorian heroine. (Shillingsburg, 2001: 81)

If Amelia does not fully fit the remit of heroine, Becky defies the very conventions that constitute one. Thackeray shows this by presenting Becky in terms of those conventions, drawing our attention to them. He applies the language of the heroine to her, highlighting, for the attentive reader, that Becky falls far from the ideal heroine, and exposing her proclivity to role-play the 'good' woman only when it is to her advantage. Here, Becky meets Joseph (Jos) Sedley, Amelia's brother and her potential beau:

> 'He's very handsome,' whispered Rebecca to Amelia, rather loud.
> 'Do you think so?' said the latter. 'I'll tell him.'

'Darling! Not for worlds,' said Miss Sharp, starting back as timid as a fawn. She had previously made a respectful virgin-like curtsey to the gentleman, and her modest eyes gazed so perseveringly on the carpet that it was a wonder how she should have found an opportunity to see him. (Thackeray, 1853: 56)

After Jos has fooled Becky into eating curry and raw chilli pepper, he protests that he 'wouldn't hurt her for the world':

'No,' said she, 'I *know* you wouldn't;' and then she gave him ever so gentle a pressure with her little hand, and drew it back quite frightened, and looking first for one instant in his face, and then down at the carpet-rods; and I am not prepared to say that Jos's heart did not thump at this little, involuntary, timid, gentle motion of regard on the part of the simple girl. (Thackeray, 1853: 65)

Thackeray piles his adjectives up one on top of another, until we are forced to recognise that he exaggerates in order to mimic Becky's teenage attempts to play the heroine: she is 'as timid as a fawn', and her gestures are respectful, virgin-like, modest, gentle, frightened, little, involuntary, timid and simple. Aware of Becky's tendency to dissemble, we cannot accept the narrator as being sincere here, and we note that his tone is ironic – even sarcastic. We are immediately aware of Becky's performance, and amused by Jos's ignorance of it. Simultaneously, this moment draws our attention to accepted conventions, and the way in which Becky flouts them, for she is described in a manner that befits a heroine, and yet she contradicts those virtues expected of one. The narrator's voice dominates the presentation of these moments, and encourages us to be aligned with its point of view.

A screenwriter wishing to adapt this to the screen must find a way to make us aware of Becky's performance, without letting other characters see through it, perhaps by recreating the presence of a narrator. Further, the way in which Becky defies the conventions of heroine, while employing those conventions for her own ends, will need to be adapted to a contemporary audience and genre.

Register[25]
In the above introduction to Amelia, the register Thackeray has chosen is important. It is sub-literary, using the vocabulary of pot-boilers and romances, and offering strictly contrasting, almost pantomine Manichaean dichotomies ('villains' and 'heroines'). Phrases like 'villains of the most sombre sort' mock a moralising tone found in other literature (such as Bunyan's *Pilgrim's Progress*), inducing us to infer that the author has his tongue in his cheek and is ambivalent about his

characters. However, the register is changeable, and draws also upon grander literary traditions, with carefully constructed sentences containing multi-syllabic words, circumlocutions, and the use of understatement and hyperbole. This play with register emphasises the constructed, fictional nature of the text (it is like a book or stageplay, not real life); indeed, at other moments, Thackeray-as-author interjects, to ruminate upon the genre he has chosen and the story he is writing.[26] Further, the literary register draws attention to the voice of the narrator, as it is a register that contrasts with the simple folk and stories being depicted and thus foregrounds the form and fact of narration.

The reader's/viewer's experience
The blurring of voices, the play with conventions of register and genre, and the resulting confusion and contradiction can create (pleasurable) uncertainty in the reader. As Shillingsburg notes,

> To know a person or writer well is to know how to take what that person says. We allow our friends and close acquaintances a far wider range of voices than we allow strangers or persons with whom our relations are strained or hostile... Thackeray's writings address the reader in so many voices and with such confidence that conventional politeness between writer and reader is stretched. (Shillingsburg, 2001: 7)

This demands that readers be 'intelligent enough, strong enough, witty enough, and confident enough to hold their own in the novel' (Shillingsburg, 2001: 71).

In creating a programme that also contains a complex mixture of voices, Andrew Davies must contend with the same challenge, but intensified. Television audiences do not necessarily expect to have to pay close attention to the nuances of the text in front of them (although the genre of classic-novel adaptations can induce a more reflective mode of engagement than many other television genres).[27] Davies is aided in this matter because, as we have seen, audiences have become more familiar with him, through his work and interviews. There is less need for Davies to make the grounds of his work clear: he does not need to state so blatantly where he is coming from, or what his philosophy is. Our familiarity with his persona and his authorship allows him to build upon what we already know about his favoured tropes of content, style and tone. We recognise his voice almost before he begins to speak.

In considering Davies's adaptation of *Vanity Fair*, then, we shall consider how the world and characters of *Vanity Fair* are recreated on screen, how the programme's use of stylistic and generic features relate to aspects of Thackeray's literary style, and how the programme employs voice(s) and tone.

Vanity Fair: the adaptation

The world of Vanity Fair is introduced in the opening shots of episode one. A close-up of the face of a plump woman as she languorously picks her nose is followed by a medium-long shot of her lying upon a chaise longue, draped in a grubby sheet, in a mock Rubenesque pose. In the background, oblivious, is a gathered rabble, drinking and carousing. A cut takes us to a child's feet walking up stone steps: we can see the hem of a tatty skirt above bare legs and muddy shoes. As the camera subsequently lingers on this girl's face, she is established as Becky, the protagonist. In long shot, we see Becky (Danielle Hawley) pouring wine from a jug into the waiting glasses of the drinkers; their hands take Becky's wrists to steady her hands as she pours. Becky's attempt to chide her father for drinking too much is dismissed by him. Finally, a cut takes us from the young girl's disappointed and disillusioned face to a brazen adult Becky (Natasha Little), now a teacher, saying her farewells to her French class with the words 'et baissez mon cous'.

Apart from proffering a history and motivation for Becky, this sequence establishes the world of *Vanity Fair* as one in which debauchery, selfishness and greed prevail, and childhood innocence is tarnished by the dominance of these values. The fat woman who mimics the pose of a buxom beauty is no oil painting: her face distorted, her manners appalling, she revels in the base pleasures of the body. This overly earthy quality is emphasised throughout the serial with the display of excessive behaviour (overeating, drunkenness, gambling, womanising). The results of this upon the human spirit are shown in the effects on the characters, some of whom sink entirely into an abyss of apathy and self-loathing: Pitt Crawley's wife, Lady Crawley (Joanna Scanlan), for example, is pictured immobile in her bed, surrounding by food scraps and indeterminate objects, while her ugly pug dogs noisily rummage through her opened boxes of chocolate (in a later scene, maggots join them). There is also an equation of humankind with animals. The hog who snuffles in the mud at the start and end of several episodes, its grunts and snorts dominating the soundtrack, is connected with various characters by direct cuts from it to them or vice versa. One character, Bute Crawley (Stephen Frost), talks more excitedly and affectionately to his dog than to his wife, whom he mostly ignores. The humans' relationship with animals is ambivalent, though. While they are like them, and while pets replace partners and children in their owners' affections, animals are also mistreated: dogs are tied up, favourite sheep are served up for dinner, dead crows are strung up to scare other birds from apparently barren fields. At the beginning of episode two, a crow is shot and takes an ungraceful and undignified nosedive, plummeting at speed headfirst into the ground, and landing half-buried, with its feet in the air. The effect is painfully comic, revealing a lack of respect for nature, and revelry in killing for its own sake.

As in the novel, however, this world is presented as a ribald rather than depraved one. It is amoral rather than immoral. Davies holds back from complete condemnation of the baser human instincts and their depicted consequences. The world in the adaptation, like that in the novel, is also a rich one, sometimes beautiful and appealing. In its occasional use of generic settings – plush interiors, impressive costumes, attractive townscapes – the serial creates a world that appeals to the senses of the viewer. This is an exciting and stimulating place, such that we can almost forgive its inhabitants their excesses and extravagances.

A similar ambivalence is present in the treatment of material possessions. Thackeray's thematic critique of commodification is re-presented as an emphasis is placed upon possessions and objects. The downward spiral implied by Bunyan and picked up by Thackeray, wherein even previously sacrosanct things become objects to be bought and sold, is presented visually here: one sequence includes a pan across Amelia's (Frances Gray) body, then across the fine uniforms of the soldiers, and finally across the pearls and jewels that decorate the ladies at their ball, clearly implying Amelia to be yet another pretty adornment, to be bartered and displayed. Yet these items are also shown, with an ambivalence typical of Thackeray and Davies, to be both visually attractive and emotionally important. Episode four opens with a shot of the small items and keepsakes lying in the bloodied mud of the battlefield, after the battle in which George Osborne (Tom Ward), Amelia's husband, has been killed. Suddenly these items are no longer fripperies but valuable, permanent reminders of ephemeral human lives. The central importance of things and the reification of life are insidiously and constantly present.

Becky Sharp
It is clear why Becky would appeal to Davies. There are clear similarities between Moll Flanders and Becky; when John Carey accurately pin-points the motivations that justify to us Becky's less noble actions, his words could apply equally to her predecessor: 'the more we learn about her, the more inclined we are to defend her against her creator's primmer assessments. Her sin, simply, is that she does everything in her power to escape from poverty and from the contempt that, she has found, it brings' (Carey, 1977: 178). As in *Moll Flanders*, Davies presents his heroine as a clever, inventive, amoral woman who finds ways to negotiate the obstacles that society places in her path.

Shillingsburg ruminates upon the appeal of Thackeray's Becky:

> The conventional eye follows [female characters like] Becky Sharp ... because they provide constant and unpredictable interruptions to conventional development for women. They are not unusual women [in real life] ... but they violate the tacit conventions for good women, and the conventional eye sees in them the behavior that is to be labeled bad. (Shillingsburg, 2001: 107)

When Shillingsburg refers to the 'conventional eye', he makes an important distinction between our judgement of real people and our evaluation of characters in fiction. The contemporary reader of Thackeray would have been likely to assess Becky as a 'bad' woman, but that judgement would have been made as much in relation to generic conventions as with reference to the mores of real life. Furthermore, such a judgement would not have meant that the reader did not like Becky. Indeed, in her flouting of conventional representations of 'good' women, Becky is intriguing. Davies needed to compensate for the fact that the modern-day viewer's 'conventional eye' probably differs from that of Thackeray's contemporaries, so that some of Becky's behaviour judged inappropriate then seems perfectly acceptable now. Yet to retain Becky's fundamental appeal, Davies needed to find a way to make her an unconventional, 'bad' woman. He did so by working with and against the conventions of the genre of classic-novel adaptations. Viewers may disagree amongst themselves with regard to what they expect of women in everyday, real life, but one is likely to find greater consistency with regards to their expectations of female characters in classic-novel adaptations.[28] Davies worked with an awareness of the generic conventions that determine expected modes of female behaviour.

Amelia is used as a counterpoint to Becky, as in the novel, which allows Davies to contrast her generically conventional behaviour against

14, 15 *Vanity Fair* (1998): Becky and Amelia; and Becky re-seduces Jos

Becky's transgressions (figure 14). In the first episode, we are introduced to Amelia and Becky together: Amelia simpers and whispers,
eager to please those around her, whilst Becky is defiant and worldly,
acting out of her own interests. Immediately, Becky's difference from
Amelia engages us.

Becky is defined as a woman who plays a series of different roles in
accordance with her changing circumstances.[29] She performs for both
the women and (particularly) the men around her, in order to extract
from them what she desires. Like Moll, her performance often consists
of playing the generic 'good' woman as seen in Amelia. When asking
Jos Sedley (Jeremy Swift) about his travels in India, she refers to an
elephant's 'big nose' so that he might gently correct her with the word
'trunk'; since her good education and broad general knowledge have
already been established, her faux naif performance is transparent to us
(but convinces the foolish Jos). Becky displays a fine awareness of psychology, performing thus so that Jos may play a role too – the role he wishes
to play, of brave adventurer and heroic slayer of tigers. It is in the ability
to allow others to present themselves as they choose that Becky excels.
In comparison to Moll, Becky is crueller (and takes more risks), for she
goes beyond the goal of achieving her ends through others, and uses
others for her own entertainment. She revels in Jos's bravura performance, 'innocently' teasing him, and pushing him to behave in an
increasingly absurd manner, solely, it appears, for her amusement.
Becky's ability to assess those around her is shown in her adaptability:
she realises that Lord Steyne (Gerard Murphy) sees through her
coquettish manipulations, for he notes that she 'drives a hard bargain',
when she is trying to conceal that she is bartering favours with him, and
later, more explicitly warns her, 'Don't overplay your hand'. However,
Becky also recognises the enjoyment Steyne derives from watching her
attempt such coups, and becomes more explicit in her game-playing
with him, using her machinations as part of her charm.

Vanity Fair offers a rather darker view of the effect of this game-
playing upon its protagonist than did *Moll Flanders*, acknowledging the
likely limitations placed upon a woman such as Becky within society.
While Moll escapes to the bright new world of America, with her
partner Jemmy, Becky finds that even if she deserts England, she cannot
escape the strictures of society that contain her. She misjudges Lord
Steyne, who finally tires of her attempts to dupe him, and she finds that
he can have her removed from a restaurant, a town, even polite society,
as he wishes. Becky is unable to overcome the judgement of others and
the constraints of her gender and class.[30]

Becky also incurs losses that result from her own choices. She loses her husband, Rawdon (Nathaniel Parker), with whom she has found a positive, mutually supportive relationship, because of her deceit, and in the end must settle for re-seducing Jos (figure 15). Most importantly, Becky finds that in constantly playing roles, she becomes 'typecast', always hiding behind an appropriate image, until she is unable to reveal (or remember) herself. She begins the serial as a fresh-faced young woman, and gradually adds more and more make-up, painting her face to conceal her increasing age; finally, at the end of the serial, she appears with a mask, concealing her identity, and presenting herself as a scarlet woman, dressed in black and red (she is no longer able to play the innocent). Becky survives to play another game, but she must start from scratch. She does not leave the table a winner. Becky is the protagonist, and ultimately our heroine, but she defies the conventions of the 'good' woman and stretches the definition of a heroine, in being both psychologically flawed and relatively unsuccessful. The exploration of the roles Becky plays, and their impact upon her, grows out of Davies's fascination with character revelation and development; he reprises this focus on role-playing in several other of his recent programmes, including *Moll Flanders*, *Daniel Deronda* and *Othello*.

Voice

The depiction of point of view and voice in *Vanity Fair* is intriguing. The camera will suddenly change views within a scene, revealing it from another angle, and implying that there are several ways to look at something. The adaptation also extends Becky's point of view and thus conveys a stronger sense of her subjectivity. In the novel, Rawdon is introduced in passing, and the meeting, courting and marriage of Becky and Rawdon seems to occur rather quickly and unconvincingly. In the adaptation, Becky is depicted as the master of her own fate; on seeing the portrait of Rawdon, she imagines him in all his liveliness, and the fact that when she meets him he matches this image suggests her power to make things happen as she chooses. Becky's subjectivity is conveyed and critiqued through both Davies's dialogue and a sympathetic directorial style. She is shown to be self-aware, but also self-deluding, refusing to admit the extent of her failings. When Rawdon discovers her deceit and leaves her, at the end of episode four, Becky at first protests 'I am innocent', seeming to believe it. Yet at the start of the episode five, which picks up at the same point, Becky has amended her plea to 'I'm not guilty'. A dawning realisation that she cannot overplay her role as the innocent, wronged woman forces her to adapt her performance, at least marginally.

The camerawork, the structuring of scenes and the editing provide a pointed narratorial commentary upon the action. Amelia's voice-over panegyric on the subject of George Osborne's virtues is played over images of her beloved eyeing up another woman. In this case the camera and editing offer a narratorial corrective to Amelia's misconceptions, showing that she is deluded. Thackeray's narratorial commentary is also displaced into the mouths of minor characters; his observation that 'If a man has committed wrong in life, I don't know any moralist more anxious to point his errors out to the world than his own relations' becomes an remark from a household servant to a visiting medic, 'Say what you will, Dr Squills, but if a man's character is to be abused, there's no-one like a relation to do the business'.

While the narratorial voice is thus claimed to be relatively 'value free', commentating apparently disinterestedly upon the action,[31] other characters' voices add more complex reflections. The manservant Samuel[32] correctly detects Becky's artifice and manipulation, and he frequently makes his distaste for Becky clear in his words and actions, yet Samuel is not a disinterested observer but one who is biased, prejudiced and self-interested (he fears that Becky will usurp him in the household). His partiality does not invalidate his opinion, but it does motivate it. In this way, the adaptation underlines the importance of evaluating the sincerity and truthfulness of every character's voice, no matter how minor the character may be. The viewer is led to interrogate the motives and interests of whomever is speaking, and not blindly to trust what is said. This corresponds with the high value that Davies places upon pluralistic (though not necessarily relativistic) debate, in which all viewpoints are given a voice and an opportunity to persuade others.

Style, genre and tone

In my comments on Thackeray's style, I noted his ironic use of various registers. Using carefully selected vocabulary and particular syntactical and stylistic features that are familiar to the reader, Thackeray plays against our expectations, offering heroes and heroines who do not fulfil their roles, narratorial commentary that cannot be trusted, and a fluctuating and unreliable authorial voice. Davies cannot employ register in the same way in the audio-visual medium of television, but he utilises an alternative frame of reference: genre.

Vanity Fair, like *Moll Flanders*, takes familiar conventions of the classic-novel adaptation genre and distorts them in a playful manner, although it does so in different ways and to different effect. The opening of the serial marks its differences from previous adaptations. A mixture of fonts in the credits conveys a sense of messiness and randomness, unlike the carefully arranged credits in the copperplate script of classic Austen adaptations, for example. The music, too, announces a very different tone from the restrained good taste and gentle nostalgia of those previous texts. It is a jolly, boisterous tune, cheery and undisciplined: played by brass and woodwind, it sounds somehow amateurish, with the flute rather windy and occasionally screechy, and the instruments not entirely in tune with one another.

In this spirit of rebellion against traditional generic features, the conventional presentation of settings is overthrown in the serial. In episode four, Becky arrives at her new employer's house, Pitt Crawley, a large country residence owned by Baronet Sir Pitt Crawley (David Bradley).[33] However, generic expectations of a lovingly maintained English country home are confounded in this scene. Having already mistaken the dishevelled baronet for a servant, Becky discovers that his home is equally dilapidated. Inside, the house appears as if it has been ravaged by marauding animals (implying the bestial and dissolute nature of its residents). The furniture is dirty, rickety or broken, and scattered randomly about the space; upturned ornaments and indistinct objects clutter every surface; pictures hang at precarious angles; and there is straw scattered along the mantelpiece. Dim lighting creates an ominous, gloomy atmosphere which is intensified by a row of mounted, stuffed animal heads affixed to the banisters – a material reminder of death within this already lifeless house. The conventions of the genre are upturned along with the contents of the house.

The tone of the serial is carnivalesque.[34] Elements of carnival are explicitly portrayed in episode one, when Amelia, George Osborne, Becky, Dobbin (Philip Glenister) and Jos attend a local fair. The opening shot is a large close-up of a man with a powdered face and absurd wig; the image is accompanied by bold, bombastic music. A series of shots follows, displaying theatrical displays and freaks of all kinds, until the frame is suddenly filled with a rear view of Jos's rather large and ungainly bottom as he descends inelegantly backwards from his carriage. The impression is of theatricalised buffoonery, and while the entertainers at the fair are paid to fulfil this role, Jos and his companions are clearly allied with them through intercutting, making them appear ridiculous. As the group sits at dinner, enjoying an intimate meal, the camera pulls back to reveal that they are seated on a podium in the centre of the fair, and are being observed (and mocked) by the crowds gathered around their stage. The implication is clear: Jos and his high society friends are no less absurd, no less base, than the travelling folk who entertain them with their exaggerated appearances and behaviour. This can be regarded as a key scene for setting the tone of the piece, as it seems to depict Vanity Fair itself, and establishes the characters firmly within that bizarre world – one far removed from the expected microcosm of the classic-novel adaptation.

The effect of the programme's stark differences from more typical adaptations is to throw into relief the usual conventions of the genre. As we watch our protagonists dine (above) we are made aware of the performances that ordinarily construct the world of the classic-novel adaptation – the manners, the restraint, the niceties – because here they are put on stage, exposed and ridiculed. A later dining scene similarly exposes the absurdities of gentility, with Baronet Crawley's obsequious butler, Horrocks (John Surman), pompously announcing the menu for the evening meal: '*potage de mouton à l'Ecossaise*, followed by *mouton aux navets*, accompanied by *pommes de terre au natural*' (roughly translated as mutton soup, followed by mutton and potatoes). The attempt to disguise dull native food in flowery French, and to gentrify the essential act of eating a meal is exposed as mere bourgeois pretension. The genre's typical emphasis on manners and gentility, and its warm, nostalgic tone, are discarded in favour of a boisterous, raucous and occasionally savage exposure of the underside of life in the nineteenth century.

This is not to suggest that the programme is mere frivolity, for it does not lack genuinely touching and moving moments. These are rare, but are all the more affecting for their rarity. A scene between Osborne's father (Tim Woodward) and Dobbin, at Osborne's graveside, is accompanied by a piano track, which adds a sentimental touch. Attentive viewers will also recall that the piano was a gift given to Amelia by Dobbin, but which she wrongly attributed to George, so this is also a poignant and rather cruel reminder of Amelia's delusions about her heroic husband, suggesting that the man being mourned was no hero.

Disruption

Such fluctuations in tone are generally managed so that they do not appear jarring, through a careful use of the episodic structure of television.[35] However, this is not always the case. The disruption of generic conventions and expectations is part of a broader pattern across the programme. Disruption is used as an aesthetic device to highlight the constructedness of the text, and to throw into relief the usual conventions of the genre and the medium. In episode two, Becky breaks down in tears when she confesses to the Crawleys her secret marriage to Rawdon. As she is comforted by Miss Crawley (Miriam Margolyes), a sentimental violin theme is played on the soundtrack; as Becky leaves the room, the music continues, appearing to build towards an emotional climax. But when the door swings shut behind Becky, the accompanying musical theme is cut brutally short, in the middle of a phrase, as if switched off by an insensitive editor keen to go home early. The effect is as if the music was not heartfelt, but was simply tacked on – a device that bore no intrinsic connection to the content of the scene. Jolting us out of our empathetic engagement with the scene, this disruption draws attention both to the falsity of Becky's performance and to the manipulations of our emotions by a musical soundtrack. Similarly, a romantic moment between Becky and Jos in episode one, as they escape from the bustle of the fair for an evening stroll, is disturbed by fireworks (and the gluttonous Jos's subsequent realisation that it is 'suppertime'). In each case, the emotional tenor of the scene is spoiled, highlighting its tenuously constructed nature.[36]

Vanity Fair therefore plays against our expectations of the television genre of classic-novel adaptations, in the way that Thackeray manipulates the traditional constructs of literary registers. To understand this adaptation one must regard it as a conversation with various schema: with the source novel, a genre, contemporary life, and common perceptions of the era depicted. The effect upon the viewer is to demand greater concentration and commitment – a fuller engagement with the text. The programme is also part of Davies's oeuvre, and to recognise this is to guide our attention to particular aspects. In *Vanity Fair*, Davies's voice does not silence that of others. Instead, it is his vision, interpreted by the crew, that shapes all aspects – dialogue, camerawork, editing, performance, and so on. It makes more sense to think of the programme as expressing Davies's sensibility – a sensibility that is utterly attuned to the televisual medium.

Wives and Daughters (1999) and *Daniel Deronda* (2002)

Wives and Daughters (1999) is adapted from Elizabeth Gaskell's novel of 1865. Although the source novel cannot be straightforwardly classified as a 'classic', the style of the adaptation ensured the programme's place within the genre of classic-novel adaptations, and in doing do possibly bestowed an enhanced critical status upon the source text in the eyes of the viewing public. This suggests the potential power of Davies and other adapters to challenge and expand literary canonicity. The programme typically places female characters at the centre, with the protagonist, Molly Gibson (Justine Waddell), providing an alternative depiction of nineteenth-century femininity: while she patiently awaits the attention of the man she loves, she also actively engages in a life of learning and exploration, and displays appealing characteristics of resilience, courage, intelligence and insight. The theme of exploring a newly discovered world (made available by imperial trade links) is central here, and picked up in Davies's excellent *The Way We Live Now* (discussed in Chapter 7). Stylistically, though, as Davies notes, the programme lacks the flair of some of his other recent work in the genre: '*Wives and Daughters* was well directed but it was like two steps backwards [after *Vanity Fair*] as it was done in a very stately way' (Davies, quoted in Ransome, 2001: 39).

In contrast, Davies's adaptation of *Daniel Deronda* (2002) benefits from a strong directorial style which makes reference to an art cinema aesthetic. The opening credits to each episode appear to mimic a renowned sequence from Terence Davies's *The House of Mirth* (2000): the camera moves across the glittering surface of a body of water, accompanied by an operatic soundtrack, establishing a languorous and reflective pace, and allowing the viewer to focus on details of the image and the music.[37] The rich visual texture of the serial complements its narrative and thematic complexity, and provides striking moments that draw attention to vital, underlying themes. The scenes in which Daniel (Hugh Dancy) first catches sight of Gwendolen Harleth (Romola Garai) and Mirah Lapidoth (Jodhi May), for example, sensitively evoke the strangeness and significance of these two interventions, in different ways.

Daniel's observation of the beautiful but conceited Gwendolen at the gambling table is presented through intercuts that reveal his overt fascination (figure 16), and Gwendolen's acute awareness of his gaze, which she regards, correctly, as a both a challenge and a criticism, rather than the kind of compliment she is accustomed to receiving. The increasingly intrusive close-ups of Gwendolen suggest the pressure of

16, 17 *Daniel Deronda* (2002): Daniel watches Gwendolen; and Gwendolen senses Daniel's gaze

his scrutiny, and expose her attempts to appear confident and indifferent as mere performance (figure 17). Mirah's introduction is contrasted with that of Gwendolen. Mirah is initially intrigued by Daniel's gaze upon her, but is ultimately self-absorbed, standing silently by the river in which she intends to drown herself. There is an air of despairing purposefulness about her, conveyed in her detachment from the world around her and enhanced by her severe appearance: swathed in black, and with black hair, she seems to have sunk already into darkness (and she thus contrasts with Gwendolen's eye-catching appearance, with her embellished emerald gown and sparkling jewels). As Daniel rows slowly past Mirah, he sings a plaintive lamentation, which seems out of place in this most English of settings. The song connects him with Mirah – with her identity as a fellow Jew, and her passion for singing – although at first he struggles to deny the former connection. Mirah is portrayed as an Ophelia, disillusioned and despairing, seeking to escape the world through a quiet, watery death. The captivating energy of Gwendolen is sharply contrasted with the desperate strength of Mirah. In each scene, though, a powerful and immediate connection is created between Daniel and the woman he espies, and as is customary in an 'art film' aesthetic, details of sound and image, and references to other texts and stories, are carefully deployed, with the effect of defamiliarising each moment, and intensifying the impact of these sequences. Notably, dialogue between these central characters is absent during these pivotal moments of their first meetings. The lack of wordiness and the concomitant reliance upon visual details to communicate the significant aspects of the scene can reasonably be attributed to Davies. As noted earlier with reference to *Middlemarch*, Davies has disagreed with several directors who wish to prioritise his dialogue over visual and aural details, for he believes the latter to be better suited to the audio-visual medium of television. The power of these two scenes lies in qualities such as the tension in a glance, the ambient sounds that reveal the world around the characters, and the rhythm and momentum created by the pattern of intercutting. In advocating more 'visual' adaptations, Davies exhibits a keen awareness of the needs, possibilities and development of the televisual medium.

The plot of *Daniel Deronda* allows Davies to present the kind of characters that he creates most successfully: individuals struggling to assert their independence and identities within a broadly oppressive, or at least restrictive, context. While Mirah is the most obvious victim in the adaptation, having suffered the loss of her family and home, and being out of place in her current situation, other characters have to deal with similar challenges. Daniel, of course, must come to terms with his true (Jewish) origins; in doing so he offers a respectful and fond, yet incisive, critique of the conventional, contemporary English male identity with which the genre is more often associated. As he says to Sir Hugo Mallinger (Edward Fox), his guardian, 'Yes, of course I want to be an English gentleman, sir, but I want to understand other points of view.' Daniel thus exhibits an understanding that the role of English gentleman is necessarily restrictive, limiting the experiences he may have, and the affiliations he may form. In short, he questions the way in which his identity is pre-constructed for him through the expectations of others who demand that he fulfil a particular, predestined role.

Unsurprisingly, though, in view of Davies's typical preoccupations and sympathies, it is the female protagonist, Gwendolen Harleth, who experiences the most difficulties in negotiating the different roles she plays. With his usual sensitive awareness of the situation of women like Gwendolen, who must deploy her beauty in order to attract an offer of marriage and subsequently a secure future for herself and her family, Davies emphasises her frustration at her limited options (she often states her boredom with a 'girl's life'), and implies that her whole existence is a series of gambles like those she takes at the gaming table. She takes a chance on the apparently charming Henleigh Grandcourt, and loses pitifully, finding that he too has been playing a role in order to obtain 'the pleasure of mastering a woman who thinks she can master me': Grandcourt correlates his husbandly subduement of Gwendolen with the practice of schooling a wayward horse; he cares nothing for her and cannot regard her as having an individual identity of her own. Gwendolen's risk-taking, which is vital for her survival, is presented alongside Daniel's principled but pious condemnation of her behaviour. Daniel judges her harshly for her gambling (both the literal and figurative kind); with sympathetic irony, Davies shows that Gwendolen, though flawed, has little choice in terms of how to behave, for her situation is unlike Daniel's own secure existence as a moneyed man. Thus Davies's liberal and sympathetic world view permeates the text, guiding our responses to the characters and the text.

Notes

1 Quoted from Davies's e-mail communication to me, sent in February 2004.
2 McFarlane proffers specific examples of how such a commentating voice might be made manifest: 'The [film-maker] may indicate adverbially the tone of voice in which a remark is made by a character; the camera, on the other hand, may register a similar effect through attention to the actor's facial expression or posture (i.e. aspects of the mise-en-scène), or by cutting so as to reveal a response to such a remark (i.e. through montage) which will guide the viewer's perception of the remark, as well as through the actor's vocal inflection (i.e. through sound-track)'

(McFarlane, 1996: 18).

3 I have chosen to ignore the conceptual category of 'implied author' here, for the sake of simplicity; I have limited my focus to the concepts that are vital to my analysis. However, for a useful discussion of the implied author, I would refer interested readers to Currie, 1995a, especially pp. 243–51.

4 Quoted from previously cited e-mail from Davies to me, February 2004.

5 Quote from my interview with Davies, 21 February 2003.

6 The term 'genre' is applied loosely here. Please see my discussion of the notion of genre in relation to classic-novel adaptations in Cardwell (2002).

7 Davies refers to this disagreement in his Huw Wheldon Memorial Lecture, and has also mentioned it in various interviews.

8 Quoted from previously cited e-mail from Davies to me, February 2004.

9 Quoted from previously cited e-mail from Davies to me, February 2004.

10 More subtle tensions are also present between these two voices, and they require us to look again at Austen's work and the characters we know so well. Davies heightens the significance of Elizabeth's response to Pemberley, making it clear that her first response to its grandeur is to realise that she could have been mistress of it had she not rejected Darcy. This makes Elizabeth appear rather more pragmatic (mercenary) than she seems in the novel, and constitutes a rereading of the source that emphasises both the contemporary contingencies facing a woman like Elizabeth Bennet and also her less virtuous, selfless qualities. This leads us to reconsider how Elizabeth's character is presented by Austen, in comparison.

11 *Pride and Prejudice* was especially typical of the 1990s classic-novel adaptation, to the extent that it consolidated the genre, because it was an Austen adaptation. As I have said elsewhere: 'Austen adaptations had by the 1990s become representative of the genre of classic-novel adaptations as a whole ... [They have] played a vital role in consolidating the traits which adaptations share ... To some extent, in the 1990s Austen adaptations became synonymous with "classic-novel adaptations", and the 1995 *Pride and Prejudice* was of particular importance because of its outstanding success. Therefore *Pride and Prejudice* serves as a consolidation of the genre ... because of its importance as an Austen adaptation in confirming the archetypal image of the genre' (Cardwell, 2002: 134).

12 This could also be understood as an 'Austenesque' observation. There is a concord in tone (sympathetic irony) between Davies and Austen. However, it is more sensible to regard this as a typically Davies moment, whose much more direct control and influence over this text (the programme) means that he must be preferred when ascertaining the author of it.

13 For a concise general account of Thackeray's life, see the biography offered in Chapter 1, 'Life', in John Carey (1977: 11–33). General readers, both contemporary and modern, would be likely to have a sense of Thackeray's broad reputation, even if they knew/know no specific details of his history.

14 I dealt with *Moll Flanders* extensively in my book *Adaptation Revisited* (Cardwell, 2002) where I considered issues such as genre, performance (including the striking use of direct address), the televisual, female representation and humour. Interested readers should consult the appropriate chapter in that book.

15 The subtitle was altered when the revised edition was published: the earlier version was subtitled *Pen and Pencil Sketches of English Society*, the later one *A Novel without a Hero*.

16 Contemporary readers would have been familiar with Bunyan's fable, and Thackeray exploits this fact and draws on that earlier text in other ways (as I mention in the section on 'register', for example). Thackeray's characters differ dramatically, however, being more fleshed out, while Bunyan's characters act as embodied symbols and templates.

17 The rich world of Thackeray's *Vanity Fair* is brought out sensitively by Carey (1977), who explores it under chapter headings such as 'food', 'drink', 'light', 'colour', 'commodities', 'theatre', and so on. This also echoes Bakhtin's notion of the carnivalesque (which I return to later in the chapter).

18 *Vanity Fair* has been adapted several times for cinema, but only once previously for television; when Davies adapted it in 1998, it would have been relatively unfamiliar to viewers.

19 Shillingsburg claims we must understand the man before we can comprehend his fiction. A biographical approach is similarly advocated by Carey, who argues that because many of the characters and situations in Thackeray's work are based on the man's real life experiences, we must be knowledgeable about the latter; in particular, Carey feels that a biographical approach can explain the noted fall in eminence of Thackeray after *Vanity Fair* (Carey, 1977: 11).

20 Though Shillingsburg refers to characters 'like ourselves', I think it is vital to recognise that their 'mixed' attributes are such not because the characters are 'life like' but because they are precisely fictional constructs that are useful for creating a fascinating story. That is, I would place greater emphasis on their careful construction within a text, rather than regarding them as 'real' people.

21 Thackeray states that Amelia is 'not a heroine' on p. 43, but five pages later he seems to have changed his mind, referring to 'the heroine of this work, Miss Sedley (whom we have selected for the very reason that she was the best-natured of all; otherwise what on earth was to have prevented us from putting up Miss Swartz, or Miss Crump, or Miss Hopkins, as heroine in her place?)' (Thackeray, 1853: 48).

22 There is ambivalence, for example, when Thackeray describes Amelia's letters to George Osborne: 'She wasn't a heroine. Her letters *were* full of repetition. She wrote rather doubtful grammar sometimes, and in her verses took all sorts of liberties with the meter' (Thackeray, 1853: 154). Thus he is critical of her correspondence (he notes later that it is too lengthy, as well as being poorly written); however, he also implies that such criticisms are petty – that Amelia's lack of literary talent is not important, for it is her expression of love for George rather than the mode of expression that matters. It is finally the expressing of emotion, not its mode of expression, that matters.

23 This is an interesting comment, given its emphasis on the visual qualities of a heroine, and implying an awareness of physical typecasting; it seems almost pretelevisual!

24 Alternatively, it implies that Thackeray's plans, his designs for the novel, were set down before the writing process and cannot now be changed.

25 I write in rather broad and imprecise terms about register here. Register is a far more complex and interesting concept than my cursory analysis implies, but a fuller consideration of it falls outside the remit of this book. Interested readers may like to refer to Butler (1999) for a more sustained discussion.

26 The interplay of different voices and registers within the novel highlights the constructed nature of the text, by commenting upon the process of storytelling, and emphasising the difference between stories and real life. Frequently, the narrator/author pauses to suggest alternative developments that might have occurred, or how else the story might progress. An excellent example of this occurs when the narrator/Thackeray questions how the story might be different if the events were the same but the novel were in a different genre, or if the characters were from a different social class (1853: 88). (Thackeray does not use the term 'genre' himself, but his comments imply such a concept.)

27 A more active, engaged attitude to texts such as classic-novel adaptations on the part of the viewer may occur for several reasons. For example, the perception of a programme as 'quality' television, and of its status as 'authored' (by Davies), leads

viewers to regard it as more carefully considered and constructed than quotidian television, and thus potentially richer in meaning. This means that additional effort expended on interpretation is likely to be rewarded, which encourages greater attention and focus upon the text.

28 Some aspects of the novel require little or no updating, though. Indeed, some features are still challenging to modern-day perceptions of femininity and appropriate female behaviour. For example, Becky shares with Moll Flanders a complete lack of interest in maternal matters. She feels no affection for her son, Rawdon, finding him a nuisance; however, knowing that some social expectations must be met, she plays the role of affectionate mother. The adaptation exposes this as mere performance. In episode four, when Rawdon turns up unexpectedly at the adults' dinner table, and reveals that he ordinarily eats not with his parents but with the servants in the kitchen, Becky bids him to come and 'kiss his mother', and whispers fiercely to him, 'Mind your tongue, you little fool. Now go back to your place.' Then she pats him kindly on the head and sends him to bed, with a demure smile to the watching guests, as she simpers, 'What would we women be without our children?' Overturning modern-day as well as contemporary views on women's 'natural' instincts, the scene also subverts our expectations of women within the genre of classic-novel adaptations.

29 In this, Becky is strikingly reminiscent of Moll Flanders, in having to play appropriate roles, and recognising the way in which others determine those roles; at the end of the serial, when she must rescue her situation, she states that 'I need to be the Becky they first knew'.

30 In *Vanity Fair*, Davies is particularly sensitive to the social constraints that bind all the characters to some degree. A general critique of hierarchical power relations within society is conveyed through the depiction of the dynamics of individual interpersonal relationships, such as in the cruel and absolute dominance of Lord Steyne over his wife. The perpetuation of such hierarchical structures is exemplified in the relationship between Osborne's father and Osborne's son, in which Osborne's father attempts to make a man of his grandson by forcing wine upon him – instead, his attempt to enforce a masculine identity upon the youngster only makes the child ill.

31 To clarify: I mean that the voice is disinterested, rather than uninterested. The voice has no vested interest – no prospect of personal gain from its narration. This is not to say that the voice lacks an opinion or a 'personality' merely because it is not a character, for it clearly exhibits both at different points.

32 The black manservant is called 'Sambo' in the source book; this name was changed to the more politically correct 'Samuel' in the adaptation.

33 A baronet is not as grand as sounds; the baronetcy has been the lowest hereditary title since 1611.

34 This echoes Bunyan's conception of Vanity Fair.

35 The opening of a new episode offers the opportunity for a change in tone; this is exploited in episode four, which opens with the death of Osborne, and Amelia's sincere and heartfelt grief, and which thus breaks away from the predominantly buoyant, witty and ironic tone that predominates throughout the serial.

36 Disruptions of a similar kind happen also in relation to other aspects of the serial. There is a curiously unsettling moment, for example, when George Osborne switches, in an instant, from light-heartedly teasing Jos Sedley about his alcohol-induced exploits, to harshly condemning that same drunken behaviour, and cruelly convincing Jos that he has lost Becky for good.

37 This echoes a beautiful invented scene from Terence Davies's film, which works to link together what was originally Parts I and II of the source novel, and transport us from Lily Bart's London home to Monte Carlo. The camera pans around

Lily's deserted drawing room, and then a cut takes us outside, where the shot moves from rain in front of trees, to rain on the surface of a river, to the sea, and across to the new location. This is accompanied throughout by an extract from Mozart's *Cosi Fan Tutte*.

Distinguishing the televisual

6

Davies has occasionally ventured into film screenwriting, and has worked on four projects that have come to fruition: *Consuming Passions* (1988), *Circle of Friends* (1995), *The Tailor of Panama* (2001) and *Bridget Jones's Diary* (2001).¹ He also continues to write books and plays. However, television remains his medium of choice, and the locus of his best-known work, primarily because of the authorial role he is permitted to play (the high level of control, creative input and freedom open to him). This chapter explores how Davies's work seeks to defines television's specificity through its relationships with other media.

The title of this chapter therefore refers to two things. The first is the distinguishing of the televisual that can be seen in Davies's recent programmes, and the second is the corresponding distinguishing of the televisual by me as a critic of his work. Increasingly, Davies's work fully exploits the medium of television; in recognition of this, the chapter places an emphasis upon that work within the specific context of its medium. While the two previous chapters focused on Davies's adaptations from literature, this chapter considers his rarer, recent adaptations from other media: from theatre and from film. These arts share more features with television than does literature, in being both visual and performed. Theatre is visual in a way that literature is not, for it can present solid objects and the performances of actors to the audience, rather than conveying these things in a symbolic fashion. Film is even closer to television in being composed of recorded moving images that bear an indexical relation to the real world. Hence when adapting material from these media, Davies is compelled to take into account the relationships, similarities and differences between television and these, its closely related cousins; he must fully exploit the particularities of the televisual medium in order to mark his adaptations' differences from their source texts.

This chapter sustains my previous focus upon authorial traits within

Davies's work, referring back to notions such as his world view, thematic concerns and voice, and continuing my emphasis on stylistic innovations and developments within his work. The difference in this chapter is that my observations are made specifically with reference to the televisual context. In each case I consider how elements in the programmes under scrutiny contribute to the televisual nature of the texts, and assert the texts' distinction from their theatrical or filmic sources. The differences in medium and type of the source material led Davies to adapt the sources differently; thematic, stylistic and tonal emphases were in some part determined by Davies's awareness of medium-specific differences between literary, theatrical, filmic and television texts. In his quest to create great television, Davies has sought to assert its differences from great literature, theatre and film.

The effect of these factors upon my critical project is significant. In the spirit of 'sympathetic disinterest' referred to in the introduction to this book, this chapter attempts to reiterate the importance of taking up an appropriate and responsive approach to the close analysis of individual works. Therefore the process referred to in the title – that of making the televisual distinct from other media – is both what Davies is doing and what the critic is required to do in order to appreciate the work responsively. When dealing with *Othello*, for example, the theatrical nature of the source text suggests a focus on how Davies has manipulated characterisation, performance and spatial aspects; when considering *Doctor Zhivago*, the programme's dual literary/filmic roots demand a consideration of its intertextual context and a reflection upon its televisuality as distinct from film as well as literature. Chapter 7 then concludes this study by reinforcing the importance of televisual aesthetics to Davies's artistic sensibility, revealing that he not only distinguishes the televisual but embraces it, and reflecting upon what this means for the television critic and scholar.

From theatre to television: characterisation, performance and space in *Othello* (2001)

William Shakespeare's *Othello* (1622) recounts the tragic downfall of its eponymous protagonist, who is driven to jealousy and murderous rage, convinced that his wife Desdemona is being unfaithful to him. In fact, she is true, but the malevolent, manipulative Iago, who was passed over for honours in favour of his old friend Othello, manufactures the situation to avenge his wounded pride. An intricate exploration of Othello's psychological turmoil forms the pivotal centre of the play. In its interest in the revelation of and interrelations between characters, and in the effect of situation upon character, the play concords with Davies's typical concerns.

Harold Bloom notes, of the play, that:

> It is Othello's tragedy, but Iago's play. I do not mean that Iago runs off with it, or that Othello's is not a great role. Iago is a dramatist who takes over his fellow characters and plots them into the play that he desires to stage. He is a theatrical improviser, making his plot up as he goes along: He imagines passions for others, and even proposes emotions for himself, which to some degree he subsequently feels ... His intellect is extraordinary: amazingly quick, endlessly resourceful. Iago is the master psychologist in all of Shakespeare, expert at manipulating everyone else in the play. His pride and analytical interest in his own technique make him also the forerunner of theatrical criticism: as he says, 'For I am nothing if not critical.' (Bloom, 1996: 5)

One can see how such a man as Iago would interest Davies. Here is a character who is clever, witty, charming, self-interested and dangerous. He yearns for power and the deference of others. He is self-aware and self-reflective, and he reveals how easy it is to manipulate the situation in order to make others play out the roles we would choose for them. There are clear resonances here of Francis Urquhart, Davies's first truly immoral protagonist, and in the emphases upon manipulation, performance and reflection, *Othello* echoes the concerns explored in many of Davies's previous works, including *Moll Flanders* and *Vanity Fair*. Further, the psychological exploration of Othello, and the way in which his situation deeply affects his state of mind, echoes Davies's ongoing concerns (one thinks particularly of his early adaptation of *The Signalman*).

Indeed, Davies drew upon some familiar techniques in his version of *Othello*. Direct address, used to such great effect in the *House of Cards* series and in *Moll Flanders*, is again employed here, with Iago speaking directly to the camera, in the presence of other characters. This is twinned with a mobile, roving camera, as in *Moll Flanders*, which draws attention to the televisual nature of the image (unlike theatre). The most obvious way in which Davies signals the modern, televisual nature of his *Othello*[2] (and simultaneously reasserts his authorship over the programme, downplaying Shakespeare's claim over the material) is in updating the story, setting it in the present day. John Othello (Eamonn Walker) and Ben Jago (the Iago character, played by Christopher Eccleston) are friends who work as senior police officers with the Metropolitan Police. Othello is appointed Chief Commissioner over Jago, partly because the appointing panel wants to make a 'positive statement' by appointing a black candidate (Othello and Jago are equally qualified for it). Jago, aware of the reasons behind this appointment, is overwhelmed with bitterness and envy, and resolves to undermine his friend and seize the job from him which he believes is rightfully his. Davies retains the basic structure and emphases of Shakespeare's plot, but in updating the play's setting, he also disposes of Shakespeare's language, and the characters use present-day speech.

Davies's *Othello* asserts on the one hand the programme's theatrical roots, and on the other its televisuality, alternating between theatrical and televisual modes in order to create dramatic emphases, both in its use of space, which I shall come to later, and in its characterisation and performance.

Ben Jago, the dramatist

The adaptation interprets the source text in the manner that Bloom does, above, placing Jago at the centre of the narrative, and highlighting his power over Othello and other characters. Jago's voice is present throughout the programme, both as a voice-over and in direct address. His words open and close the serial, 'It was about love, that's what you've gotta understand. Don't talk to me about race; don't talk to me about politics. It was love. Simple as that.' The exact repetition of these words, placed on either side of a tale that belies their inaccuracy emphasises both their disingenuous nature and Jago's fundamental unreliability as a narrator. Repetition is used elsewhere in the serial, troubling any assumptions we may have regarding the transparency of language – or at least its ability to provide us with access to truths about a character. Jago's repeated avowal of sympathy, 'I've been there', and his overuse of words such as 'honesty' and 'trust', betray his lack of human compassion; he seems incapable of feeling empathy with others, despite figuring out how to manipulate their thoughts and emotions.

At the opening of the serial, it briefly appears that Jago might be a partial, yet relatively reliable, observer of the narrative. He plays the role of confidant, encouraging us to accompany him ('Come on!' he entreats, as he gestures the camera onwards; the camera dutifully follows), and offering us 'useful advice' on the action (he suggests we dismiss a minor character from our minds with the words, 'Yesterday's man – forget about him'). For this reason we are inclined to take seriously what he has to say. Indeed, his more general, accurate reports about the upcoming narrative have the ring of a theatrical chorus, for they imply sagacity and an awareness of the story to come; of 'Dessie' (Desdemona, played by Keeley Hawes) and Othello, he says, 'She loved him as well as she knew how. He loved her more than any man should love a woman.' Correctly and playfully identifying the form of the drama (and thus referentially acknowledging Shakespeare's source), Jago says of the impending events, 'Tragedy, right? No other word for it.' It is only when he adds the words, 'I loved him too, you know!', that the full extent of his insincerity, and the complexity of his relationship with Othello, is revealed. This encourages us to weigh up his words with great care, never trusting them. After the disastrous meal out, in which Othello flies into an irrational rage, Jago asks 'So what do you think? I know, I feel it too. I'm almost sorry I started this. Too late now – it's up and running. It's beyond my control'. At that moment, we are asked to consider the possibility that Jago is not being utterly insincere, but is expressing some small measure of regret – but we cannot be certain either way. We are also asked to question not just his words but his actions, even the smallest details of performance; this alters the way in which we relate to the character. When Jago breaks down in tears, in sympathy with a contrite, weeping suspect, we regard the moment as a successful performance on his part. The result is a troubling and engaging uncertainty regarding Jago's character, which demands constant attention and reconsideration from us.

Jago's eye contact with the camera, direct address and voice-over, utilise specific features of the television medium. The intimacy that a camera permits, allowing us to come face to face with a character, is something that is difficult to recreate in the theatre, and direct address is a technique we tend to associate with television rather than with film, where it is far less common. However, its use in drama, as noted in Chapter 4, is rare, and the consequence of this is to create a sense of theatricality, especially when other characters on screen remain oblivious to the soliloquy being performed within their hearing. In this way, the presentation of Jago is simultaneously televisual and theatrical.

Sometimes, we hear Jago's thoughts in voice-over rather than in direct address (such as when he is in conversation with Othello, and the soundtrack presents both his insincere, overt dialogue and his true feelings, in voice-over, implied to be in his head). This technique does not disrupt the dominant naturalistic traditions of television drama to the same degree as Jago's asides to camera, for we understand that Othello remains oblivious to Jago's thoughts and that we are being offered privileged access to them. At other moments, though, the programme slips into a 'theatrical' mode. Consider the intense, angry speech that Jago offers to the camera later in the programme. What begins as an internal monologue (voice-over on the soundtrack) moves to Jago speaking the words we hear, and builds to an impressive, furious tirade as Jago storms down a corridor in the Met, smashing swinging doors open so that they crash behind him, pounding the walls with his fists, and aggressively advancing on the camera. In this moment, television drama's typical dependency upon naturalism is suspended, as Jago's rant goes unnoticed by any of those around him, and the camera pulls back from its intimate close-up on Jago's face, as if to approximate a relation to him more like that of a theatre-going audience.

Yet the televisual medium is cleverly exploited even in this 'theatrical' moment: immediately after this speech, there is an advertisement break, and when we return to the programme, Jago seems to have taken the few minutes of real time that we were away from him to check his temper and collect his thoughts. 'What a performance – I quite surprised myself!' he exclaims. In its use of the real time of the advertisement break, the programme exploits the nature of television broadcasts, differentiating this moment as televisual rather than theatrical or indeed filmic. The scene is successful because we are taken away from Jago for a few minutes, long enough for the character to recover, but we are not offered another scene; the moment is suspended through the break, and we are willing to accept that the duration of the break is representative of the 'real' time it took Jago to curb his emotions. If this had been attempted on stage or film, another scene, or possibly an interval, would have had to be inserted, disrupting the diegetic temporality, and reducing the powerful connection between the two moments.

Jago's reference to his 'performance' is a typical Davies trait, as we have seen in previous chapters; it is also a reference both to the performative nature of television (he draws attention to the practice of 'acting') and, in implying the over-dramatic, exaggerated nature of that particular moment of his performance, to theatricality as not being 'real'. Thus the more televisual performances – naturalistic, and in which expressiveness is often constituted out of tiny details, captured in close-up – are contrasted with the rather exaggerated mode of theatrical performances, where the former are often presented as offering the more truthful perspective (a claim, perhaps, for the greater perspicacity and intimacy of television over theatre). Again, the source medium and the adaptive medium (theatre and television) are utilised to create a unique, reflexive aesthetic.

Intersubjectivity

Jago's tireless attack on Othello's balance of mind is captured in a moment when he is teasing Othello with the photographs of Dessie and Michael Cass (Richard Coyle). Having cruelly aroused Othello's suspicions. Jago leans back insouciantly, and casually suggests, 'Maybe all this is just in your head.' Then, in an apparently casual but terrifyingly portentous gesture, he touches Othello's head and gently pushes it to one side. It is a powerful, physical expression of the control he is gaining over Othello's mind.

At a more insidious level, the power of Jago over Othello is presented through the use of shot juxtaposition, cutting from Jago to Othello in a way that implies a causality between the two (i.e. Jago is determining Othello's responses). This utilises television's specific visual qualities to imply intersubjectivity (the merging of two or more characters' subjectivities) in a way that theatre cannot. An example of this is when the scheming Jago is deciding upon his next machination, and he looks upwards towards the light on the ceiling. The camera moves with his point of view, so that the screen is filled with powerful, bright white light; a cut takes us underwater to Othello's swimming pool, just as Othello dives in. The strong sense of movement within the shots – upwards in the first, with Jago's gaze, and downwards in the second, with Othello's trajectory into the water – links the two shots; there is a sensation that as Jago rises Othello falls, and that Jago's upward movement causes the fall of Othello, as if he has thrown an object into the air and it must inevitably come crashing to earth. As in Davies's other work, inter-subjectivity is also used to cast doubt upon the objectivity of scenes; as rioters gather noisily after news of a black suspect's death at the hands of the police, we cut to Dessie, who abruptly awakes, as if the preceding scene, which is so significant for her and her husband, was her nightmare, rather than reality. The merging of reality and dreams presages Othello's future state of mind and the severe consequences of this for Dessie.

Framing is also used to convey Jago's constant, threatening presence, as he insinuates himself into every situation. He is even revealed to be present when we least expect it. When Dessie retreats to the home of Lulu (Rachael Stirling), her closest friend, and Jago's wife, after Othello's sudden outburst of anger, an intimate two shot shows the two women sitting at the dining table, talking about Othello's changed temperament. The intimacy of the moment is disturbed and undermined when the camera moves to reveal that Jago is present at the table too. He advises Dessie to return home to Othello, despite the women's fears, and thus hastens the final tragic scene of Dessie's murder by her husband.

Media images

Updating Shakespeare's play, Davies replaces the fragile 'proofs' of Desdemona's infidelity (the handkerchief, for example) with the ostensibly more 'reliable', scientific proof that modern-day technology can provide us with. In doing so, he reveals that the most up-to-date innovations are equally dangerous in the wrong hands: Jago's e-mail precipitates the attack on Dessie's flat; the photographic 'evidence' of Dessie and Cass's relationship is misinterpreted by a jealous Othello; and Jago exploits Othello's blind faith in science and in him when he reports that DNA testing of Othello's robe has proved Dessie's infidelity with Cass. Othello overvalues the truth-telling potential of modern science, and underestimates the ways in which modern, objective technologies can be manipulated and used against him.

Most saliently, the adaptation foregrounds the media – television, radio and newspapers – and the role that they can play in a modern-day tragedy like Othello's. All the central characters are aware of the imbrication of the media within their lives; the omnipresence of the media is highlighted towards the beginning of the programme when Lulu is watching television – she sees Jago ring their home doorbell, and then gets up to greet him at the door. There is no escape from the attentions of the press.

At first, it seems that Othello is canny about the media. He chooses to address the enraged rioters alone, knowing that, as a high-profile black officer, he is best able to present the right image to both protestors and the media. He is aware of the connotations of his image and how to manipulate them. It is his argument about media presentation that convinces the protestors to behave peacefully; he points to the television cameras trained upon them and asks how they want to be seen. His reward is positive press coverage.

Yet Jago is far more shrewd. He mocks Othello's naïve attempts to 'manage' his image, mimicking the *Hello!*-style interviews that Othello and Dessie engage in, parroting their words back to the television screen. He sneers at Othello's official photographs in his Chief Commissioner's uniform (though embraces the same for himself in the end). He poses the question to his wife, 'But are they *too* good?', referring not to their actual 'goodness' but to how they are perceived – the way in which they appear. It is not their real moral standards that he is interested in questioning, but the moral aspects of the image they have chosen to publicise. Jago recognises an important truth which Othello overlooks (or at least underestimates): that if one man is lauded, there will always be another who wishes to topple him from his pedestal. The programme re-presents this element of Shakespeare's play and successfully updates it by revealing how the games played by modern-day celebrities and the media perpetuate an ancient cycle of hero worship, envy, calculated backstabbing and the ultimate undoing of a once-admired paragon.

Davies resists a simplistic division between good and evil, however. It must be observed that Othello's attempts to look the part and say the right thing are not presented as entirely laudable. In particular, his use of clichéd, New Labour neologisms (such as in his speech on 'zero tolerance') suggests that he is not the free-thinking individual he hopes to appear, but is a somewhat willing tool of the establishment. Perhaps this is the reason that Jago is able to encourage Othello to play into the hands of the media. Significantly, in a programme concerned with its own televisuality, Othello's downfall is captured on television. Othello undertakes a television interview, but he is beginning to fall apart. He is unable to answers the interviewer's questions, and instead turns and gazes directly into the camera; unlike Jago's direct gaze, his holds no power, only confusion and despair – it is an appeal for help. Othello is silent, unable to speak. We cut to a boiled egg being cracked open, and then pull back to see Jago at breakfast, holding up a copy of the *Daily Express*, on which is emblazoned the headline 'Police chief cracks up on TV'. Unable to control his own image, Othello is crushed by the media. Television revels in his ruin.

Spatiality

Theatrical and televisual spaces differ in many regards, and those differences are exploited in *Othello* (just as distinctions between filmic and televisual spaces are recalled in the later *Doctor Zhivago*).

The potential for a focus on minute details is one of the things that differentiates filmic and televisual spatiality from theatrical space. Tiny spaces can be explored. The opening of *Othello* declares its televisual nature by utilising this. A big close-up of Dessie's closed eyes, her eyelids twitching with the rapid eye movement of deep sleep, is followed by a similarly framed close up on her lips, which flutter slightly as she murmurs indistinguishable words. A further close-up presents Othello's

18 *Othello* (2001): hands

and Dessie's hands intertwined, black upon white, their hands fore-grounded within the frame, the background sparse (figure 18). Television historically paints with broader brushstrokes than film (arising from its initially much poorer and smaller images); here, that tradition is sustained, allowing a focus on a few specific details. The consequence of this is that we tend to read the images symbolically, assuming a figurative aspect to their content. Othello's obsession with Dessie's dreams, and his fears about what those dreams might contain, is captured in his close attention to her eyes and lips; we too attempt to read what she says in her sleep, seeking clues to a mystery that does not really exist. The fact that Othello and Dessie are of different races and colours is also foregrounded in the hands shot; again, this issue is vital to the upcoming story.[3] All three shots (eyes, lips, hands), and the shots of Othello watching Dessie in her sleep, contain important seeds of future developments and complications, seeds that are nourished and nurtured by Jago in the pursuit of his own ends.

At other times, the programme opens up 'theatrical spaces' – that is, the spaces seem somehow unnaturalistic and exaggerated in size or style. When Othello confronts the rioting crowd, he positions himself at the top of a flight of steps, looking down upon the people; one protester stands his ground on the roof of a car, defiantly mirroring Othello. Thus the lone, elevated protester comes to personify Othello's opponents, in the way that theatre often presents a singular person to represent many. This dramatic use of vertical and horizontal space, combined with vivid lighting and powerful dialogue, brings a theatrical air to this moment of overt conflict which is so fundamental to the story. A similar sensation is conveyed when Othello and Cass fight each other in an underground car park; the space is lit in blue, so that the colours, though plausible, are non-naturalistic, implying a more symbolic, significant dimension to the clash. Another key scene, in which Othello loses his temper with his friends and lashes out at Cass and at Dessie, is presented in a strange, exaggeratedly gothic space (we assume it is a private room in a restaurant, though this is unclear), implying that the scene is not to be read merely literally. The theatricality of the scene is enhanced by the falseness of the setting (the fake painted walls and so on), intensifying the strange, threatening atmosphere within the group.

The programme also utilises the televisual medium to create fractured and symbolic spaces.[4] There is a repeated, curious image of the block of flats in which Othello and Dessie live, shown inverted, reflected in the river below. At the simplest level, this suggests the way in which their world is turned upside down by Jago's machinations. Beyond this, though, this shot connects with another repeated motif – that of Othello swimming underwater. In this way, it is made clear that Othello is the one who dives into that inverted world, embracing it of his own accord, whilst Dessie remains outside it. The role of Jago in creating the topsy-turvy world that finally ruins Othello is emphasised at the end of the serial: Jago, standing outside Othello's flat, is pictured inverted, reflected in the water, while Lulu, who stands with him, is depicted the right way up (not reflected). The water comes to represent the obscene world that Jago has created for Othello, and in which Othello eventually drowns. Again, this wholly exploits the potential of television to present spaces not easily available to theatre, and to direct our attention to them in a way that heightens their symbolic potential.

Through elements as varied as performance style, narrative concerns, symbolic motifs, framing, spatial composition and language, Davies's *Othello* reshapes Shakespeare's text to reveal the interrelations and differences between television and theatre, and exploit the potential of television as an art form compatible with, but ultimately distinct from, its theatrical relation.

From novel to film to television: embracing intertextuality in *Doctor Zhivago* (2002)

When Davies chose to adapt *Doctor Zhivago* for television, he had to contend with the existence of two major sources: Boris Pasternak's 1956 novel (published in English in 1958) and David Lean's well-known film adaptation of 1965. While this provided the potential for greater richness of reference, meaning and affect, it also meant that the serial had to contend with the viewers' familiarity with these previous texts and their affection for them. In every choice made, from the narrative structure, to the selection of cast and locations, to stylistic decisions regarding framing, editing and the use of sound and music, there was the risk, or the opportunity, of stimulating viewers' memories of the other *Zhivagos*. The television adaptation also drew upon another key source: original archive footage of street scenes filmed in Russia between 1897 and 1917, thus further extending the programme's referential context.

Zhivago is therefore usefully considered in terms of its relationship with Pasternak's source novel and with Lean's film version (and with reference to its use of archive footage); in short, we are concerned with the programme's different levels and types of intertextuality. The presence of two major antecedent texts, one of which is audio-visual, demands that we modify the approach taken to Davies's other adaptations, and engage in intertextual criticism, as distinct from source criticism. This allows an emphasis on the dialogue between the three texts, and the resonances created within them by their references to earlier texts. John Frow expresses the essence of this approach:

> Intertextual analysis is distinguished from source criticism both by this stress on interpretation rather than on the establishment of particular facts, and by its rejection of a unilinear causality (the concept of 'influence') in favour of an account of the work performed upon intertextual material and its functional integration in the later text. (Frow, 1990: 46)

Given *Zhivago*'s 'dual origin' (the preceding novel and film), it is particularly important to consider the adaptation in relation to both sources. As Frow implies, intertextual analysis traces the connections between texts but also values each text as an independent and individually conceived artwork, rejecting fidelity criticism. And as Brian McFarlane contends, intertextual criticism might offer a route out of the abiding problem of 'fidelity criticism' – the comparison of an adaptation to its source novel, usually undertaken in terms that denigrate the former's independence and achievements as an artwork: 'Modern critical notions of intertextuality represent a more sophisticated approach, in relation to adaptation, to the idea of the original novel as a "resource"' (McFarlane, 1996: 10).

I have previously noted that adaptation poses particular challenges for critical evaluation; these are complicated and exacerbated by the second level of intertextuality found in Davies's *Zhivago*: its references to the film, another audio-visual text. There seems to be an implicit critical consensus that recreations of audio-visual texts in the same or similar media pose special problems for evaluation, as the derogatory term 'remake' implies. Questions that arise in relation to adaptation are intensified in this case; for example, what is to be gained from recreating a work in the same or a very similar medium (e.g. film to film, or film to television)? How might we conceptualise the remake in terms of its relationship to its source(s)? Finally, how might we evaluate it, given the importance of longstanding (if contentious) criteria such as originality and artistic/authorial integrity to the evaluation of artworks?

In *Zhivago*, Davies and director Giacomo Campiotti asserted the televisual nature of their production by building and then manipulating particular relationships with the two previous texts and their media (literature and film). Through close attention to the programme, it is possible to ascertain how an awareness of the other *Zhivago*s determined details of the programme: how the programme echoes, remembers, or attempts to erase the memory of those previous texts, and how the serial claims its difference from the other texts, both by avoiding intertextual references and by re-forming them, forging its own imprint of *Zhivago*. In exploring a problematic instance of a serial made in the shadow of a celebrated and adored novel as well as a much-loved film, one must recognise the problems of evaluation created by intertextuality in remakes and adaptation, but it is important also to affirm the potential created through the use of intertextual references to attain originality, and artistic and authorial integrity.

Pasternak's novel

> On they went, singing 'Eternal Memory', and whenever they stopped, the sound of their feet, the horses and the gusts of wind seemed to carry on their singing. (Pasternak, 1958: 13)

The opening lines of Boris Pasternak's novel *Doctor Zhivago* encapsulate the book's themes and expressive form, conveying a wealth of meaning in a few simple words. All at once we are aware of the intimate and inextricable relationship between people, their environment, and nature; this is a world in which, when people can sing no longer, their feet, their horses and the wind that accompany them sustain their song. Inherent within this image is a sense of eternity, echoed in the song's title, incorporating the past, present and future of the people and the wider world. The importance of the gathering of people in a group is also vital here: 'on *they* went', we are told. There is a sense of solidarity and stoicism, as well as a feeling of inevitable forward movement, if not progression; the people press on, continuing their journey, never standing still. From the outset we are made aware of the importance of communality, community and collective destiny, which are built upon a foundation of shared emotions and customs: grief at the death of one of their group (for the novel opens with the funeral of Zhivago's mother), and a long-established mode of expression – the singing of popular songs. There is a profound and obscure connection established here between the collective group, shared emotion, the natural world, and time. These are the fundamental notions that are thrown into question by the revolutionary world depicted in the novel. The changing social and political environment inhabited by Zhivago, Lara and other characters is interrogated through the ideas, beliefs and values implicit within the novel's opening sentence, and the book thus offers a sensitive, engaged, and reflective exploration of the reasons, motives and ideologies that lay behind the Russian revolution.[5]

Pasternak's prose[6] is typically heavy with significance, yet his choice of simple vocabulary and his uncomplicated sentence structures avoid the pitfalls of portentousness or pretentiousness. Indeed, his writing is beautiful: careful, understated, tender and thoughtful. His style is plain and unfussy, but the conceptual and emotional significance of the images his sentences create is profound. Structurally, the novel is multi-faceted and intricate. *Zhivago* is no straightforward love story set against a backdrop of revolutionary Russia, with historical events relegated to the background. Nor is it a political novel – a narrow indictment of the stark political developments at that time. The characters' lives and loves are interwoven with their historical circumstances – and necessarily so. Zhivago loves not just Lara but also Tonya, not just women but also poetry, and he respects, understands, and to some degree condones, the motives for revolution (even if he does not approve of its consequences). Nor is Zhivago the pivot around which the story turns. There are many characters, major and minor, whose tales are as important. In short, this is a novel that manages to convey complexity. The novel is immense – not just in length but in scope and significance, in tone and style. Nothing is simplified, nothing is black and white, no one aspect of the story is presented as more important than another.

Lean's film

One can see how such a novel presents particular problems for the adapter who wishes to convey something of its scope and tone. From depicting the full range of events in the narrative, to conveying the wide range of characters and the careful characterisation, to revealing the intricate and intimate relationships between history, the natural world, the social world and the people that constitute it, the adapter faces a difficult task in selecting and representing the material on the screen. David Lean's famed film adaptation, released in 1965, may not have achieved 'fidelity' to the novel, but Lean's love for the novel is clear, and the elements he chose to adapt and convey created memorable film history.

The stylistic choices facing Lean were perhaps the most tricky. Pasternak's style is constituted by words; Lean was working within an audio-visual medium, which opened up a range of stylistic elements not available to Pasternak. Lean's film displays the stylistic features found frequently across his work, and shared in particular by his other epic film *Lawrence of Arabia*. Alongside the use of extreme long shots cut against close-ups, *Zhivago* employs splashes of colour and light to draw attention to symbolic details:

Lean has often been called a great craftsman, and his films do indeed speak of a meticulous attention to detail: in the careful composition of each frame, in the precise and expressive use of sound and music, and in the nuanced performances drawn from each member of the cast. However, Lean's expressive use of mise-en-scène moves beyond mere craftsmanship; the themes and concerns of each film are articulated variously through dialogue and plot, sound, colour, editing, music, chiaroscuro and lighting ... his films are concerned with the integration of style and theme, with the expression of character, emotion, mood and the particularities of space, place and period. (Cardwell, 2003)

The film's opening scene shows General Yevgraf Zhivago (Alec Guinness), Yury Zhivago's surviving half-brother, attempting to find his niece, Tanya, who is Yury and Lara's daughter, amongst the girls who work at the factory he supervises. The entire story is then presented in flashback, introduced by this character as he relates it to Tanya. Typically of Lean, the style of this sequence is not foregrounded through camera movement, the camera remaining relatively still within shots, but through two dominant long-take long shots that are typical of Lean's 'epic' style. The film opens with Yevgraf looking down upon the workers as they leave work, and the second shot of the film is a salient one that sets the scene and tone. The long duration of this shot gives the viewer time to take in details of sound and image. We see, in extreme long shot, the dark interior of a building, lit only by the natural light that filters through the darkness from a bright arched entranceway, shaped like a train tunnel, at the centre of the screen. The light seems to be stifled by the darkness, so that the majority of the mid- and foreground of the scene is almost black. Near this limited light source we can see an endless trail of workers marching through the entrance way and along what appears to be a high, fenced corridor; other workers stream down some steps below the entrance. Both columns of people disappear into darkness, but the sounds of their feet and their voices persist, echoing around the cavernous area. The only bright colour in the image is a bright red communist star which is proudly displayed in the space above the tunnel entrance. The hundreds of workers are indistinguishable as individuals here, but when the camera cuts back to the workers, it is in mid shot, and as they pass the camera we note the camaraderie between them, their orderliness (they pass two by two, crocodile style), and also their differences – individual faces, mannerisms, coloured clothes. The mass is humanised. This is a motif that is repeated throughout the film: the presentation of 'the people' as a unified mass, and then the revelation of individuals within the group.[7] Indeed, the first shot of the main backstory echoes this: an extreme long shot of bare Russian landscape – snowy mountains in the background, the blue-black rock of their bases in the middle distance, and bare sandy coloured terrain at the bottom of the screen, nearest us. A small black huddle moves slowly across this immense terrain. The next (mid) shot reveals this black huddle to be a collection of people – a funeral procession.

Thus Lean utilises his own stylistic predilections for long shots and grand pictures, and his own thematic preference for character-based melodramas about love, to present one of the novel's key tensions – that between regarding the individual as a person and perceiving the people as a unified mass. His expressive style, which rejects naturalism in order to foreground emotional salience, is also employed to convey something of the novel's relationship between people, nature and history. Lean uses colour to highlight, expressively, what is significant, such as the red star that hangs over and dominates the factory workers in the second shot of the film. Utilising film's capacity for sound and image, he makes what appears to be a direct reference to the opening lines of the novel, as the sounds of the factory workers continue after they have disappeared from view. Even more pointedly, the dirge that dominates the soundtrack in the funeral scene appears to be sung extra-diegetically – none of the processors is visibly singing. Thus the song's importance extends beyond this particular instance (this single funeral) and seems to arise of its own accord from the people's grief and their history; it is symbolically removed from a specific historical moment, just like the song 'Eternal Memory', cited in the novel's opening lines. Repeated shots of the wind blowing the autumn leaves from the trees as the mourners stand around the grave of Zhivago's mother also imply the liveliness of nature – its vital role within the people's world. When the dirge has ceased, the introduction of Russian folk music over these shots implicates the social world within the natural world – almost as if the people's music moves the branches of the trees and stirs the wind to blow.

Davies's television serial

When Davies embarked upon his adaptation of *Zhivago*, broadcast on BBC television in 2002, the project was ambitious not just in taking on such a masterpiece of literature but also because comparisons with the earlier, much loved film by Lean were inevitable. Davies was free to choose his perspective on the novel, and he has said (with reference to the choice of a foreign director for the project):

> We felt there was a whole new version of it to be told. I suppose I felt that it needed a different sensibility. Because the film itself is regarded pretty much as a British classic, even though it's a Russian novel, I really didn't

want to do something that would feel ... that would make any direct
appeal as though they were walking in the shadow of the great David
Lean, and I think a lot of British directors inevitably felt that – didn't
want to be compared to him.[8]

As Davies was clearly aware, most viewers of the television adaptation would not have had an in-depth knowledge of the novel; indeed,
many of them would not have read it. But the enduring popularity of
Lean's film meant that Davies was aware of the comparisons that would
be drawn with it: he said the project was 'daunting because everyone
wonders how you can do better than the David Lean film' (source
unknown), and that 'what you've got to do is try and make people forget
about the film' (Davies, interviewed by Ransome, 2001: 39). Further, as
the earlier film was made in a comparable audio-visual medium to
television, memories of the film (in contrast to the book) would be
audio-visual – in terms of images, sounds, music. Watching the new
adaptation of *Zhivago* would certainly bring the book to mind in those
viewers who had read it, but it was even more likely to bring to mind
notable and familiar moments from the earlier film. As Hans Matheson,
who played *Zhivago*, notes: 'For a lot of people it's a film rather than a
book'.

However, that is not to downplay the programme's relationship with
Pasternak's text. The producer, the director and members of the cast
expressed a genuine love of the novel. Sam Neill (who played Komarovsky), asserted that 'We're not doing David Lean here, we're doing a great
novel. And we're revisiting the novel, not revisiting David Lean's film.
We're having another look at the novel.' Therefore both sources are
important to the programme's intertexuality. The television adaptation
was revisiting familiar territory not just in terms of the book but also in
terms of key memorable images from the film, and it is clear that
screenwriter Davies and director Giacomo Campiotti bore these inter-
texts in mind when they made their artistic choices, as a comparison of
particular scenes and more general style and structure makes clear. It
was important that the art work demarcate itself from the earlier version,
lest the adaptation be accused of mimicry, of being a pale imitation, of
being no more than a remake.[9] Yet the adaptation could also use the
viewers' knowledge, their familiarity with the preceding texts, to add
resonances and echoes to the contemporary one.

Davies and Campiotti made very different stylistic choices from Lean,
and these led to different thematic emphases and fluctuations in mood.
Also, they were working on television, and had different limitations of
the medium to consider. During the production process, Davies
complained that 'Granada, who are doing it, have always been stingy

about budgets, and you can't do *Zhivago* without trains and snow and armies and stuff. There's a limit to what you can do with close-ups!' It is interesting to see, however, how television's limited budget and consequent dependence upon 'close-ups' had a constructive impact upon the filming of key scenes (such as the Bloody Sunday scene I shall look at in more detail later).

Style

The opening of the television adaptation exhibits striking aspects of style that work both to establish the text's concerns, themes and sensibility and to differentiate the programme from the film. It is revealing to compare it with the opening of Lean's film. Choosing a different starting point, the programme opens just after Yury's father has thrown himself from a train, leaving Yury an orphan. We see a snowy landscape, with a train track leading from the foreground and curving away into the distance, to the right. In the background is a wood. The shot is taken from ground level, and deep focus means that we can see clearly into the distance, following the route of the track. At first there is no music – only a howling wind and eerie animal noises emanating, we assume, from the forest. Then we hear muffled shouts, and a small boy (Yury, played by Sam MacLintock) appears from the right, running along the railway track towards us, pursued by two men. The next cut takes us behind the two men, and is a hand-held camera shot, as if the camera operator is running behind them. We hear the laboured breathing of the men as they pursue Yury. The effect is to disturb the rather numbed, muffled atmosphere of the previous shot, placing us at the centre of the action and movement. This kind of contrast is one that the director uses throughout the serial, and it emphasises different perspectives on the same action: one that is distanced, observing, muted, passive, and another which is participatory, energetic, emotional, involved. Picking up a different aspect of the novel, then, this style highlights the two ways in which history is presented in the novel and understood by its characters – as a story, in which one observes individuals playing their transient parts, and as life, lived by individuals whose own stories are usually more important to them than the bigger picture.

Campiotti's eye for structure and shape is clear in this adaptation, and his concern for dramatic formal composition is similar to Lean's. Indeed, the first shot of the funeral procession (this time for Yury's father, following his suicide) is reminiscent of Lean's: in a long shot snowy landscape, the procession is merely a series of black dots moving slowly from left to right, and the only colour here is the bright red title *Doctor Zhivago*. However, adapting to the smaller screen of television,

Campiotti moves away from Lean's expressive, impressive style, mostly eschewing extreme long shots except for a few of Russia's beautiful snowy landscapes. He makes good use of close-ups, as we shall see, and also employs medium-long to long shots to great effect; he plays with form, composing images in patterns: looking down on the crowd gathered around Yury's father's grave, the mourners form a near-perfect circle, with the grave at the centre. The pleasing uniformity of such images – their prettiness – means that they appear as tableaux: still, almost frozen in time. There is an air of unreality about them so that, contra Lean, they do not prioritise emotional content and expression but an appreciation of form, conveying simultaneously the sense of a fragile community on the edge of change. In these shots, there is a sense of distance from events and from the communities depicted, almost as if one were seeing them as history. The use of cinefilm enhances this feeling.

The use of cinefilm
The way in which history – or historical context – is presented is notable. Original cinefilm material of Russia from 1897 onwards[10] is inserted into the narrative, constituting an additional intertextual reference. The first time this occurs is when we see a street scene of Moscow taken in the late 1800s or early 1900s. The images are accompanied by apparently diegetic sound – horses' hooves in the snow, people talking and their feet crunching the snow underfoot, shouts and laughter. This sequence begins after the previous scene has finished, so it is not arbitrarily inserted, but the switch to black and white cinefilm is nevertheless a jolt to the viewer. After a few moments, colour gradually bleeds into the final shot of the sequence – a black and white shot of a snow-covered square, in which a horse and carriage wait – and this shot is revealed to be contemporary (i.e. part of the diegesis). Through placing new images alongside the cinefilm, there is an attempt to make a claim for the veracity of the circumstances presented – a claim not that the story is 'true' but that the depiction of historical context is realistic. We are asked to believe that if these streets, these houses could have been filmed with today's technology in 1897, this is what we would have seen.

Of course, this makes use of the particular environment of the televisual context, as we might expect of a Davies programme. Contemporary television provides us with documentary footage in a way that contemporary film does not; we associate newsreels and actuality footage with television. Further, the drama-documentary and the documentary-drama, in which fictional sequences are often presented alongside documentary ones, is a television form and is rare on the cinema screen. This distinguishes the television *Zhivago* from Lean's cinematic version, utilising a striking and unusual formal device that marks its style as different from Lean's expressive and melodramatic mode of presentation. The inclusion of such material simultaneously claims a greater relation to historical truth and accuracy. The black and white cinefilm images are powerful – a reminder that although *Zhivago* is a fictional story, the experiences of the characters within their particular socio-political historical moment were shared by millions of real people. In bleeding colour back into those images, moving from the real moment to the representation of it, this *Zhivago* appears to bring the past to life, to present the past to us. While the effect of the cinefilm is partly to historicise the action and distance it from us as something past, its integration into the narrative through this blurring effect has the result of communicating our potential connection to those past events and times.

Three depictions of a scene: the Bloody Sunday massacre

One of the most interesting instances that crystallises what has been discussed so far is recreation of the massacre of Bloody Sunday, 22 January 1905, when the Imperial Guards of Tsar Nicholas II charged at and fired upon a peaceful assembly of marchers protesting for better working conditions.[11] Hundreds of protesters were killed outside the gates of the Winter Palace in St Petersburg.

Pasternak's treatment of the episode is curious and accomplished, exhibiting familiar stylistic traits. Lean's depiction of the scene is one of the most memorable moments from the film, and is often cited by viewers as one of the most impressive and awful scenes. Davies was aware of both Pasternak's rendition and the special status of Lean's interpretation of this incident, and had to find a way to reinterpret the scene differently, without losing any of its undeniable emotional power. The way in which he resolved this challenge is explored below.

Pasternak's version

> After all the walking and singing, people were glad to sit quietly for a bit and let others do their work for them, shouting themselves hoarse. The speakers, who agreed on most points, seemed all to be saying the same thing; if there were any differences between them they were overlooked in the relief of sitting down and having a rest. In the end it was the worst orator of the lot who received the most enthusiastic welcome. People made no effort to follow him and merely roared approval at every word, no one minding the interruptions and everyone agreeing out of

impatience to every word he said. There were shouts of 'Shame!' and a telegram of protest was drafted; then the crowd, bored with the speaker's droning voice, stood up as one man and, forgetting all about him, poured out in a body – cap to cap and coat to coat – down the stairs and out into the street. The procession continued.

While the meeting had been taking place indoors, it had started to snow. The street was white. The snow fell thicker and thicker.

When the dragoons charged, the marchers at the rear at first knew nothing about it. A swelling noise rolled back to them as of great crowds shouting 'Hurrah!' and individual screams of 'Help!' and 'Murder!' were lost in the uproar. Almost at the same moment, and borne, as it were, on this wave of sound along the narrow corridor which formed as the crowd divided, there appeared the heads of riders and their horses, manes and swinging swords carried swiftly and silently above the crowd.

Half a platoon galloped through, turned, re-formed and cut into the tail of the procession. The killing began. (Pasternak, 1958: 42–3)

Pasternak proffers an intriguing depiction of this incident. If one considers the relatively small number of words he uses to convey this pivotal moment – the moment that many consider played a vital role in triggering the revolution of 1917 – it may appear that he seems almost to gloss over the incident. Yet it is through his understated and simple language that he conveys the plain, undeniable truth of the events and the controlled manner in which the troops killed many innocent civilians. His brevity is ironically clinical.

In Paskernak's rendition, considerably more time is devoted to establishing the events preceding the actual massacre. The extract above picks up after preceding paragraphs have described the meandering, babbling crowd wandering from building to building, bickering about where they should go. The leaders of the group, who have been warned of the impending attack, try to warn the people, but in the confusion and general bustle they are ignored. The meeting itself is no organised revolutionary assembly – it is presented as happening almost unexpectedly: 'The fact of stopping and going inside a building was taken as an invitation to an impromptu meeting, which in fact began at once' (Pasternak, 1958: 42). The protestors are depicted as a disorganised band of people, literally and figuratively unclear about where they wish to go, wandering from location to location until they settle on a lecture hall which has the advantage of being relatively warm and having places for them to sit down. These are not political animals or dangerous revolutionaries; they are a group enjoying the communal event of meeting and venting their feelings and frustrations to one another. It is clear from Pasternak's view that there was nothing rabidly political about the meeting, nor were there angry words or open dissent. Indeed, he adopts a humorous, slightly mocking attitude to these simple people and their messy assembly.

The tone changes, however, when Pasternak writes of the snow; tension builds up just as the snow does. The contrasting silence of the scene outside is ominous, as if anticipating the bloodshed to come. When the charge on the group begins, Pasternak focuses on the sense of confusion and misunderstanding – the disbelief – that is the first response of the crowd. Still naïve, still failing to comprehend the situation, the crowd is at the mercy of the dragoons, whose actions exhibit military precision. The riders 'galloped through, turned, re-formed': the sequence of verbs sounds like a military drill, executed perfectly and unfeelingly, and their lack of passion or emotional engagement is emphasised by their silent swiftness as they ride through the crowd. Then there is the simple statement: 'The killing began' – the words bluntly presenting the truth, and the gerund conveying a more active and striking image than a straightforward noun. The sentence that follows the extract above begins 'A few minutes later the street was practically empty.' Nothing of the actual massacre is thus described, though the aftermath is. In presenting the most important moment – the massacre – in so few words (indeed, only in the word 'killing' is it directly presented) Pasternak manages to convey the horrific nature of the attack. It is presented as if in the historical context such a callous action was almost expected, quotidian – not worth lingering on. One feels the need to reread what one has just read, unsure that that is truly what is being revealed. The short, sharp response of the dragoons to such a disorganised, unimportant meeting is out of all proportion, and the inverse proportions of the amount of time expended describing them employs dramatic irony to highlight the enormity of the event.

Lean's version
Lean's depiction of this scene is rightly famous. Unlike Pasternak, he conveys explicitly the enormity of the event, and emphasises what a travesty the attack was and its human cost. The marchers are shown moving quietly through Moscow streets, singing and carrying their banners. They are shown in long shots, from eye level and from a high-angle perspective (from Zhivago's point of view, from his balcony), moving slowly across the clean surface of the snow, and the high-angle shot reveals empty space in front of them, implying action to come that will fill it. This shot is intercut with the mounted guards, gathered in the darkness, whose horses scuffle quietly in the snow, as they await the marchers. Thus the premeditated nature of the attack is emphasised. As in the novel, the silence of the streets is ominous, with only the singing

piercing the night. The most well known moment is the charge of the dragoons. There is a point of view shot from the front row of the marchers, where Pasha stands, and the singing falters and gradually stops as a vague rumbling sound gradually arises on the soundtrack. It is unclear at first what the noise is, and the visual image gives little aid – there is snow, and darkness, and in the distance a series of glittering spots of light, which appear to be bobbing up and down. Like Pasternak's protesters, these marchers cannot understand what they are seeing and hearing – and as we are placed amongst them, we share their confusion. Gradually the sound becomes clearer, and then we recognise it: the sound of horses' hooves galloping over snow towards the camera and the crowd; simultaneously, the glittering dots are revealed as the reflections of light off the unsheathed swords of the dragoons.[12] It is unclear at first at what speed the horses are moving, for the deep-focus long shot means that the horses take a very long time to traverse even a short distance. The terrible truth dawns just as the horses reach the camera and marchers, and the swords swish down, slicing into the heads, shoulders and arms of the protesters.

Lean thus chooses to emphasise two key aspects of Pasternak's depiction: the ruthlessness of the disproportionately powerful dragoons in attacking the unarmed protestors, and the crowd's slowly dawning realisation of what is happening. Sharing the protesters' perspective, we experience for ourselves their misapprehension, uncertainty and then horror.

The scene is highly dramatic. It exhibits a terrible beauty. The charging horses and the glittering swords, though dreadful, are also impressive – filmed in long shot and from a low angle, they are overwhelming, and awful in both contemporary and archaic senses. Lean's eye for grandeur is apparent here. He conveys the significance of the event by making it enormous, impressive, overwhelming. He uses cinema's wide screen and deep focus, combining them with long takes, to communicate the ruthlessness of the action (the dragoons must charge from a distance, without losing speed, without taking the opportunity to pull up their horses, to slow down, to shout and warn the marchers). This is a most cinematic sequence; whilst it communicates the seriousness of the situation, one is left wondering whether it somehow mitigates its callousness by drawing viewers' attention to cinematic mastery (the careful and expressive use of sound and image).

Davies's version

Given that many viewers would have memories of this pivotal moment in Lean's film, Davies needed to find a way to present the sequence differently, but without losing the power of either Pasternak's or Lean's versions. Working with Campiotti, he achieved this by two methods: first, he implicitly recalled Lean's depiction, amending its context and therefore making it work differently within his presentation; secondly, he overtly countered the familiar images of Lean's film with images that contrasted in content, style and tone, drawing on different aspects of the novel. The resulting sequence reflects Davies's feelings about Lean's film: 'It does the spectacle very well ... and the politics ... but not the relationships. With a little bit more time, and with the concentration that television has on faces in intimate close up ... I thought you could say more about [them].'

The television adaptation offers two instances of the guards' slaughter, thus proffering two points of view on the events of that day. First, we see a gathering of protesters looting a bakery or, as Pasha (Kris Marshall) describes it 'liberating the means of production'. One of the revolutionaries makes an impromptu speech, ending with the famous words 'bread, land and freedom'. There is a cut here to what appears to be original cinefilm recordings of the 1905 attack. The first shot is a high-angle, almost aerial shot that is reminiscent of the point of view shot of Zhivago in Lean's film, as he observes the charge from his balcony. The programme thus subtly asserts its advantage over Lean's film in showing us actual footage from the period (simultaneously, of course, it reveals the close links between Lean's depiction of the events and real historical events). Other cinefilm shots follow, some high-angle, some from the ground, showing the dragoons charging on immense crowds. On the soundtrack are pseudo-diegetic sounds of guns firing, screams, shouts and footsteps. This actuality footage is integrated into the next fictional sequence by means of a crossover shot: this shot, faded into colour from black and white as usual, is of a man filming events with an old cinefilm camera – a postulated source of the preceding cinefilm sequence. The effect of this is to forge a close connection between the 'filmed' reconstruction and the actuality footage that is presented as being filmed by the same man. Similarly, the soundtrack continues across both types of material, reinforcing their common subject matter.

The adaptation goes on to provide another alternative view, though. After more shots of fighting in the large main street, which clearly recall both Lean's film and the actuality footage, another scene is presented. Here, in contrast with Lean's use of wide, open spaces, Davies chooses to situate a key attack in a small, cramped courtyard between buildings. Indeed, the exact configuration of space remains unclear, as the use of hand-held camera and fast editing as the marchers push into the area fails to give the kind of overview that Lean's long shot offered. A sense of tension is thus built up differently: we are aware that when the attack comes, there will be few routes of escape for the marchers. Later, when the mounted guards enter the space, they seem to block entirely the only exit from the scene.

The protestors gather in a side street and are engaged in a mixture of earnest but light-hearted discussion and the harmless banter of slogans. The sound of gunfire in the distance is noticed by some of the people, whose anxious faces reflect their concern – however, the speakers are jubilant and oblivious to what is happening in the streets, and the cheers of those at the front of the crowd drown out the concerned muttering of those near the back (echoing both Pasternak's and Lean's versions of how this moment was perceived and grasped by those involved). From a perspective standing at the back of the group, we see a guard on horseback enter the foreground of the shot, and some of the crowd turn as they hear his arrival. Tension mounts. Utilising television's usual reliance on close-ups and mid shots, Davies constructs a conversation between Pasha and the marchers and the dragoons who have now joined their general. Pasha and his comrades attempt to lighten the tone of the moment, breaking the silence that has fallen, by jollying the dragoons along, encouraging them to 'get down off their high horses' and join them. This attempt to ameliorate a tense situation is greeted with silence; then the chief guard makes a forward gesture and foot soldiers armed with muskets and bayonets filter through the mounted dragoons and kneel at the front of the group, pointing their weapons at the massed people (figure 19).

In choosing to use television's close-ups and mid shots, Davies creates a different atmosphere from that created by Lean's cinematic, impressive style. The physical proximity of the guards to the marchers suggests a possible intimacy, or at least a potential connection between the two groups. Lean's dragoons did not look their victims in the eye; they did not hear them speak. Here, we momentarily believe that the

19 *Doctor Zhivago* (2002): firing on the crowd

guards cannot attack the group standing only a few feet in front of them, and Pasha's brief levity creates a fluctuation in tone – a moment of hope that the situation can be saved. This is supported by our memories of the preceding scene, in which, during the street fighting, Zhivago refused to leave a wounded man he was tending even when the mounted soldier pulled out his gun and ordered him to do so. Zhivago's direct gaze and his reply – 'You won't shoot. We're not savages yet' – causes the guard to put his gun away. We therefore feel it is possible that the same will occur here.

Suddenly the chief guard gives a signal, 'Open fire', and the foot soldiers shoot directly into the crowd, at almost point blank range. After waiting a few seconds for the panic to spread, as several members of the crowd fall wounded or dead to the ground, the same guard orders 'On', and the horses charge at the crowd, trampling many people underfoot, and scattering those at the edges into doorways and narrow alleyways in their attempt to escape. Again, as in Lean's film, and unlike in the novel, the attacks upon individuals are emphasised, with gruesome images of swords slicing at individual's faces, arms and shoulders.

The sequence thus chooses to refer to both Pasternak's and Lean's texts, as well as incorporating another new intertext: the original film footage. It uses a similar fluctuation of tone to that found in Pasternak's novel, with the hope that the situation can be saved by humour and naivety, then cruelly crushing those hopes as the attack is ordered. The programme also implicitly recalls Lean's text, repeating the aerial shot which in Lean's film is a point of view shot from Zhivago's balcony, and in a sense it pays tribute to that previous representation, valuing it for its accuracy, for the actuality footage reveals that Lean's dramatic long shot was no directorial excess but influenced by real footage of the event. Historical accuracy, in addition to emotional vividness, is thus ascribed to Lean's version. However, the use of documentary footage creates a striking, jarring style which contrasts vividly with viewers' memories of Lean's depiction of the same scene, claiming greater veracity and directness. And the setting of the sequence that follows in a small, compressed space is a direct counterpoint to Lean's film. The scene is powerful because it employs conventions of television with which we are familiar (documentary, the intimacy between characters created by mid shots and close-ups, restricted spatiality). The televisual aspect of this presentation is thus highlighted. Television usually bring us news of the outside world, but presents it in terms of issues that are related to home and to 'us', unlike the epic event of cinema. Depicting the events of 22 January 1905 within this context underlines the attacks as travesties of trust, decency and human intimacy.

The question of evaluation and critical practice

Finally, questions relating to the kind of critical project undertaken in this book lead us towards the discussion offered in the conclusion (Chapter 7). Does the example of Davies's *Zhivago* help us to clarify the grounds for and techniques of critical practice? What does the presence of intertextuality in its various forms mean for our interpretation and evaluation of the texts here? 'Adaptation' and 'remake' have long been loaded terms, implying the superiority of one text over another. An intertextual approach to adaptation is said to demote fidelity criticism and offer greater potential for appreciating an artwork in its own right. Can this argument be supported?

In terms of how one interprets adaptations such as *Doctor Zhivago*, I would argue for intertextual criticism as a viable alternative to fidelity criticism. A simple comparison of the television *Zhivago* with Pasternak's novel would ignore the equally salient references made to Lean's film and other sources (such as the cinefilm). It would be equally limiting to assume that the programme stands entirely alone, unrelated to other texts. An intertextual approach takes into account all that is there in the adaptation, rather than focusing on one privileged source and neglecting other features of the programme – it also recognises the importance of the programme's artistic and cultural contexts.

However, whilst it is clear that intertextual criticism aids us in interpretation, we are left with the tricky question of evaluation. The notion of intertextuality has its own evaluative connotations. Whilst artworks have made reference to preceding texts throughout history, intertextuality as a critical term is relatively recent, and has been somewhat hijacked by postmodern theorists, who often repackage it as pastiche, neglecting other ways of conceptualising interrelations between texts (see Cardwell, 2002: 92–3). In the worst cases, intertextuality has been deployed to dismiss summarily questions of value and critical judgement, granting equal but different status to all texts, or at least refusing to assess them against one another. Old-fashioned criteria such as artistic or authorial originality and integrity are disregarded in favour of a low-commitment approach to interpretation – one in which one needs to make no critical judgement.

There is not enough space here to address these concerns in full. Instead, I shall briefly ask how one might evaluate the television *Zhivago*, which can be regarded not only as an adaptation but as a remake. Can it make any claims for originality and artistic/authorial vision? What, in short, was the point of making it? Davies utilises the medium of television in order to create a new perspective on the tale of *Zhivago*.

Limited by budget and technology, he and Campiotti exploit apparent constraints to create a distinctive and appropriate style for the project. Using television's narrower focus, they manipulate fine details to represent the story. Far from being restricted by television's smaller screen size and different ratio, he exploits these features of television to focus attention on important details and to inflect the story differently.

Perhaps the most interesting feature of this programme is that it achieves originality through its intertextuality – its recycling of pre-existing images and texts. Through revisiting both Pasternak's and Lean's work, and archive footage, the programme offers a reading of the earlier texts in which each becomes an intertext, informing our reading of the others. It is in the combination of the texts and the interplay established between them that Davies and Campiotti are able to say something new about *Zhivago*, Russia and Bloody Sunday 1905.

Of course, intertextual criticism depends upon an active and engaged reader or viewer. Worton and Still argue that

> a text is available only through some process of reading; what is produced at the moment of reading is due to the cross-fertilisation of the packaged textual material (say, a book) by all the texts which a reader brings to it. A delicate allusion to a work unknown to the reader, which therefore goes unnoticed, will have a dormant existence in that reading. On the other hand, the reader's experience of some practice or theory unknown to the author may lead to a fresh interpretation. (Worton and Still, 1990: 1–2)

Admittedly, the argument is not flawless.[13] However, it does shed some light upon the experience of watching the television *Zhivago*. It emphasises the potential breadth of intertextual criticism: it is only after watching the archive footage in the television version, including the aerial shot that echoed Lean's film, that I became aware of the references that Lean's film knowingly or unknowingly made to actual footage of the event he was depicting. Thus our experience of an earlier text may be enhanced by the experience of a later one – something that fidelity criticism would not admit. Finally, Worton and Still's emphasis upon 'fresh interpretation' and the revisiting of earlier texts offers us the opportunity to evaluate a text within the context of intertextual criticism. Davies and Campiotti chose to present their view not just of Pasternak's tale of *Zhivago*, but also of the story as it had been told by Lean; they also chose to explore the historical context of the story. In doing so they added to our understanding of the story of *Zhivago*, its origin and resonances, fleshing it out with alternative perspectives. Whilst we might conclude that the television version fails in particular areas (historical fidelity, or Keira Knightley's casting as Lara), we must conclude that in its ability to reach out and affect other renditions of the same story and events, in its many references to other texts, recalling to mind the complexity of history and of the novel through its presentation of another point of view upon them, it displays a level of intertextual richness that marks it out as an artwork worth more than a cursory consideration.

Furthermore, in its extensive, intelligent and sensitive use of attributes of the medium of television, *Zhivago* distinguishes televisual aesthetics from those of literature and film, just as *Othello* consciously manipulates the differences between theatre and television. It is perhaps in this celebration of the potential power of the televisual that Davies's contemporary artistic sensibility can be found.

Notes

1 All these films are adaptations of some sort. *Consuming Passions* (1988) is based on a Monty Python television play called *Secrets*, which was written by Michael Palin. The film is a predictably surreal comedy that follows the tribulations of a novice management trainee who works at Chumley's chocolate factory. The film was not critically acclaimed, and Davies himself calls it, in retrospect, 'appalling' (in an e-mail communication with me, April 2004). *Circle of Friends* (1995) and *The Tailor of Panama* (2001) are adapted from Maeve Binchy's and John le Carre's novels, respectively; both films were relatively well received by the public and critics. *Bridget Jones's Diary* (2001), and the sequel, *Bridget Jones: The Edge of Reason* (forthcoming 2004) were adapted from Helen Fielding's books about the eponymous character. Davies worked with Richard Curtis on these two films, and was responsible for the overall structure of the first film, and its use of the narrative construction of *Pride and Prejudice*.

2 The title of the programme is actually written 'otheLLo', which emphasises the serial's rewriting of the original, and its breaking of conventions.

3 The question of race is foregrounded in the adaptation much more than in the source play, and its treatment is updated, so that related issues such as positive discrimination, political correctness and racial histories are also addressed.

4 There is also the fractured image created by the use of several mirrors, in the scene in which Othello and Dessie talk of their past and how she was 'different' before she met him. However, this technique is not an original one, and has been used in many films and programmes before, so here I have focused on the use of the river reflections, instead, which I consider more intriguing and unusual.

5 The 'Russian revolution' was not a singular event but a series of uprisings and conflicts and two distinct revolutions. However, as it is usually simply referred to as the 'Russian revolution' I shall use the term here.

6 Out of necessity, I refer throughout to Pasternak's novel in translation (translated in 1958 by Max Hayward and Manya Harari), not to his original Russian prose. This makes my comments on his vocabulary, sentence structure and style somewhat illegitimate as literary criticism, but valid in terms of my exploration of the novel as intertext, since for English-speaking readers, that is how they will have read and remembered his novel.

7 This alternation in viewpoint – regarding members of a group as individuals at one moment, and in the next moment the group as mass – is echoed in the

conversation in this scene between Yevgraf and his colleague as they watch the workers. Yevgraf asks 'What are they like, these girls?', emphasising his symbolic as well as literal distance from them. Subsequently, the two of them discuss the workers in apparently sympathetic, yet somewhat detached and dispassionate terms, seeing them as massed individuals, and attempting to reconcile the two aforementioned viewpoints: 'Jobs like this [that the women do] ... they're degrading. You shouldn't use human beings to move earth. And it's not efficient. If they were to give me two more excavators I'd be a year ahead of the plan by now.'

8 This comment from Davies is taken from his interview on the DVD of *Doctor Zhivago* (2003), as are subsequent comments from the actors in the programme.

9 The makers of the television *Zhivago* therefore chose to focus on different aspects of the narrative and to make careful decisions about casting, amongst other things. For example, Campiotti, the director, stated that they chose to change the final scene as it was shown in Lean's film, because it was 'too good' in Lean's version. Also, they wanted relatively unknown actors so that they could 'recreate their roles afresh'. However, they also cast Keira Knightley as Lara – someone with a physical resemblance to Julie Christie (Lara in Lean's film), rather than a resemblance to Pasternak's Lara. Both actors have striking long, blonde hair, for example, whereas Pasternak's Lara is a brunette. This is clearly an echo of the film rather than the novel.

10 I have been unable to find further details about the origins of this material. The footage shown in the Bloody Sunday sequence appears to present the actual events of that particular day – the massacre outside the Winter Palace – but I have not been able to confirm that this is the case. However, the material is presented in a way that stakes a claim for its authenticity.

11 In real life, this march was led by priest George Capon, though this is not mentioned in any of the *Zhivago*s.

12 The glittering swords of the dragoons, a notable feature of Lean's presentation, also seem to refer to a comparable moment in Eisenstein's *October* (about the 1917 October revolution), in which the guards of the provisional government prepare to fight the Bolshevik revolutionaries.

13 For example, they refer to an allusion that has a 'dormant existence in that reading'. However, an allusion that exists only dormantly (as they describe), nevertheless exists in the text, not in the reading, for an allusion cannot be dormant within a reading made by a reader who is unaware of the existence of that allusion. Instead the allusion remains dormant within the text, to be discovered by the knowing reader.

Conclusion: Davies, television, criticism and authorship

7

In this final chapter, I conclude by drawing together the strands of thought presented in this book. I begin with a brief look at one of Davies's most accomplished programmes, *The Way We Live Now*. Continuing the theme of Chapter 6, the televisuality of the serial is elucidated; further, its innovative and expressive use of the televisual form is regarded as evidence of Davies's continuing development as an artist and his unique authorial sensibility. I also reflect upon what approach such a programme entreats the critic to take, considering briefly the referential contexts that might be pertinent to an analysis of the tele-visual work. The purpose of this brief case study is to offer a reflection upon the broader critical project that this book constitutes, exploring the potential and desirable relationship between work and critic, and ruminating upon how each text may determine the appropriateness of particular approaches or methodologies to be used in its analysis. Finally, I return to the question of Davies's authorship, and consider what this project may have contributed to an understanding of this tricky matter.

Embracing the televisual: *The Way We Live Now* (2001) in context(s)

I have undertaken different kinds of criticism in this book. In response to the shape of Davies's oeuvre, most of the programmes I have con-sidered herein have been adaptations – indeed, three of the four preceding critical chapters cover adapted works. In the past, adaptations have posed particular problems for critics, and have led to reliance on fidelity criticism, which I have avoided. I have argued elsewhere that we should reject comparison with source novels, for the purposes of interpretation and evaluation of adaptations (films and programmes). At worst, comparison leads us to false expectations about the film's intentions and form, blinding us to what it is trying to achieve in itself, and prejudicing us against the adaptation from the outset, judging it by the standards of the book. At best, our close attention to the novel is restrictive: it shapes our reception of the adaptation, leading us to focus too narrowly on some aspects over others, and to ignore other relevant contextual factors. Both interpretation and evaluation are therefore affected, and our attentive responsiveness to the film as an artwork is reduced. Comparison undermines the potential for 'sympathetic disinterest'.

And yet, despite this stance, I have undertaken in previous chapters to make references to and comparisons with source texts. I have done so because I felt that to explore elements of the source text could help to throw into relief specific elements of the adaptation (as suggested at the end of Chapter 2), and not to pursue a judgement of one against the standards of the other. I hope I have also shown that the approach one takes to a programme ought to be dependent upon the material being assessed. I want to conclude by examining a sequence from one of Davies's finest adaptations, *The Way We Live Now* (2001), and by emphasising, very briefly, how a recognition of the numerous contexts within which a work exists is vital to responsive criticism. These contexts have all been discussed within this book; they include the generic context, the authorial context (Davies) and the televisual context.

The Way We Live Now is based on Anthony Trollope's book (1875). The serial displays many virtues that can be associated with Davies's authorial signature: superb, subtle, credible characterisation; humour and sharp observation; joyful energy and ironic sympathy for its protagonists. Most notably, though, the programme is strikingly innovative, playing with and subverting conventions of the classic-novel adaptation genre, and fully embracing the televisual medium. There is a sense of visual power in the programme, which simultaneously draws upon features of movement and performance that are crucial to television's appeal. In this programme, one sees the familiar aspects of Davies's authorial signature (his world view, his voice) become so fully ingrained within the text that one could propose it exhibits a coherent 'sensibility', whereby style and content cannot be separated, and one perceives that the programme is recognisably by Davies (whilst simultaneously accepting that this is achieved by the efforts of a team working together).

The opening moments of the serial

The serial opens differently from the book, which begins with an introduction of the characters; a new scene depicting Melmotte's arrival at his new home in Grosvenor Square is created. This sequence relates most closely to the introduction of Melmotte in the book.[1] It opens with what appears to be an abstract shot composed of a number of vertical lines, some of which seem to be moving across the screen; as the shot progresses, the actual content becomes clearer: a polished door that reflects streams of light from an unknown source is being opened, and creates a mirror image (thus the curious kaleidoscopic effect as the door moves). Two views of a man's head appear, his head being duplicated in the image as it is mirrored in the door (he thus appears to be looking in two different directions). It is unclear which of the images is real, and which is the reflection.

The next shot is a long shot, symmetrically framed, showing a grand room empty of furniture, yet warm, in honey-coloured tones. The man (a servant) crosses the room from left to right, to the heavy, closed curtains that shroud the tall windows. In medium shot, he briskly pulls the curtains open, and a cloud of dust whooshes towards him; bright light pours into the room as he gazes outside.

There is a sharp disjunction as the next cut takes us outside, to an apparently unrelated location (this is not implied to be a point of view shot): a low-angle shot looks up at horses and then a carriage as they cross the screen from right to left. Another cut takes us to a big close-up of the very top of a globe, so that we see the curve of its surface and part of its frame and axle. The colours are minimal – hues of brown and yellow – so that the image is a rather abstract one, focusing on tiny details. Movement in the background and the sound of rolling wheels alerts us to the fact that the globe is moving across the floor. The next shot is of the underside of the globe, as it passes an ornately carved piece of furniture; this is followed by a low-angle close-up of the globe, which appears enormous, and of the two men who are moving it and who, because of extremely bright back-lighting, appear only as black shapes either side of the globe. They leave the globe at the centre of the screen.

A low-angle shot shows a servant's feet moving towards the back of a covered wagon, and then he pulls a dust sheet from a huge black chair being transported within it. An aerial shot shows the chair being unloaded by two men.

A medium long shot of the entrance of a country house reveals servants assembling at the doorway; they line up on either side of the front door in orderly fashion, and anxiously and hurriedly adjust their clothing. In long shot, a carriage arrives at the house. In mid shot, a servant approaches the carriage's door, and unfolds the steps to allow the travellers to disembark. Raised women's voices can be heard from inside the carriage as we look again at the waiting servants; a young woman (Marie Melmotte, played by Shirley Henderson) stumbles ungracefully from the carriage, almost as if shoved rudely from inside; a woman (her mother, Mme Melmotte, played by Helen Schlesinger) follows her. The two stand framed by the lines of servants, looking uncertain and embarrassed. They part, and seem to join the two lines, one on each side, and everyone turns to look at the carriage (i.e. to look at the camera).

A long take follows: the camera moves rather unsteadily down from the carriage, up the front steps, and into the hallway of the house (this is implied to be a person's point of view – actually Augustus Melmotte's); just as he enters the hallway, an aerial shot catches his figure crossing the floor, and swoops down to a rather odd angle, just missing Melmotte's face and instead capturing a young servant pushing another globe across the floor, followed by Melmotte's wife and daughter.

As the camera follows closely behind Melmotte, the screen is almost filled with the dark outline of his broad, hunched shoulders as he marches onwards; then a reverse shot shows the front of him, but again he is only a black shape, with only the faint glow of his cigar visible, and with glimpses of the second globe behind him. A close-up of Melmotte's black-gloved hands pulls back into a mid shot, showing him sliding a concertina door open: this is shown first from one side of the door and then the other, creating a jump cut sensation as the sliding movement changes direction. There is a close-up of the hand in which Melmotte holds his glowing cigar, surrounded by a cloud of smoke; then, a full-length shot of him as he turns to us and we finally see a clear shot of his face (and we see that the actor is David Suchet). He stands off-centre in an empty room, and the camera moves in to a low-angle, medium close-up of his face. He declaims, 'Well, let us see what we can do here.' Immediately the screen cuts to black, and the title of the programme is shown: *The Way We Live Now*, carved out on a block of grey-black stone, in raised capital letters. The music which has accompanied the entire sequence, and which I refer to below, ends at this point with a dramatic chord.

Adaptive context?

One could choose to regard this programme as an adaptation, and compare it with the source novel, and to do so highlights some differences and similarities between the two. The programme foregrounds Melmotte more than the book does, establishing him as the central character. Like the book, though, the programme reveals Melmotte's effect upon those around him, and his reputation, before it shows the man himself and his appearance (his reputation precedes him, as it were). The sense that he is a go-getter, an entrepreneur who rushes at things, is implied through the fact that the household is not yet ready to receive him – he is there before they know it. This can be correlated with the sentence 'All this had been done within twelve months'. The description of Melmotte's appearance corresponds closely to David Suchet's appearance, but in the novel this is an opportunity to introduce Melmotte in relation to his wife and daughter – in the adaptation he is a more solitary figure. The importance of travel and building up his global empire is implied by the presence of two globes – one is at the house, and one is with him, as if he cannot rest from marking out potential new territories upon it.

Looking briefly at the source novel in comparison then, our attention is drawn to the presentation of Melmotte and his characterisation, and this appears not incompatible with the adaptation's concerns in this scene. However, I would argue in keeping with my previous contention: that to take this approach is to ignore the programme's own agenda, its artistic choices, its emphases and voice. To comprehend the sequence as part of an artwork necessitates appreciating more fully its references to its artistic and cultural contexts and its medium. In choosing to draw upon earlier texts, an artwork does not need to be regarded as secondary, derivative, or intending to take up an attitude of fidelity to the earlier works. Much attention has been paid to the problem and status of literature-to-screen adaptation, which can be regarded as a foregrounded, privileged form of intertextuality.[2] Yet, as I argued in Chapter 6 regarding *Zhivago*, it is important to consider the intertextuality of an adaptation more generally and not simply to focus upon and privilege its relationship with a singular source novel.[3] The other contexts within which an adaptation exists must also be recognised. In the case of *The Way We Live Now*, the programme's locus within three contexts could be considered: its generic context, its authorial context, and its televisual context. Finally the sequence's aesthetic particularities need to be established – what defines it, how it is composed, shaped, inflected. And actually, once this has been done, as we shall see, it becomes clear that this sequence's most important aesthetic concerns can be neither reduced to the presentation of Melmotte nor related to the novel. They are quite separate.

Generic context

This programme stands within the popular genre of (British) classic-novel adaptations. Its generic identity is marked by broad indicators, some of which are extra-textual (for example, it was advertised as such, and Davies's authorship is foregrounded) and some of which are intra-textual (for example, the costumes and the locations, which indicate a sense of the past; the presence of well-known British character actors; the overt use of symmetry as a compositional device; and the high production values). However, this programme also declares itself as belonging to a new breed of costume dramas, following in the footsteps of other Davies adaptations such as *Vanity Fair* and *Moll Flanders*, with its camerawork (hand-held, wobbly, with partial views); its music, which is not sedate but lively, almost lurching, and which is employed in the manner of a commentary rather than as a mood-inducer in the background; and its focus on small details rather than large landscapes. Thus *The Way We Live Now* clearly makes reference to recent examples of the genre of British television classic-novel adaptations, as well as to Davies's established oeuvre.

This referential context is important because the programme refers to its membership of this genre more than to its relationship with the source book. This genre provides its framework, its ground rules, and a set of expectations for the audience. Most viewers will know this genre better than they will know the source book. They will have preconceptions about representations of the past, of gender and class in this genre; they will expect certain narrative and formal conventions. The opening of the serial conforms with some expectations and not others: it is like using the sonnet form but experimenting within it. One cannot fully interpret a sonnet without being aware of the form/genre it uses; the same applies here. The adaptation's compliances with, differences from, and contrasts with generic norms give us clues for interpretation here. For example, we notice Melmotte's wife and daughter's undignified descent from the carriage and their trepidation in meeting the servants. This conveys the sense of their being outsiders, which is emphasised by associating wobbly views to Melmotte's point of view, highlighting his unstable, disruptive influence in this ordered, formal world. Similarly, Melmotte's musical theme is defiantly slower than the dominant theme, disrupting its timing, persistently forcing the music to slow down. This echoes Melmotte's forceful insistence on doing things his own way, on forging onwards against the tide. It is the programme's use of generic conventions, rather than any references to the source novel, that are of significance here.

Authorial context: Davies

Furthermore, specific expectations are raised regarding the programme's authorial context. Its place in the context of Davies's other recent work will give rise to certain expectations in the knowing viewer: a certain tone or point of view that can be broadly understood as detached, sympathetic irony. As we have noted, Davies's recent adaptations tend to have great sympathy for often unsympathetic or wicked protagonists; to use these protagonists to reflect upon the iniquities and double standards of the world which judges them; to be amusing and amused; and to exhibit a sense of ironic humour, which often arises from details of the programme, and from characters' performances. So the programme's place within, first, the genre and, secondly, Davies's oeuvre says more about its tone, intentions and our engagement than the source book can tell us about the adaptation.

Televisual context

The third pertinent context is that of television, and here it is useful to distinguish this television adaptation from film adaptations. First, attention is drawn in this adaptation to the use of framing and an emphasis on singular details. Historically, television has painted with broad brushstrokes, not over-filling the frame, but focusing attention on a few salient details in each shot, which, as I have implied previously, no doubt arises from its historically poorer and smaller image. The same is true here, leading us to observe details for their significance. Further, the pace of television is said to be faster than that of film, as it must grab and hold the viewer's attention. Although the shot lengths here are generically fairly slow, the pace appears faster because of the spatial disconnection between cuts – the striking movement from one place to another.

Finally, *performance*, which could be understood to be a defining characteristic of television,[4] seems to be vitally important to the tone and structure of this sequence. The preparations for Melmotte's arrival take place in an empty house: the floor is cleared as if a space is being prepared for action – the servants are like stage hands awaiting the starring actor. Melmotte's face is hidden from us at first, as he walks purposefully to the large room, pushes back the doors, opens up the space, takes centre stage, and dramatically announces: 'Well, let us see what we can do here.' We then cut to the programme title. This sequence thus forms a prologue before the action, and enhances the theatrical mood. There is an emphasis on awaiting the presence of both Melmotte and David Suchet as the star, so that Suchet's line becomes something with extra-diegetic significance. As if calling upon a troupe of actors to begin, he opens the performance. The emphasis on performance is again important in establishing the programme's links with other recent Davies adaptations, reasserting its connections with those. It does not refer to Melmotte's presentation in the novel. Indeed, in the novel Melmotte is presented by the author – he is not permitted to present himself in this way. The particular style of presentation employed here marks out the importance of the televisual context to the aesthetic choices of the adaptation.

Responsive criticism: aesthetic concerns and questions

Finally, and briefly, for a full and responsive interpretation of this adaptation we need to consider the aesthetic features that define its formal and tonal distinctiveness. The overriding air here is one of anticipation. This is created and sustained by partial views: the first shot is unclear – what are we seeing? Then we hear the wheels of the globe as it moves across the floor – what are we hearing? Then we sense the preparations – for whom are we preparing? And finally we are denied sight of Melmotte's face – who is he (with reference to both star and character)? Some details are notable: the way in which the music shapes the sequence, creating momentum, pace and tension and governing its duration; the creation of rhythm and intrigue through the use of spatial disorientation, jump cuts, and sudden changes in the direction of movements; and the manner in which details are valued not just for their narrative significance but also for the visual pleasure they provide – their texture, sensuality and form.

It is vital to recognise that, in terms of where we might wish to develop our study of this adaptation, the programme raises its own questions – which are unrelated to the source novel because they arise from its own aesthetic specificities. For example, one of the most striking features here is the familiar sense of sympathetic but ironic detachment from Melmotte that one expects from a Davies adaptation. But it is rather more difficult to analyse how this is achieved. As I have shown above, it is fairly easy to pinpoint details in the sequence that confirm Melmotte as an outsider and a rather unpleasant man. Yet we are drawn to him, and the adaptation seems to be presenting him sympathetically; it is this latter aspect that is hard to analyse. Reference to the source book is of no help to us in understanding this. The novel presents a much blander relationship with the character. An explicit point of view on Melmotte is offered: referring to the 'wonderful look of power about his mouth and chin', the author notes: 'This was so strong as to redeem his face from vulgarity; but the countenance and appearance of the man were on the whole unpleasant, and, I may say, untrustworthy' (Trollope, 1875: 31). The redemption from vulgarity implies, of course, the risk of it, and 'unpleasant' and 'untrustworthy' are damning adjectives. Also, the parenthetical 'I may say' implies an embedded narrator offering an explicit point of view.

But this does not help us, when we come to the adaptation, to look beyond details of physionomy and performance. To discover the attitude of this sequence to Melmotte, we must discard the book and focus on what is before us on the screen. Close attention to the details of the sequence reveals a sense of *collusion* between the camera and Melmotte. As we see from his chair in this sequence, Melmotte is egotistical and showy. He would have chosen to make a grand entrance and take centre stage. The sequence lets him do so. Indeed, the camerawork facilitates this, just missing his face when it could show it – allowing him to remain absent until he declares the action open. So the music (which is playful and bombastic, and creates a jaunty pace and rhythm) and the focus on ironic details (the globes and chair) foreground the presence of a narrative point of view that is sarcastic and ironic, commenting on the man. But the camera is also sympathetic to him, allowing him his pleasures, colluding with his performance. The novel's explicit view – 'I may say' – becomes much more diffuse and complex, being presented through different facets such as camerawork, editing, music, framing, and so on. Here, then, comparison with the novel is ultimately unproductive. References to contexts other than the adaptive context help to restore the text's autonomy. But finally, it is close attention to the details of the programme that moves us towards the goal of responsive, sympathetic, disinterested criticism, which is one of the key aims of this book.[5]

Critical reflections: my role as critic

Davies opened his Huw Wheldon Memorial Lecture by explaining, in characteristic tongue-in-cheek fashion: 'Mostly what I'm going to do is tell a lot of little stories, and what I hope is that a meaningful pattern with emerge, which will solve the mystery of life for you all' (Davies, 1994). Though I never hoped to discover the meaning of life, this project has certainly undertaken the former aim: to seek a 'meaningful pattern' within Davies's work. The patterns, echoes and motifs in content, style, voice and tone that I have found are necessarily those to which I am instinctively drawn. I have sought the pleasures I find in Davies's work and focused on what they are and from what they arise, and have overlooked other aspects, other patterns, that do not interest or impress me. Thus the analysis offered in this book is always open to supplementation by others, and indeed to disagreement and dissent. Others may return to the texts I have referred to here and enhance or dispute my interpretations and evaluations of them. Criticism is an ongoing and shared practice. In particular, I hope that the texts that I wished to explore in more detail but had no time to (including *A Rather English Marriage, Daniel Deronda* and *The Way We Live Now*), and the few earlier programmes that I was unable, finally, to locate, may be given some further attention by others.

While restrictions on the amount of work I could cover here are only to be expected, it is important to admit the limitations that have arisen from my particular choice of focus and methodology. In particular, my own predilections and notions of value have come dangerously close to undermining the ideal stance of 'sympathetic disinterest'. I have chosen to draw upon a well-established tradition of close analysis that prioritises particular textual qualities over others. Victor Perkins summarises these aptly: 'The meanings which are contained most securely within a film [or programme] are those formed at the deepest level of inter-relation and synthesis ... If we agree in making qualities of organization and coherence a primary issue in critical judgement, complexity and subtlety are vindicated as highly relevant criteria' (Perkins, 1972: 177, 118). Moving from this understanding, I have sought in Davies's work a close integration of style and meaning, coherence, complexity and subtlety. However, this creates problems for my evaluation of particular genres like the romance (see the end of Chapter 4), intensifying my criticism of the work Davies has done within them, and even contributing to my personal distaste for such programmes. While I stand by the evaluations I offered, it is possible that another scholar may wish to contest my analyses on the grounds that it is not 'sympathetic' – that is, it displays the flaw that Perkins warns against: 'The weakness of much criticism is its insistence on imposing conventions which a movie is clearly not using and criteria which are not applicable to its form' (Perkins, 1972: 188). In seeking subtlety, profundity and intellectual challenge in genres that do not regard these qualities as part of their artistic project, it could be argued that the criticism I offer is invalid, for it disallows the approbation of any text that works fully within the conventions of such genres. I leave this potential question open.

Having offered some reflections upon the critical practice undertaken herein, there is the second aspect of this project to consider: the question of Davies's authorship.

Davies's authorship

Has a conceptualisation of 'authorship' proved useful in considering Davies's oeuvre? What has this project discovered (or uncovered) about Davies's authorship?

The validity of conceiving of Davies as a television 'author'

Various arguments can be proffered against the broad notion of a television author, with the most salient relating to the collaborative nature of television production, which undermines the notion of a singular, expressive author behind a text. In the context of Davies's work, it is imperative that the input of those who have participated in creating his oeuvre be considered. Particular, fruitful relationships between Davies and producers such as Louis Marks and Sue Birtwistle, and directors such as Paul Seed, Ben Bolt and Simon Langton have been vital in aiding Davies's development as an artist.

It should not be assumed, however, that the work of these facilitators undermines Davies's authorial claim over the programmes they made together. As Davies's career has progressed, he has managed to establish, sustain and indeed develop an identifiable authorial signature. The collaborative history of his work can be regarded as the pursuit of a closer, sympathetic understanding between Davies and the casts and crews, especially the directors of his programmes, which has led to a more responsive and coherent interpretation of Davies's screenplays by these personnel, and consequently a greater synthesis of style and meaning within his work.

At the outset, it appeared that the eclecticism of Davies's oeuvre, and the adapted status of so many of his programmes, might have worked against typical conceptions of consistent, original authorship. However, Davies's commitment to self-expression through audio-visual techniques has aided him and allowed his unique authorial signature to flourish. His concern for visual and symbolic expression rather than blatant expression through dialogue has been foundational in shaping his work, so that recent work exhibits greater subtlety and complexity and a fuller exploitation of the audio-visual televisual medium. He has moved from overtly depicting a world view, consisting of specific preoccupations and types of characters and situations, to developing a recognisable authorial voice (an attitude that could be called 'sympathetic irony'), to expressing a more comprehensive authorial sensibility which fully utilises the features of television to present an authorial vision that is both appropriate and sensitive to the particular text and also shares concerns with other examples of his work. He has attained a televisual sensibility.

So what, finally, is the usefulness of notions of authorship in the context of a critical project like this? Some doubts were expressed in Chapter 2 regarding the conjunction of a critical overview with an exploration of the concept of authorship. In that chapter I proposed that in sustaining an emphasis on Davies's work, rather than on Davies the man, or on authorship as a theoretical construct, a sound critical response to his work could be achieved alongside some pertinent observations about how television authorship is constructed, understood and received. 'Sympathetic disinterest' can be sustained alongside an awareness of authorship. The important thing is not to be seduced by theories that either laud or dismiss the 'author'. Within the field of television studies, there is great ideological investment in theories both for and, especially in the present context, against authorship. Yet a sensible and sensitive awareness of television authorship can be attained through recognising the context of television production, which provides limited but actual possibilities for 'authorship'. Indeed, common language may have more to tell us about the importance of authorship to television as an art than many of the more popular theories that fail to engage with the actualities of television production, reception and criticism.

Seeking Davies's authorial signature: characters and tone of voice

Initially, I aimed to detect Davies's world view within his oeuvre. I found a recurrence of particular themes (education, history and the past, freedom versus conformity, the individual within the institution, and so on), which implies an organising, consistent consciousness behind the work. However, if a world view is discernible in Davies's work, it can be found presented most vividly in the centrality of his characters, and the way in which Davies reveals, explores and develops them (his 'tone of voice'). *Observer* columnist Vanessa Thorpe asserts that 'for Davies, his Becky Sharp, his Emma Woodhouse, and his Elizabeth Bennett are all real people, to be defended with vigour. The social and political aspects of a work, in contrast, mean almost nothing to him' (Thorpe, 2002: 27). While Thorpe correctly weights the strength of Davies's commitment to, and engagement with, his characters over his interest in broader social and political critique, she overlooks the fact that his characters nevertheless function to communicate and explore some of these wider concerns. At a relatively straightforward level, many of the most memorable characters in Davies's work stand for, and speak out in support of, particular values to which Davies seems to ascribe. It is through our engagement with these characters that we may become connected to the work, and thus indirectly aligned with Davies's preoccupations and world view. One might think of Joe Peck (*Bavarian Night*), David Powlett-Jones (*To Serve*) and Stephen Daker (*Peculiar Practice*), for example. David and Stephen are especially representative of Davies's sensibility, in that they stand for compassion and connectivity with their fellows, valuing human beings and their interrelationships above (but not to the neglect of) institutional affiliations. They also prize the principles upon which a civilised society stands: education, freedom of speech (and just as importantly, the freedom to argue, to debate, to counter others' views while expressing one's own), respect for the past and for history, and hope for the future. These figures value humanity, above all else.

But Davies's characters are rarely two-dimensional mouthpieces for his own views; rather, as his work has developed, characters have become less singular and heroic, and are deeply affected by other people around them and the situations in which they find themselves. The interactions between characters reveal the profound impact that we have upon one another, across time, and our power both to hurt and to heal through our interpersonal relationships (consider *The Water Maiden, Time after Time, The Old Devils, Inappropriate Behaviour, A Rather English Marriage*, and so on). Further, an emphasis is placed upon the close relationship between character and environment. This is not just part of Davies's attempt to investigate facets of human psychology (which he achieved so successfully in *The Signalman* and *Othello*, for example); it also functions reflexively, providing a commentary upon characters' situations. Thus *A Private Life* explores the insidious impact of apartheid upon family relationships; *Peculiar Practice* offers a sustained critique of contemporary British education in the late twentieth century, and its detrimental effects upon those working and studying within it; and programmes such as *Moll Flanders, Vanity Fair, Emma, Daniel Deronda* and *The Way We Live Now* expose the iniquities and double standards of their respective periods, which are so often idealised in the genre of classic-novel adaptations. The converse power of changed situations to offer redemptive comfort and consolation is also expressed, as in *To Serve*, or *A Rather English Marriage*, although it is typically people, rather than places per se, who are responsible for enacting change.

Relatedly, Davies has shown an enduring interest in the playing of roles – the performances we put on for those around us. This implies the powerful influence of environment upon character: we are the people we must be, as determined by our situation. This is particularly true of female characters like Marianne in *The Water Maiden*, Alice in *Bavarian Night*, Morgan in *King Arthur*, Moll Flanders and Becky Sharp. It is striking that Davies's recent adaptations in particular (but also his earlier and non-adapted programmes) are full of strong female protagonists who find they must shift for themselves in a world which limits their possibilities, and that their method of coping is frequently to play the roles the world wishes them to play, while retaining a sense of self-identity behind these performances. Within the context of classic-novel adaptations, this subverts our expectations of generic conventions relating to the presentation of 'heroines', asking us to apprehend the social situations of the women and appreciate their need for ingenuity and canny manipulation. Davies thus demonstrates that he is not lacking in social conscience and is fully aware of, and sensitive to, the socio-historical contexts that limit people's ability to act freely in their own interests. Although individuals are central to Davies's work, and form the emotional focus of his programmes, these individuals are not entirely autonomous but are constrained, shaped and even determined by their environments.

Davies's central characters are also not 'heroes' in a simple sense. The characters privileged as protagonists, to whose thoughts and words we are given most access, are not necessarily upstanding, straightforward or trustworthy. They frequently constitute unreliable narrators who mislead us with their apparently insightful reflections (consider the duplicitous Francis Urquhart, the dissembling Moll and Becky, the malicious Ben Jago). It also appears that, alongside Davies's continuing commitment to strong female protagonists, there is also discernible in his oeuvre a tradition of strong, 'bad', male characters – and in his recent work, characters like Komarovsky in *Doctor Zhivago* and Grandcourt in *Daniel Deronda* have verged dangerously close to diverting the viewer's affections from their virtuous counterparts (Zhivago and Deronda, respectively). Indeed, Davies recognises the fundamental appeal of a melodramatic male villain, especially within the context of an ordinarily demure genre such as the classic-novel adaptation. He himself experiences the seductive and captivating power of amoral or immoral male protagonists, just like that of his femme fatales; he states that 'there are some [characters] I particularly enjoy inhabiting – often brutally articulate right-wing characters like Bob Buzzard in *Peculiar Practice*, or Francis Urquhart'.[6] This comment endorses Davies's commitment to the inclusion of dissenting and politically incorrect voices within his work; he is able to inhabit and enjoy points of view that contradict his own instinctive proclivities, expose their fundamental appeal to us, and thus create the distinctive and powerful medley of voices that I noted previously.

Davies's voice is constituted not just by his concerns and preoccupations, but also by the way in which he speaks about them and the attitude he takes to his characters and their stories. His work displays boldness in addressing uncomfortable subject matters and reshaping hallowed texts. Watching his work, I have become increasingly aware of Davies's genuine sense of enjoyment in creating, innovating and experimenting within contemporary television. He is bold in updating cherished sources, arguing that 'we are right to read for ourselves, in our own time, and for our own purposes', and entreating budding adapters that to 'know [the adaptation is] going to be of its time, so why not embrace it?'[7] Davies displays a comparable commitment to a full intellectual and emotional engagement with the source texts upon which his adaptations are based, and regards their protagonists as very much present to him, here and now. Natasha Little has spoken of her reasons for taking on the part of Becky Sharp in *Vanity Fair*: she was at first reluctant to do a 'period piece', and had reservations about her ability to engage with the character; however, on reading the script, she came across a stage direction written by Davies – 'Becky thinks, "Oh, fuck it!"' Suddenly, Little found that Becky was less a historic figure in a classic text, and more a modern woman dealing with familiar problems. She accepted the role. The anecdote reveals the way in which Davies regards Becky as contemporary, in the sense of being present to him while he is writing, and the level of his close sympathetic engagement with her character, situation and motivations. I have characterised Davies's attitude to both his stories and his characters as 'sympathetic irony', and this may be considered his tone of voice – the manner in which he speaks about them. This tone of voice defines his world view and his work as much as its content does; it unites the best of his programmes across different production periods, genres and adaptive sources. It is present in Davies's script, and enhanced by responsive direction.

Davies's status as author, and his role in this critical project

Having reached the final stages of writing this book, I asked Davies whether he felt there was such a thing as a world view expressed in his work. His response was this:

> I don't think much about world view when I'm writing, though sometimes I think I can see one when I've finished. A recurring theme is something like Yeats's 'the best lack all conviction, while the worst are full of passionate intensity'. [This was] explored through comedy in *A Very Peculiar Practice*, which got increasingly serious, and it comes up again I think in *Game On!* ... My political views were formed a long time ago, roughly New Statesman in the mid-fifties, modified by Karl Popper

(piecemeal social engineering preferable to Utopian socialism) and as the years go by, increasing cynicism about institutions of all kinds.[8]

It is intriguing to note Davies's mention of elements that have indeed risen to the surface in this study of his work: the appeal of the morally dubious protagonist over the 'good' man; the attempt to find a balance between 'lack of conviction' and 'passionate intensity'; the use of comedy to offer ideological critique; the commitment to rigorous, intelligent, pluralist debate; the valuing of the human, the individual, the personal, over systems and institutions. Davies's reflections upon his world view enhance my general observations with greater particularity, and add weight to my interpretations through their concurrence with my conclusions. However, the reason for my waiting until the project was nearly completed before asking Davies about such matters was that I have been basing my critical project upon *embodied intentions* (as outlined in Chapter 2). I began with his texts, made inferences based upon what could be found within them, and then, out of curiosity, sought confirmation of my findings from Davies. I did not begin with a detailed knowledge of Davies the man and then attempt to seek him out within his work. This is what distinguishes the approach taken in this book from a biographical or strong auteurist approach. The texts – the programmes themselves – are at the centre of this project; Davies's authorship of them is crucial, but in the context of this critical study, it is his authorship and artistry that concern me, not his life or personality.

In order to clarify the practical implications of my concern with embodied intentions, it is worth considering the status of Davies's known intentions within this critical project. Some traditions of textual analysis place paramount importance upon the author's original intentions, going so far as to claim that 'the ideal of textual criticism is to present the text which the author intended' (Thorpe, 1972: 50). That is not an ideal to which I have adhered in this book. I have sought to explore the details of the texts through which the author(s) successfully communicated his (their) meanings, and have also given consideration to interpretations that may not have been intended by any 'author' of the text at all. Davies's consciously stated intentions therefore have a curious status within this interpretative context. For example, Davies mentioned in passing that 'I do think that a lot of romantic/sexual relationships can be seen as student/teacher relationships, e.g. Stephen and Lyn's in *A Very Peculiar Practice* – she is teaching him to trust and be tactile, etc.'[9] However, I failed to see this connection between Davies's interest in education/teaching and his preoccupation with interpersonal (romantic) relationships; it did not appear clear to me that his work contained this. Therefore his comment adds something to my understanding of his work, but the existence of this idea within his work has yet to be supported by valid interpretations of what is actually present, embodied within the text. Thus the author's intentions are an interpretation of the work, but are not determining (interpretations must derive from what is present in the text).

There are thus disparities between Davies's and my perceptions of his work. Indeed, at a conceptual level, there are considerable and overt disagreements between our views on adaptation and authorship. I have spent considerable time arguing that Austen and Eliot have no logical claim to authorship over his adaptations of their novels,[10] and Davies seems often to support this, claiming that fidelity is a 'futile quest', and undermining both the notion of an 'original' and the privileged status of adaptation: 'I would say that there is no original ... Every reading of a book is an adaptation of that book.'[11] On other occasions, though, Davies speaks of his desire to be faithful to his source, and avers that 'I'd still say the original author's is one of the best claims over the material' (quoted in Ransome, 2001: 35). Our differences of opinion on this matter undoubtedly arise because Davies is committed to the creative act of adapting, and I am committed to the logical act of conceptualising adaptation. He is speaking of his feelings towards the authors of the source texts he adapts; I am speaking of my thoughts regarding questions of authorship and the integrity of individual artworks.

Whether you are is convinced by either Davies's or my understanding of the authorship of adaptation depends primarily upon the kind of answer you seek, and your affiliations and interests. What is clear, though, is that Davies's views upon his work – specific texts, or broader practices – do not necessarily constitute the last word, nor are they able, on their own, to confirm or undermine the criticisms and conceptualisations that have been offered in this book. Davies's status within this project is therefore not one of a final 'authority', whose relationship with the texts is paramount, and whose intentions are sacrosanct. Criticism cannot be founded upon recourse to the views of the author of its texts; it must be founded upon the texts themselves, the details they make available to the critic, and upon transparent and persuasive argumentation.

Evaluating Davies: moving from criticism to pleasure

Finally, a few words on the evaluation of Davies as author or artist are necessary. While not all of his projects have been successful, as I have noted, Davies's commitment to his art is unquestionable. Many critics have noticed the way in which he dominates 'quality' television, especially in the genre of classic-novel adaptations. On noting the clash in broadcast times between *Deronda* and *Zhivago*, one reviewer wrote, 'The truth is, though, it would be hard to find a place to put any Andrew Davies-branded product where it did not vie with another one for its audience' (Thorpe, 2002: 27). Davies's output is prolific because he has boundless enthusiasm for his work, not because he regards television as mere entertainment or a means to make a living. When Alan Yentob asked him to write between 48 and 52 fifty-minute episodes of 'something like' *Peculiar Practice*, Davies responded that 'It seemed almost unkind to explain to him that works of genius are not like that. You can't order them up like rolls of carpet' (Davies quoted in O'Brien, 1996: 30). Davies respects television's potential as an art form, deploring the new trends, in which fresh ideas become stale

> because of the absolute necessity to produce more and more, and longer and longer, runs of proven successes ... What follows, we all know: shows that seem fresh and bright and sparky when we first saw them are flogged relentlessly, until the last dodgy plot possibility flops exhausted on the living room carpet, to bleed to death, and the baffled couch potatoes turn to each other and say 'Oh, I dunno ... it's gone off a bit, hasn't it?' (Davies, 1994)

Within the context and constraints of contemporary television production, Davies persists in his desire to innovate and experiment, always wanting to push ahead with something new, as one can see from *Is That Your Body, Boy?*, *The Signalman* and *A Few Short Journeys of the Heart*, through *The Old Devils*, *Moll Flanders* and *Vanity Fair*, to *Othello*, *Doctor Zhivago*, *Daniel Deronda* and *The Way We Live Now*. He exploits the specificities of television (its serial form, its employment of direct address, its intimate position within our homes) to engage us in new and unpredictable ways. As this book goes into production, we await the broadcast of his second Trollope adaptation, *He Knew He Was Right*, and confirmation of the rumours that he is remaking that television classic, *Brideshead Revisited*.[12]

Davies has an unshakeable confidence in his vocation as a writer, and holds strong views on the process and purpose of writing. He argues that 'being a writer is all about trusting your own feelings and your own perceptions, rather than other people's' (Davies, 1994). While this may sound solipsistic, Davies is keen to emphasise his commitment to the audience's enjoyment, stimulation and development. He wishes to share his view of the world with the viewers of his programmes:

As an audience, we're hungering for something that gets at the essence of our lives, shows us something we've never seen before, but we recognise it when we see it ... Life is always different from the official version – usually funnier and stranger and scarier – and most of my writing has been stimulated by this thought – that it's not like you think it is, it's like *this*. (Davies 1994)

He thus places an emphasis on the ordinary, the everyday – the people, relationships and situations that are quotidian and shared by many; however, he desires to reveal the familiarities to us afresh, just as he refigures and transforms familiar source texts and genres. In this way, his programmes incorporate reflections upon the characters and events they present, and they simultaneously gesture towards Davies's particular view of the world.

In Chapter 3, I cited T. S. Eliot's notion of impersonality as a admirable quality in an artwork. But Eliot went further, in his description of the developing, progressing artist: 'What happens is a continual surrender of himself as he is at the moment to something which is more valuable. The progress of an artist is a continual self-sacrifice, a continual extinction of personality' (Eliot, 1919: 76). Yet this is to deny one of the fundamental pleasures of knowing an artist's work. As his oeuvre has developed, Davies has successfully 'erased' the more obvious references to himself and his life which marred some of his earlier work. But he has retained a sense of his world view, his voice, his sensibility. In his work we may find traces of these, glimpsing also qualities of his personality: his humour, energy, passion, insight and intelligence. Having watched so much of Davies's work, I now find great pleasure in the moments in which he makes himself known within the programmes: the scenes that convey the truthful tension that exists within personal relationships, or the moments when his contemporary sensibility offers a new perspective on a cherished source text. (I recall, for example, the wonderfully sharp moment in *Daniel Deronda*, when Sir Hugo Mallinger playfully teases the rather prim Deronda about his 'flirting with the women again'; the comment causes us to regard Daniel from a novel standpoint, and alters our view of his behaviour.) In this way, a perception of Davies's ever advancing authorship, which is in one sense an erasure of self, and in another sense an endurance of self, is also a source of pleasure for the viewer of his texts. It may be that this study has demonstrated to readers that an awareness of authorship can enhance the critical study of television programmes; I also hope to persuade those readers that such an awareness may intensify the pleasure of experiencing those programmes.

Notes

1 This sequence from the novel is given in Appendix 2.
2 Indeed, Jim Collins explicitly correlates adaptation with intertextuality in his study of the novel and film of *The English Patient*. He regards adaptation as part of what he calls 'cineliterary culture', and characterises it as fundamentally intertextual (Collins, 1999).
3 I have also made this argument in more conceptual terms, elsewhere (Cardwell, 2002: 6–8).
4 I propose 'performance' as a fundamental feature of television in *Adaptation Revisited*; see in particular the section on 'television and performance' (pp. 87–92) and chapter 7 (*Moll Flanders*).
5 My purpose here is to explicitly interpret and implicitly evaluate this programme. Within that remit of interpretation and evaluation, there is no need for comparison. Everything I need to see I can see in the programme, and it is not relevant to my aims to undertake a comparison with the book. Other purposes require alternative methodologies, of course; some projects rightfully require a comparative approach.
6 Quoted from Davies's e-mail communication to me, sent in February 2004. Davies also notes that he even incorporates such a character into the sitcom format of *Game On!*: 'Martin is nice but a loser – Matthew is appalling, probably very disturbed, but somehow much more attractive.'
7 Quote from my interview with Davies, 21 February 2003.
8 Quoted from previously cited e-mail from Davies to me, February 2004.
9 Quoted from previously cited e-mail from Davies to me, February 2004.
10 The most sustained version of this argument is offered in *Adaptation Revisited* (Cardwell, 2002).
11 Quote from my interview with Davies, 21 February 2003.
12 Davies is also working on an adaptation of *Falling*, a thriller by Elizabeth Jane Howard; he is undertaking this project with his daughter, who is a script editor. *Bridget Jones: The Edge of Reason*, the sequel to *Bridget Jones's Diary*, is currently in post-production.

List of programmes, films and other texts

Programmes and films

The information provided on each programme/film is presented in the following format:

> *Title of programme/film*, television channel on which it was transmitted [name of general series if appropriate, e.g. 'Play for Today', 'Screen Two'] (production company/companies), date of transmission, director.
> Details of source text, if the programme/film is an adaptation.

Some earlier television programmes do not list the 'director' in the credits. When a 'director of photography' is named instead, I have given this person's name. When neither a director nor a director of photography is named, I have noted this.

Publication dates for written texts in both this list and the bibliography refer to the first year in which the book was published in full in English.

Television: serials and series

Anglo Saxon Attitudes
Channel 4 (Thames Television/Euston Films Ltd), 1992, dir. Diarmuid Lawrence.
Based on the novel *Anglo Saxon Attitudes* (1956) by Angus Wilson.

Boudicca
ITV (Box Films and TV/WGBH Boston/Carlton International/Mediapro Pictures), 2003, dir. Bill Anderson.

Daniel Deronda
BBC (WGBH Boston/BBC), 2002, dir. Tom Hooper.
Based on the novel *Daniel Deronda* (1876) by George Eliot.

Diana
BBC (BBC), 1983, dir. Richard Stroud and David Tucker.
Based on the novel *Diana* (published in two parts: *There was a Fair Maid Dwelling*, 1960, and *The Unjust Skies*, 1962) by R. F. Delderfield.

Doctor Zhivago
ITV (Granada Television/Evision/WGBH Boston), 2002, dir. Giacomo Campiotti.
Based on the novel *Doctor Zhivago* (1958) by Boris Pasternak.

Eleanor Marx
BBC (BBC Colour), 1976, dir. Jane Howell.
Based on the biography *The Life of Eleanor Marx 1855–1898* (1967) by Chushichi Tsuzuki.

Final Cut, The
BBC (BBC/WGBH Boston), 1995, dir. Mike Vardy.
Based on the novel *The Final Cut* (1995) by Michael Dobbs.

Fortunes and Misfortunes of Moll Flanders, The
ITV (Granada Television/WGBH Boston), 1996, dir. David Attwood.
Based on the novel *Moll Flanders* (1722) by Daniel Defoe.

Game On!
Co-writer Bernadette Davis. BBC (Hat Trick productions), 1995–98, dir. John Stroud.

Harnessing Peacocks
LWT (Meridian Broadcasting Ltd), 1992, dir. James Cellan Jones.
Based on the novel *Harnessing Peacocks* (1985) by Mary Wesley.

He Knew He Was Right
BBC (BBC Wales), 2004, dir. Tom Vaughan.
Based on the novel *He Knew He Was Right* (1869) by Anthony Trollope.

House of Cards
BBC (BBC), 1990, dir. Paul Seed.
Based on the novel *House of Cards* (1989) by Michael Dobbs.

Legend of King Arthur, The
BBC (BBC TV/Time-Life Television), 1979, dir. Rodney Bennett.

Middlemarch
BBC (BBC), 1994, dir. Anthony Page.
Based on the novel *Middlemarch* (1872) by George Eliot.

Mother Love
BBC (BBC TV in association with WGBH Boston), 1989, dir. Simon Langton.
Based on the novel *Mother Love* (1983) by Domini Taylor.

Old Devils, The
BBC2 (BBC Wales), 1992, dir. Tristram Powell.
Based on the novel *The Old Devils* (1986) by Kingsley Amis.

Pride and Prejudice
BBC (BBC/A&E), 1995, dir. Simon Langton.
Based on the novel *Pride and Prejudice* (1813) by Jane Austen.

Take a Girl Like You
BBC (BBC/WGBH Boston), 2000, dir. Nick Hurran.
Based on the novel *Take a Girl Like You* (1960) by Kingsley Amis.

Tipping the Velvet
BBC (BBC), 2002, dir. Geoffrey Sax.
Based on the novel *Tipping the Velvet* (1998) by Sarah Waters.

To Play the King
BBC (BBC), 1993, dir. Paul Seed.
Based on the novel *To Play the King* (1992) by Michael Dobbs.

To Serve Them All My Days
BBC (BBC TV with the Australian Broadcasting Commission), 1980, dir.
    Ronald Wilson.
Based on the novel *To Serve Them All My Days* (1972) by R. F. Delderfield.

Vanity Fair
BBC (BBC/A&E), 1998, dir. Marc Munden.
Based on the novel *Vanity Fair* (1848) by William M. Thackeray.

Very Peculiar Practice, A
BBC (BBC Pebble Mill), 1986, 1988, dir. David Tucker.

Way We Live Now, The
BBC (BBC), 2001, dir. David Yates.
Based on the novel *The Way We Live Now* (1875) by Anthony Trollope.

Wilderness
Co-writer Bernadette Davis. ITV (Carlton UK Television), 1996, dir. Ben
    Bolt.
Based on the novel *Wilderness* (1991) by Dennis Danvers.

Wives and Daughters
BBC (BBC/WGBH Boston), 1999, dir. Nicholas Renton.
Based on the novel *Wives and Daughters* (1865) by Elizabeth Gaskell.

Television: single plays and films

Ball-Trap on the Cote Sauvage
BBC (BBC), 1989, dir. Jack Gold.

Bavarian Night
BBC ['Play for Today'] (BBC), 1981, dir. Jack Gold.

Emma
ITV (Meridian/A&E), 1996, dir. Diarmuid Lawrence.
Based on the novel *Emma* (1816) by Jane Austen.

Fearless Frank
BBC (BBC), 1978, dir. Colin Bucksey.
Based on the biography *Frank Harris* (1975) by Philippa Pullar.

Few Short Journeys of the Heart, A
BB2 ['Performance'] (BBC), 1994, dir. Paul Tickell.
Based on the short story *Dirty Faxes* by Andrew Davies (published in his
    collection of short stories *Dirty Faxes*).

Filipina Dreamgirls
BBC1 ['Screen One'] (BBC Wales), 1991, dir. Les Blair.

Getting Hurt
BBC2 ['Obsessions'] (BBC), 1998, dir. Ben Bolt.
Based on the novel *Getting Hurt* (1989) by Andrew Davies.

Grace
BBC ['Thirty Minute Theatre'] (BBC), 1975, dir. Brian Parker.

Happy in War
['Velvet Glove'] (1977). No further details available.

Headcase
Anna Lee pilot. ITV (LWT Productions), 1993, dir. Colin Bucksey.
Based on the novel *Headcase* (1985) by Liza Cody.

Heartattack Hotel
BBC (BBC Films), 1983, dir. Mike Vardy

Imp of the Perverse, The
BBC ['Centre Play'] (BBC), 1975, dir. not known.
Based on the short story *The Imp of the Perverse* (1850) by Edgar Allan Poe.

Inappropriate Behaviour
BBC2 ['Screen Two'] (BBC), 1986, dir. Paul Seed.

Is That Your Body, Boy?
BBC ['Thirty Minute Theatre'] (BBC), 1970, dir. Claude Whatham.

Lucky Sunil
BBC2 ['Screen Two'] (BBC), 1988, dir. Michael Caton-Jones.
Based on a story by Tariq Yumus.

Martyr to the System, A
BBC2 ['Playhouse'] (BBC), 1976, dir. not known.

No Good Unless It Hurts
BBC ['Sporting Scenes'] (BBC), 1973, dir. not known.

Othello
ITV (Canadian Broadcasting Corporation/LWT/WGBH Boston), 2001,
    dir. Geoffrey Sax.
Based on the play *Othello* (written 1604; published 1622) by William
    Shakespeare.

Private Life, A
BBC2 ['Screen Two'] (Totem Productions Ltd), 1988, dir. Francis Gerard.

Prizewinner Cowboy in the White House
1977. No further details available.

Pythons on the Mountain
BBC ['Playhouse'] (BBC), 1984, dir. Mike Vardy.

Rather English Marriage, A
BBC (Wall to Wall Television Ltd), 1998, dir. Paul Seed.
Based on the novel *A Rather English Marriage* (1992) by Angela Lambert.

Renoir, My Father
['Play of the Week'], 1978. No further details available.

Signalman, The
BBC (BBC Colour), 1976, dir. Lawrence Gordon Clark.
Based on the short story *The Signalman* (1866) by Charles Dickens.

Time after Time
BBC2 ['Screen Two'] (BBC), 1985, dir. Bill Hays.
Based on the novel *Time After Time* (1983) by Molly Keane.

Very Polish Practice, A
BBC1 ['Screen One'] (BBC), 1992, dir. David Tucker.

Water Maiden, The
BBC ['Bedtime Stories'] (BBC Colour), 1974, dir. Kenneth Ives.

Who's Going to Take Me On?
BBC (BBC), 1967, dir. not known.

Television: work for children

Baby, I Love You
Teen drama. BBC (BBC), 1985, dir. not named.

Bill's New Frock
Educational video. (Channel Four Schools), 1997, dir. Pete Travis.

Boot Street Band, The
Co-writer Steve Attridge. BBC, 1993, dir. John Smith.

Danger: Marmalade at Work
ITV (Thames Television), 1984, dir. Peter Duguid.

Educating Marmalade
ITV (Thames Television), 1982, dir. John Stroud.

Look and Read: 'Badgergirl'
BBC (BBC), 1969, dir. Colin Cant.

Look and Read: 'Dark Towers'
BBC (BBC), 1967, dir. not known.

Marmalade Atkins in Space
1981. No further details available.

Cinema-release films

Bridget Jones: The Edge of Reason
Co-writers Adam Brooks, Richard Curtis, and Helen Fielding. Working
   Title Films/Universal Pictures/Miramax/Little Bird Ltd/Studio Canal,
   forthcoming 2004, dir. Beeban Kidron.
Based on the novel *The Edge of Reason* (1999) by Helen Fielding.

Bridget Jones's Diary
Co-writers Helen Fielding and Richard Curtis. Little Bird Ltd/Studio
   Canal/Working Title Films, 2001, dir. Sharon Maguire.
Based on the novel *Bridget Jones's Diary* (1996) by Helen Fielding.

Circle of Friends
Price Entertainment/Lantana, 1995, dir. Pat O'Connor.
Based on the novel *Circle of Friends* (1990) by Maeve Binchy.

Consuming Passions
Co-writer Paul D. Zimmerman. Euston Films, 1988, dir. Giles Foster.
Based on the television play *Secrets* (1973) by Michael Palin and Terry Jones.

Tailor of Panama, The
Columbia Pictures Corporation/Merlin Films, 2001, dir. John Boorman.
Based on the novel *The Tailor of Panama* (1996) by John le Carré.

A selection of other texts

Radio plays

Accentuate the Positive, 1980.
Campus Blues, 1984.
Curse on Them, Astonish Me!, 1970.
Day in Bed, A, 1967.
Getting the Smell of It, 1967.
Hospitalization of Samuel Pellett, The, 1964.
Innocent Eye, The, 1971.
Shortsighted Bear, The, 1972.
Steph and the Man of Some Distinction, 1971.
Steph and the Simple Life, 1972.
Steph and the Zero Structure Lifestyle, 1976.

Stage plays

Battery, 1979.
Brainstorming with the Boys, 1978.
Can Anyone Smell the Gas?, 1972.
Diary of a Desperate Woman, 1979.
Fearless Frank, 1978.
 Based on Davies's television play *Fearless Frank* (1978).
Filthy Fryer and the Woman of Mature Years, 1974.
Going Bust, 1977.
Linda Polan: Can You Smell the Gas?; What Are Little Girls Made Of?, 1975.
Prin, 1990.
Randy Robinson's Unsuitable Relationship, 1976.
Rohan and Julia, 1975.
Rose, 1980.
Shortsighted Bear, The, 1972.
Teacher's Gone Mad, 1977.

Books for adults

B. Monkey
 London: Lime Tree, 1992.
Dirty Faxes
 London: Methuen, 1990.
Getting Hurt
 London: Minerva, 1989.
New Frontier, The
 Novelisation of second series of *A Very Peculiar Practice*.
 No publication details available.
Very Peculiar Practice, A
 Novelisation of the first series of the television serial, London: Coronet Books, 1986.

Books for children

Alfonso Bonzo
1986. No publication details available.

Boot Street Band, The
1993. No publication details available.
Novelisation based on the television series.

Conrad's War
London: Blackie, 1978.

Educating Marmalade
London: Puffin, 1995.
Novelisation based on the television series.

Fantastic Feats of Doctor Boox, The
London: Collins, 1972.

Marmalade and Rufus
New York: Crown, 1980; London: Random House, 1983. Later reissued as
   Marmalade's Dreadful Deeds. London: Puffin, 1995.

Marmalade at Work
1984. No publication details available.
Novelisation based on the television series.

Marmalade Hits the Big Time
London: Puffin, 1995. Hardcover version published 1996 by Blackie
   Children's Books; audio version published 1997 by Chivers Audio Books.

Marmalade in Space
London: Blackie Books, 1986.
Novelisation based on the television series.

Poonam's Pets
With Diana Davies. 1st American edn – New York: Viking, 1990.

Other programmes and films cited in this book

B. Monkey
Miramax Films, Scala Productions, Synchronistic Pictures, 1998, scr.
   Chloe King, Michael Radford, Michael Thomas, dir. Michael Radford.
Based on the novel *B. Monkey* (1992) by Andrew Davies.

House of Mirth, The
Arts Council of England/FilmFour/Granada Film Productions/et al.,
   2000, scr. and dir. Terence Davies.
Based on the novel *The House of Mirth* (1905) by Edith Wharton.

Loneliness of the Long Distance Runner, The
British Lion Film Corporation/Bryanston Films Ltd/Woodfall Film
   Productions, 1962, dir. Tony Richardson.
Based on the novel *The Loneliness of the Long Distance Runner* (1959) by
   Alan Sillitoe.

Singing Detective, The
BBC (BBC), 1986, scr. Dennis Potter, dir. Jon Amiel.

Stand up, Nigel Barton
BBC ['The Wednesday Play'] (BBC), 1965, scr. Dennis Potter, dir. Gareth
   Davies.

Vote, Vote, Vote for Nigel Barton
BBC ['The Wednesday Play'] (BBC), 1965, scr. Dennis Potter, dir. Gareth
   Davies.

Appendix 1
The Signalman (1866)
by Charles Dickens

'Halloa! Below there!'

When he heard a voice thus calling to him, he was standing at the door of his box, with a flag in his hand, furled round its short pole. One would have thought, considering the nature of the ground, that he could not have doubted from what quarter the voice came; but instead of looking up to where I stood on the top of the steep cutting nearly over his head, he turned himself about, and looked down the Line. There was something remarkable in his manner of doing so, though I could not have said for my life what. But I know it was remarkable enough to attract my notice, even though his figure was foreshortened and shadowed, down in the deep trench, and mine was high above him, so steeped in the glow of an angry sunset, that I had shaded my eyes with my hand before I saw him at all.

'Halloa! Below!'

From looking down the Line, he turned himself about again, and, raising his eyes, saw my figure high above him.

'Is there any path by which I can come down and speak to you?'

He looked up at me without replying, and I looked down at him without pressing him too soon with a repetition of my idle question. Just then there came a vague vibration in the earth and air, quickly changing into a violent pulsation, and an oncoming rush that caused me to start back, as though it had force to draw me down. When such vapour as rose to my height from this rapid train had passed me, and was skimming away over the landscape, I looked down again, and saw him refurling the flag he had shown while the train went by.

I repeated my inquiry. After a pause, during which he seemed to regard me with fixed attention, he motioned with his rolled-up flag towards a point on my level, some two or three hundred yards distant. I called down to him, 'All right!' and made for that point. There, by dint of looking closely about me, I found a rough zigzag descending path notched out, which I followed.

The cutting was extremely deep, and unusually precipitate. It was made through a clammy stone, that became oozier and wetter as I went down. For these reasons, I found the way long enough to give me time to recall a singular air of reluctance or compulsion with which he had pointed out the path.

When I came down low enough upon the zigzag descent to see him again, I saw that he was standing between the rails on the way by which the train had lately passed, in an attitude as if he were waiting for me to appear. He had his left hand at his chin, and that left elbow rested on his right hand, crossed over his breast. His attitude was one of such expectation and watchfulness that I stopped a moment, wondering at it.

I resumed my downward way, and stepping out upon the level of the railroad, and drawing nearer to him, saw that he was a dark sallow man, with a dark beard and rather heavy eyebrows. His post was in as solitary and dismal a place as ever I saw. On either side, a dripping-wet wall of jagged stone, excluding all view but a strip of sky; the perspective one way only a crooked prolongation of this great dungeon; the shorter perspective in the other direction terminating in a gloomy red light, and the gloomier entrance to a black tunnel, in whose massive architecture there was a barbarous, depressing, and forbidding air. So little sunlight ever found its way to this spot, that it had an earthy, deadly smell; and so much cold wind rushed through it, that it struck chill to me, as if I had left the natural world.

Before he stirred, I was near enough to him to have touched him. Not even then removing his eyes from mine, he stepped back one step, and lifted his hand.

This was a lonesome post to occupy (I said), and it had riveted my attention when I looked down from up yonder. A visitor was a rarity, I should suppose; not an unwelcome rarity, I hoped? In me, he merely saw a man who had been shut up within narrow limits all his life, and who, being at last set free, had a newly-awakened interest in these great works. To such purpose I spoke to him; but I am far from sure of the terms I used; for, besides that I am not happy in opening any conversation, there was something in the man that daunted me.

He directed a most curious look towards the red light near the tunnel's mouth, and looked all about it, as if something were missing from it, and then looked at me.

That light was part of his charge? Was it not?

He answered in a low voice, – 'Don't you know it is?'

The monstrous thought came into my mind, as I perused the fixed eyes and the saturnine face, that this was a spirit, not a man. I have speculated since, whether there may have been infection in his mind.

In my turn, I stepped back. But in making the action, I detected in his eyes some latent fear of me. This put the monstrous thought to flight.

'You look at me,' I said, forcing a smile, 'as if you had a dread of me.'

'I was doubtful,' he returned, 'whether I had seen you before.'

'Where?'

He pointed to the red light he had looked at.

'There?' I said.

Intently watchful of me, he replied (but without sound), 'Yes.'

'My good fellow, what should I do there? However, be that as it may, I never was there, you may swear.'

'I think I may,' he rejoined. 'Yes; I am sure I may.'

His manner cleared, like my own. He replied to my remarks with readiness, and in well-chosen words. Had he much to do there? Yes; that was to say, he had enough responsibility to bear; but exactness and watchfulness were what was required of him, and of actual work – manual labour – he had next to none. To change that signal, to trim those lights, and to turn this iron handle now and then, was all he had to do under that head. Regarding those many long and lonely hours of which I seemed to make so much, he could only say that the routine of his life had shaped itself into that form, and he had grown used to it. He had taught himself a language down here, – if only to know it by sight, and to have formed his own crude ideas of its pronunciation, could be called learning it. He had also worked at fractions and decimals, and tried a little algebra; but he was, and had been as a boy, a poor hand at figures. Was it necessary for him when on duty always to remain in that channel of damp air, and could he never rise into the sunshine from between those high stone walls? Why, that depended upon times and circumstances. Under some conditions there would be less upon the Line than under others, and the same held good as to certain hours of the day and night. In bright weather, he did choose occasions for getting a little above these lower shadows; but, being at all times liable to be called by his electric bell, and at such times listening for it with redoubled anxiety, the relief was less than I would suppose.

He took me into his box, where there was a fire, a desk for an official book in which he had to make certain entries, a telegraphic instrument with its dial, face, and needles, and the little bell of which he had spoken. On my trusting that he would excuse the remark that he had been well educated, and (I hoped I might say without offence) perhaps educated above that station, he observed that instances of slight incongruity in such wise would rarely be found wanting among large bodies of men; that he had heard it was so in workhouses, in the police force, even in that last desperate resource, the army; and that he knew it was so, more or less, in any great railway staff. He had been, when young (if I could believe it, sitting in that hut, – he scarcely could), a student of natural philosophy, and had attended lectures; but he had run wild, misused his opportunities, gone down, and never risen again. He had no complaint to offer about that. He had made his bed, and he lay upon it. It was far too late to make another.

All that I have here condensed he said in a quiet manner, with his grave dark regards divided between me and the fire. He threw in the word, 'Sir,' from time to time, and especially when he referred to his youth, – as though to request me to understand that he claimed to be nothing but what I found him. He was several times interrupted by the little bell, and had to read off messages, and send replies. Once he had to stand without the door, and display a flag as a train passed, and make some verbal communication to the driver. In the discharge of his duties, I observed him to be remarkably exact and vigilant, breaking off his discourse at a syllable, and remaining silent until what he had to do was done.

In a word, I should have set this man down as one of the safest of men to be employed in that capacity, but for the circumstance that while he was speaking to me he twice broke off with a fallen colour, turned his face towards the little bell when it did NOT ring, opened the door of the hut (which was kept shut to exclude the unhealthy damp), and looked out towards the red light near the mouth of the tunnel. On both of those occasions, he came back to the fire with the inexplicable air upon him which I had remarked, without being able to define, when we were so far asunder.

Said I, when I rose to leave him, 'You almost make me think that I have met with a contented man.'

(I am afraid I must acknowledge that I said it to lead him on.)

'I believe I used to be so,' he rejoined, in the low voice in which he had first spoken; 'but I am troubled, sir, I am troubled.'

He would have recalled the words if he could. He had said them, however, and I took them up quickly.

'With what? What is your trouble?'

'It is very difficult to impart, sir. It is very, very difficult to speak of. If ever you make me another visit, I will try to tell you.'

'But I expressly intend to make you another visit. Say, when shall it be?'

'I go off early in the morning, and I shall be on again at ten to-morrow night, sir.'

'I will come at eleven.'

He thanked me, and went out at the door with me. 'I'll show my white light, sir,' he said, in his peculiar low voice, 'till you have found the way up. When you have found it, don't call out! And when you are at the top, don't call out!'

His manner seemed to make the place strike colder to me, but I said no more than, 'Very well.'

'And when you come down to-morrow night, don't call out! Let me ask you a parting question. What made you cry, "Halloa! Below there!" to-night?'

'Heaven knows,' said I. 'I cried something to that effect –'

'Not to that effect, sir. Those were the very words. I know them well.'

'Admit those were the very words. I said them, no doubt, because I saw you below.'

'For no other reason?'

'What other reason could I possibly have?'

'You had no feeling that they were conveyed to you in any supernatural way?'

'No.'

He wished me good-night, and held up his light. I walked by the side of the down Line of rails (with a very disagreeable sensation of a train coming behind me) until I found the path. It was easier to mount than to descend, and I got back to my inn without any adventure.

Punctual to my appointment, I placed my foot on the first notch of the zigzag next night, as the distant clocks were striking eleven. He was waiting for me at the bottom, with his white light on. 'I have not called out,' I said, when we came close together; 'may I speak now?' 'By all means, sir.' 'Good-night, then, and here's my hand.' 'Good-night, sir, and here's mine.' With that we walked side by side to his box, entered it, closed the door, and sat down by the fire.

'I have made up my mind, sir,' he began, bending forward as soon as we were seated, and speaking in a tone but a little above a whisper, 'that you shall not have to ask me twice what troubles me. I took you for some one else yesterday evening. That troubles me.'

'That mistake?'

'No. That some one else.'

'Who is it?'

'I don't know.'

'Like me?'

'I don't know. I never saw the face. The left arm is across the face, and the right arm is waved, – violently waved. This way.'

I followed his action with my eyes, and it was the action of an arm gesticulating, with the utmost passion and vehemence, 'For God's sake, clear the way!'

'One moonlight night,' said the man, 'I was sitting here, when I heard a voice cry, "Halloa! below there!" I started up, looked from that door, and saw this some one else standing by the red light near the tunnel, waving as I just now showed you. The voice seemed hoarse with shouting, and it cried, "Look out! Look out!" And then attain, "Halloa! Below there! Look out!" I caught up my lamp, turned it on red, and ran towards the figure, calling, "What's wrong? What has happened? Where?" It stood just outside the blackness of the tunnel. I advanced so close upon it that I wondered at its keeping the sleeve across its eyes. I ran right up at it, and had my hand stretched out to pull the sleeve away, when it was gone.'

'Into the tunnel?' said I.

'No. I ran on into the tunnel, five hundred yards. I stopped, and held my lamp above my head, and saw the figures of the measured distance, and saw the wet stains stealing down the walls and trickling through the arch. I ran out again faster than I had run in (for I had a mortal abhorrence of the place upon me), and I looked all round the red light with my own red light, and I went up the iron ladder to the gallery atop of it, and I came down again, and ran back here. I telegraphed both ways, "An alarm has been given. Is anything wrong?" The answer came back, both ways, "All well."'

Resisting the slow touch of a frozen finger tracing out my spine, I showed him how that this figure must be a deception of his sense of sight; and how that figures, originating in disease of the delicate nerves that minister to the functions of the eye, were known to have often troubled patients, some of whom had become conscious of the nature of their affliction, and had even proved it by experiments upon themselves. 'As to an imaginary cry,' said I, 'do but listen for a moment to the wind in this unnatural valley while we speak so low, and to the wild harp it makes of the telegraph wires.'

That was all very well, he returned, after we had sat listening for a while, and he ought to know something of the wind and the wires, – he who so often passed long winter nights there, alone and watching. But he would beg to remark that he had not finished.

I asked his pardon, and he slowly added these words, touching my arm, –

'Within six hours after the Appearance, the memorable accident on this Line happened, and within ten hours the dead and wounded were brought along through the tunnel over the spot where the figure had stood.'

A disagreeable shudder crept over me, but I did my best against it. It was not to be denied, I rejoined, that this was a remarkable coincidence, calculated deeply to impress his mind. But it was unquestionable that remarkable coincidences did continually occur, and they must be taken into account in dealing with such a subject. Though to be sure I must admit, I added (for I thought I saw that he was going to bring the objection to bear upon me), men of common sense did not allow much for coincidences in making the ordinary calculations of life.

He again begged to remark that he had not finished.

I again begged his pardon for being betrayed into interruptions.

'This,' he said, again laying his hand upon my arm, and glancing over his shoulder with hollow eyes, 'was just a year ago. Six or seven months passed, and I had recovered from the surprise and shock, when one morning, as the day was breaking, I, standing at the door, looked towards the red light, and saw the spectre again.' He stopped, with a fixed look at me.

'Did it cry out?'

'No. It was silent.'

'Did it wave its arm?'

'No. It leaned against the shaft of the light, with both hands before the face. Like this.'

Once more I followed his action with my eyes. It was an action of mourning. I have seen such an attitude in stone figures on tombs.

'Did you go up to it?'

'I came in and sat down, partly to collect my thoughts, partly because it had turned me faint. When I went to the door again, daylight was above me, and the ghost was gone.'

'But nothing followed? Nothing came of this?'

He touched me on the arm with his forefinger twice or thrice giving a ghastly nod each time:–

'That very day, as a train came out of the tunnel, I noticed, at a carriage window on my side, what looked like a confusion of hands and heads, and something waved. I saw it just in time to signal the driver, Stop! He shut off, and put his brake on, but the train drifted past here a hundred and fifty yards or more. I ran after it, and, as I went along, heard terrible screams and cries. A beautiful young lady had died instantaneously in one of the compartments, and was brought in here, and laid down on this floor between us.'

Involuntarily I pushed my chair back, as I looked from the boards at which he pointed to himself.

'True, sir. True. Precisely as it happened, so I tell it you.'

I could think of nothing to say, to any purpose, and my mouth was very dry. The wind and the wires took up the story with a long lamenting wail.

He resumed. 'Now, sir, mark this, and judge how my mind is troubled. The spectre came back a week ago. Ever since, it has been there, now and again, by fits and starts.'

'At the light?'

'At the Danger-light.'

'What does it seem to do?'

He repeated, if possible with increased passion and vehemence, that former gesticulation of, 'For God's sake, clear the way!'

Then he went on. 'I have no peace or rest for it. It calls to me, for many minutes together, in an agonised manner, "Below there! Look out! Look out!" It stands waving to me. It rings my little bell –'

I caught at that. 'Did it ring your bell yesterday evening when I was here, and you went to the door?'

'Twice.'

'Why, see,' said I, 'how your imagination misleads you. My eyes were on the bell, and my ears were open to the bell, and if I am a living man, it did NOT ring at those times. No, nor at any other time, except when it was rung in the natural course of physical things by the station communicating with you.'

He shook his head. 'I have never made a mistake as to that yet, sir. I have never confused the spectre's ring with the man's. The ghost's ring is a strange vibration in the bell that it derives from nothing else, and I have not asserted that the bell stirs to the eye. I don't wonder that you failed to hear it. But I heard it.'

'And did the spectre seem to be there, when you looked out?'

'It WAS there.'

'Both times?'

He repeated firmly: 'Both times.'

'Will you come to the door with me, and look for it now?'

He bit his under lip as though he were somewhat unwilling, but arose. I opened the door, and stood on the step, while he stood in the doorway. There was the Danger-light. There was the dismal mouth of the tunnel. There were the high, wet stone walls of the cutting. There were the stars above them.

'Do you see it?' I asked him, taking particular note of his face. His eyes were prominent and strained, but not very much more so, perhaps, than my own had been when I had directed them earnestly towards the same spot.

'No,' he answered. 'It is not there.'

'Agreed,' said I.

We went in again, shut the door, and resumed our seats. I was thinking how best to improve this advantage, if it might be called one, when he took up the conversation in such a matter-of-course way, so assuming that there could be no serious question of fact between us, that I felt myself placed in the weakest of positions.

'By this time you will fully understand, sir,' he said, 'that what troubles me so dreadfully is the question, What does the spectre mean?'

I was not sure, I told him, that I did fully understand.

'What is its warning against?' he said, ruminating, with his eyes on the fire, and only by times turning them on me. 'What is the danger? Where is the danger? There is danger overhanging somewhere on the Line. Some dreadful calamity will happen. It is not to be doubted this third time, after what has gone before. But surely this is a cruel haunting of me. What can I do?'

He pulled out his handkerchief, and wiped the drops from his heated forehead.

'If I telegraph Danger, on either side of me, or on both, I can give no reason for it,' he went on, wiping the palms of his hands. 'I should get into trouble, and do no good. They would think I was mad. This is the way it would work, – Message: "Danger! Take care!" Answer: "What Danger? Where?" Message: "Don't know. But, for God's sake, take care!" They would displace me. What else could they do?'

His pain of mind was most pitiable to see. It was the mental torture of a conscientious man, oppressed beyond endurance by an unintelligible responsibility involving life.

'When it first stood under the Danger-light,' he went on, putting his dark hair back from his head, and drawing his hands outward across and across his temples in an extremity of feverish distress, 'why not tell me where that accident was to happen, – if it must happen? Why not tell me how it could be averted, – if it could have been averted? When on its second coming it hid its face, why not tell me, instead, "She is going to die. Let them keep her at home"? If it came, on those two occasions, only to show me that its warnings were true, and so to prepare me for the third, why not warn me plainly now? And I, Lord help me! A mere poor signal-man on this solitary station! Why not go to somebody with credit to be believed, and power to act?'

When I saw him in this state, I saw that for the poor man's sake, as well as for the public safety, what I had to do for the time was to compose his mind. Therefore, setting aside all question of reality or unreality between us, I represented to him that whoever thoroughly discharged his duty must do well, and that at least it was his comfort that he understood his duty, though he did not understand these confounding Appearances. In this effort I succeeded far better than in the attempt to reason him out of his conviction. He became calm; the occupations incidental to his post as the night advanced began to make larger demands on his attention: and I left him at two in the morning. I had offered to stay through the night, but he would not hear of it.

That I more than once looked back at the red light as I ascended the pathway, that I did not like the red light, and that I should have slept but poorly if my bed had been under it, I see no reason to conceal. Nor did I like the two sequences of the accident and the dead girl. I see no reason to conceal that either.

But what ran most in my thoughts was the consideration how ought I to act, having become the recipient of this disclosure? I had proved the man to be intelligent, vigilant, painstaking, and exact; but how long might he remain so, in his state of mind? Though in a subordinate position, still he held a most important trust, and would I (for instance) like to stake my own life on the chances of his continuing to execute it with precision?

Unable to overcome a feeling that there would be something treacherous in my communicating what he had told me to his superiors in the Company, without first being plain with himself and proposing a middle course to him, I ultimately resolved to offer to accompany him (otherwise keeping his secret for the present) to the wisest medical practitioner we could hear of in those parts, and to take his opinion. A change in his time of duty would come round next night, he had apprised me, and he would be off an hour or two after sunrise, and on again soon after sunset. I had appointed to return accordingly.

Next evening was a lovely evening, and I walked out early to enjoy it. The sun was not yet quite down when I traversed the field-path near the top of the deep cutting. I would extend my walk for an hour, I said to myself, half an hour on and half an hour back, and it would then be time to go to my signal-man's box.

Before pursuing my stroll, I stepped to the brink, and mechanically looked down, from the point from which I had first seen him. I cannot describe the thrill that seized upon me, when, close at the mouth of the tunnel, I saw the appearance of a man, with his left sleeve across his eyes, passionately waving his right arm.

The nameless horror that oppressed me passed in a moment, for in a moment I saw that this appearance of a man was a man indeed, and that there was a little group of other men, standing at a short distance, to whom he seemed to be rehearsing the gesture he made. The Danger-light was not yet lighted. Against its shaft, a little low hut, entirely new to me, had been made of some wooden supports and tarpaulin. It looked no bigger than a bed.

With an irresistible sense that something was wrong, – with a flashing self-reproachful fear that fatal mischief had come of my leaving the man there, and causing no one to be sent to overlook or correct what he did, – I descended the notched path with all the speed I could make.

'What is the matter?' I asked the men.

'Signal-man killed this morning, sir.'

'Not the man belonging to that box?'

'Yes, sir.'

'Not the man I know?'

'You will recognise him, sir, if you knew him,' said the man who spoke for the others, solemnly uncovering his own head, and raising an end of the tarpaulin, 'for his face is quite composed.'

'O, how did this happen, how did this happen?' I asked, turning from one to another as the hut closed in again.

'He was cut down by an engine, sir. No man in England knew his work better. But somehow he was not clear of the outer rail. It was just at broad day. He had struck the light, and had the lamp in his hand. As the engine came out of the tunnel, his back was towards her, and she cut him down. That man drove her, and was showing how it happened. Show the gentleman, Tom.'

The man, who wore a rough dark dress, stepped back to his former place at the mouth of the tunnel.

'Coming round the curve in the tunnel, sir,' he said, 'I saw him at the end, like as if I saw him down a perspective-glass. There was no time to check speed, and I knew him to be very careful. As he didn't seem to take heed of the whistle, I shut it off when we were running down upon him, and called to him as loud as I could call.'

'What did you say?'

'I said, "Below there! Look out! Look out! For God's sake, clear the way!"'

I started.

'Ah! it was a dreadful time, sir. I never left off calling to him. I put this arm before my eyes not to see, and I waved this arm to the last; but it was no use.'

Without prolonging the narrative to dwell on any one of its curious circumstances more than on any other, I may, in closing it, point out the coincidence that the warning of the Engine-Driver included, not only the words which the unfortunate Signal-man had repeated to me as haunting him, but also the words which I myself – not he – had attached, and that only in my own mind, to the gesticulation he had imitated.

Appendix 2
The introduction of Melmotte in *The Way We Live Now* (1875) by Anthony Trollope

The giver of the ball was Augustus Melmotte, Esq., the father of the girl whom Sir Felix Carbury desired to marry, and the husband of the lady who was said to have been a Bohemian Jewess. It was thus that the gentleman chose to have himself designated, though within the last two years he had arrived in London from Paris, and had at first been known as M. Melmotee. But he had declared of himself that he had been born in England, and that he was an Englishman. He admitted that his wife was a foreigner, – an admission that was necessary as she spoke very little English. Melmotte himself spoke his 'native' language fluently, but with an accent which betrayed at least a long expatriation. Miss Melmotte, – who a very short time since had been known as Mademoiselle Marie, – spoke English well, but as a foreigner. In regard to her it was acknowledged that she had been born out of England, – some said in New York; but Madame Melmotte, who must have known, had declared that the great event had taken place in Paris.

It was at any rate an established fact that Mr. Melmotte had made his wealth in France. He no doubt had had enormous dealings in other countries, as to which stories were told which must surely have been exaggerated. It was said that he had made a railway across Russia, that he provisioned the Southern army in the American civil war, that he had supplied Austria with arms, and had at one time bought up all the iron in England. He could make or mar any company by buying or selling stock, and could make money dear or cheap as he pleased. All this was said of him in his praise, – but it was also said that he was regarded in Paris as the most gigantic swindler that had ever lived; that he had made that City too hot to hold him; that he had endeavoured to establish himself in Vienna, but had been warned away by the police; and that he had at length found that British freedom would alone allow him to enjoy, without persecution, the fruits of his industry. He was now established privately in Grosvenor Square and officially in Abchurch Lane; and it was known to all the world that a Royal Prince, a Cabinet Minister, and the very cream of duchesses were going to his wife's ball. All this had been done within twelve months.

There was but one child in the family, one heiress for all this wealth. Melmotte himself was a large man, with busy whiskers and rough thick hair, with heavy eyebrows, and a wonderful look of power about his mouth and chin. This was so strong as to redeem his face from vulgarity; but the countenance and appearance of the man were on the whole unpleasant, and, I may say, untrustworthy. He looked as though he were purse-proud and a bully.

References

Abrams, M. H. (1953), 'Literature as a revelation of personality' (extract), in John Caughie (1981) (ed.), *Theories of Authorship*, London: Routledge, 17–21.

Amis, Kingsley (1986), *The Old Devils*, London: Hutchinson.

Austen, Jane (1816), *Emma*. All page references are to the Penguin Classics edn, London: Penguin, 1966.

Barry, Peter (1995), *Beginning Theory*, Manchester: Manchester University Press.

Barthes, Roland (1968), 'The death of the Author', in R. Howard (ed. and trans.), *The Rustle of Language* (1986), Oxford: Basil Blackwell, 49–56.

Bloom, Harold (1996) (ed.), *William Shakespeare's 'Othello'*, Broomall, Pa.: Chelsea House.

Bonnycastle, Stephen (1996), *In Search of Authority: An Introductory Guide to Literary Theory*, 2nd edn, Peterborough, Ont.: Broadview Press.

Bordwell, David (1989o), *Making Meaning: Inference and Rhetoric in the Interpretation of Cinema*, Cambridge, Mass./London: Harvard University Press.

Bunyan, John (1678), *The Pilgrim's Progress*. All page references are to the Henry Frowde end, Oxford: Oxford University Press, 1912.

Burke, Sean (1995) (ed.), *Authorship: From Plato to the Postmodern – A Reader*, Edinburgh: Edinburgh University Press.

Buscombe, Edward (1973), 'Ideas of authorship', *Screen*, 14:3 (Autumn), 75–85.

Butler, Lance St John (1999), *Registering the Difference: Reading Literature through Register*, Manchester: Manchester University Press.

Cardwell, Sarah (2002), *Adaptation Revisited: Television and the Classic Novel*, Manchester: Manchester University Press.

Cardwell, Sarah (2003), 'David Lean', BFI website: screenonline.org.uk/home.stm.

Carey, John (1977), *Thackeray: Prodigal Genius*, London: Faber and Faber.

Carroll, Noël (2000), 'Art and the domain of the aesthetic', *British Journal of Aesthetics*, 40:2, 191–208.

Caughie, John (1981a), 'Preface', in *Theories of Authorship: A Reader* (ed.), London: Routledge, 1–6.

Caughie, John (1981b) (ed.), *Theories of Authorship: A Reader*, London: Routledge.

Caughie, John (2000), *Television Drama: Realism, Modernism, and British Culture*, Oxford: Oxford University Press.

Collins, Jim (1999), 'Miramaxing the literary: the cine-literary culture of the 90s', in Ib Bondebjerg and Helle Kannik Haastrup (eds), *Intertextuality and Visual Media*, Sekvens 99, University of Copenhagen Department of Film and Media Studies

Cook, John R. (1995), *Dennis Potter: A Life on Screen*, Manchester: Manchester University Press.

Cooke, Lez (2003), *British Television Drama: A History*, London: BFI Publishing.

Corner, John (1999), *Critical Ideas in Television Studies*, Oxford: Clarendon Press.

Coward, Rosalind (1987), 'Dennis Potter and the question of the television author', *Critical Quarterly* 29:4, 79–87.

Currie, Gregory (1995a), 'The interpretative problem', in *Image and Mind: Film, Philosophy and Cognitive Science*, Cambridge: Cambridge University Press, 225–59.

Currie, Gregory (1995b), *Image and Mind: Film, Philosophy and Cognitive Science*, Cambridge: Cambridge University Press.

Davies, Andrew (1994), 'Prima Donnas and Job Lots', Huw Wheldon Memorial Lecture to the Royal Television Society (videotape).

Dickens, Charles (1866), *The Signalman*. This short story can be found as Appendix 1 in this book.

Dickie, George (1997a), 'The institutional theory of art', in *Introduction to Aesthetics: An Analytic Approach*, Oxford: Oxford University Press, 82–93.

Dickie, George (1997b), 'Intentionalist criticism', in *Introduction to Aesthetics: An Analytic Approach*, Oxford: Oxford University Press, 97–105.

Eagleton, Terry (1996), *Literary Theory: An Introduction*, 2nd edn, Oxford: Blackwell Publishers.

Eliot, T. S. (1919), 'Tradition and the individual talent', in Sean Burke (1995) (ed.) *Authorship: from Plato to the Postmodern – A Reader*, Edinburgh: Edinburgh University Press, 73–89.

Frow, John (1990), 'Intertextuality and ontology', in Michael Worton and Judith Still (eds), *Intertextuality: Theories and Practices*, Manchester: Manchester University Press, 45–55.

Gaut, Berys (1997), 'Film authorship and collaboration', in Richard Allen and Murray Smith (eds), *Film Theory and Philosophy*, Oxford: Clarendon Press, 149–72.

Harris, Margaret (1995), 'Whose *Middlemarch*? The 1994 British Broadcasting Corporation's television production', *Sydney Studies in English*, 21, 95–102.

Hawthorn, Jeremy (1987), 'Genesis', in *Unlocking the Text: Fundamental Issues in Literary Theory*, London: Edward Arnold, 64–87.

Hilmes, Michele (ed.), (2003), *The Television History Book*, London: BFI Publishing.

Hirsch, E. D. (1967), 'Validity in interpretation' (extract), in Sean Burke

(1995) *Authorship: from Plato to the Postmodern – A Reader*, Edinburgh: Edinburgh University Press, 108–16.

Hughes, Kathryn (2002), 'Making *Daniel Deronda* work', *Prospect*, December, 64–5.

Jeffries, Stuart (2002), 'Portrait: Mr Television', *Guardian*, Features, 2 Oct, 7.

Lehman, Peter and William Luhr (2003), *Thinking about Movies: Watching, Questioning, Enjoying*, Oxford: Blackwell Publishing.

Livingston, Paisley (1997), 'Cinematic authorship', in Richard Allen and Murray Smith (eds), *Film Theory and Philosophy*, Oxford: Clarendon Press, 132–48.

Lyas, Colin (1992), 'Criticism and interpretation', in Oswald Hanfling (ed.), *Philosophical Aesthetics: An Introduction*, Milton Keynes: Open University Press, 381–404.

McFarlane, Brian (1996), *Novel to Film: An Introduction to the Theory of Adaptation*, Oxford: Clarendon Press.

Maskell, Duke and Ian Robinson (2001), *The New Idea of a University*, London: Haven Books.

Nelson, Robin (1997), *TV Drama in Transition: Forms, Values and Cultural Change*, Basingstoke: Macmillan.

O'Brien, Stephen (1996), 'Andrew Davies: an interview', *Faze* [amateur fanzine], 3 (Jan./Feb.), 26–30.

Olsen, Stein Haugom (1987), *The End of Literary Theory*, Cambridge: Cambridge University Press.

Palmer, Jerry (1991), *Potboilers: Methods, Concepts and Case Studies in Popular Fiction*, London: Routledge.

Pasternak, Boris (1958), *Doctor Zhivago*, trans. Max Hayward and Manya Harari. First published in English in 1958. All page references are to the Vintage edition, London: Vintage, 2002.

Perkins, Victor (1972), *Film as Film*, London: Penguin.

Ransome, Nic (2000), 'Tipping the Eng. Lit.: interview with Andrew Davies', *ScriptWriter* (Nov.), 16–19.

Ransome, Nic (2001), 'A very polished practice: an interview with Andrew Davies', *European English Messenger*, 10:1, 34–41.

Salwak, Dale (1992), *Kingsley Amis: Modern Novelist*, Hemel Hempstead: Harvester Wheatsheaf.

Shillingsburg, Peter (2001), *William Makepeace Thackeray: A Literary Life*, Basingstoke/New York: Palgrave.

Shubik, Irene (2000), *Play for Today: The Evolution of Television Drama*, Manchester: Manchester University Press.

Stoddart, Helen (1995), 'Auteurism and film authorship theory', in Joanne Hollows and Mark Jancovich (eds), *Approaches to Popular Film*, Manchester: Manchester University Press, 37–58.

Thackeray, William Makepeace (1853), *Vanity Fair*. All page references are to the Penguin edn, London: Penguin, 1968.

Thorpe, James (1972), *Principles of Textual Criticism*, San Marino: Calif.: Huntingdon Library.

Thorpe, Vanessa (2002), 'Universal adaptor', *Observer* (22 Sept.), 27.

Trollope, Anthony (1875), *The Way We Live Now*. All page references are to the World's Classics edn, London: Oxford University Press, 1951.

Wimsatt, W. K. and Monroe C. Beardsley (1954), 'The intentional fallacy' (extract), in Sean Burke (1995) *Authorship: From Plato to the Postmodern – A Reader*, Edinburgh: Edinburgh University Press, 90–100.

Worton, Michael and Judith Still (1990), 'Introduction' to *Intertextuality: Theories and Practices*, Manchester: Manchester University Press, 1–44.

Index

Note: Literary works can be found under authors' names. Page numbers in *italic* refer to illustrations. 'n.' after a page reference indicates the number of a note on that page.